VOLUME ONE

Answers to All Your Questions

D. J. Herda

Elektra Press, LLC
Salt Lake City

Copyright ©2021 D. J. Herda
ALL RIGHTS RESERVED. No part of this book may be reproduced or transmitted in any form or by any means, electronic or mechanical, including photocopying, recording, or any information storage and retrieval system without permission in writing from the Publisher. Address requests for permissions to Elektra Press, LLC, Rights and Permissions Department, 929 W. Sunset Blvd., Ste. 21-285, St. George, UT 84770.

Printed in the United States of America

Library of Congress Cataloging-in-Publication Data is available on file.
ISBN 978-1-63732-347-2

Table of Contents

ALSO by D. J. Herda 7

INTRODUCTION: In Truth We Trust 9

ONE: The Mechanics of Writing 13

TWO: The Structure of Writing 87

THREE: The Editing of Writing 161

FOUR: The Secrets of Writing 177

AFTERWORD 223

BIBLIOGRAPHY 225

ALSO by D. J. Herda

Here are just a few of the latest volumes of fiction and nonfiction by one of the most prolific writers working today. You'll find more of his work on the Website, www.djherda.org, and at book retailers and online sellers everywhere. To contact the author, please e-mail him via Elektra Press LLC at editors@elektrapress.com, and we'll see that your message is forwarded.

FICTION

Chi-Town Blues—A shady landlady with a half-dozen skips on her hands, a suburban contractor in the Mob's cross-hairs, a nearly frozen fisherman with a sloe-eyed, murderous blonde to heat things up—they're all here. From the well-healed Near North Side and the chimera of Rush Street to the city's plebeian suburbs, this is a cross-section of Chi-Town's most secretive, seductive, and seditious characters.

The Last Wild Orchid—When a mother-and-son research team gets too close to the grizzly truth, one of them must die. But which? With the cold-blooded murderer still on the loose, a young man sets out to avenge his mother's death. But how will he recognize the killer? And what will he do when he does?

Solid Stiehl: The Death and Life of Hymie Stiehl—Hymie Stiehl learns that pal Jungle Jim Alavera has disappeared and knows what he must do. Realizing that Alavera is still alive but in growing danger, Stiehl fakes his own death only to emerge in drag to try to locate his ball-player compadre. After Stiehl's snitch tracks Alavera to a small brownstone in New Town, Hymie decides to pay the jock a surprise visit. But when he walks into a ransacked apartment with the water still warm in the bathtub, he realizes things are getting serious. And

ABOUT WRITING RIGHT

that everything points to murder. And that the cops are going to want a fall guy.

Soon!

NONFICTION

Etta Place: Riding into History with Butch Cassidy and the Sundance Kid—After she met Harry Longabaugh (the Sundance Kid) and Robert Parker (Butch Cassidy), the Wild Bunch gang set off on a spree of bank, stagecoach, and train robberies. With the law hot on their heels, they rode up to Robber's Roost in southwestern Utah where they laid low until word reached local authorities of their whereabouts. On the run again, Place accompanied Longabaugh to New York City where, on February 20, 1901, the couple joined Parker, Posing as Etta's brother, and sailed for Buenos Aires ... and infamy.

Everything You Always Wanted To Know About Writing Right (four-volume series of eBooks)—Here is everything you always wanted to know about writing but were afraid to ask in eBook format. These are the honest, unvarnished, authoritative responses to questions from writers around the world from one of the leading grammatical authorities and most widely published authors, teachers, editors, and book doctors working today. Recognizing that the need for precise information has never been greater, the author draws upon half a century of know-how and experience to provide honest, relevant answers to questions such as how to beat "writer's block," how to get motivated to write, how to create a dynamic opening line, and how to find a literary agent or publisher. He talks about self-publishing vs. conventional publishing; locating a good professional editor, and writing efficiently and effectively. He brings unique and wide-ranging experiences to the table, drawing upon his years as a book, magazine, and newspaper editor as well as a college-level instructor of everything from analytic grammar and business correspondence to Creative Writing Workshop. As one of his students remarked, "If D. J. doesn't have an answer, the question doesn't exist."

Fascinating reading and invaluable information--that's what the About Writing Right series has to offer. Broken down into easily assimilated chapters, it's a classic resource, an invaluable reference work, and a sheer joy for writers and readers of all backgrounds and ages.

INTRODUCTION: In Truth We Trust

The World Wide Web. The source of all good. And maybe just a little evil. But is it also the source of accurate information that it often presents itself to be? You've got to be kidding.

The strength of the Internet as a tool for greater learning is exactly the weakness of the Web: Anyone can post anything on the Internet anywhere at any time. In blogs, on private and public Websites, in question-and-answer sites such as Quora, Facebook, and Twitter, in book reviews on Barnes & Noble and elsewhere, in Amazon product reviews, in questions about specific products, and even on various shopping sites, from Amazon and eBay to Wayfair and Zappa. The list is endless. Unfortunately, so are the erroneous entries masquerading as truth.

That's because there is no central clearing house for the accuracy of information posted online, which is both a good and a bad thing. Such an agency would undoubtedly overstep its boundaries in reaching arbitrary (and not necessarily correct) conclusions. Want proof? Take a look at Facebook and Twitter or even *The Washington Post* and the *New York Times* and all the inaccurate information they publish *constantly*. Have you ever heard the phrase, "fair and balanced"? Well, you wouldn't hear it for long if we turned all our news sources over to a central clearing house before allowing information to see the light of print. The result would be a serious dampening of the flow and exchange of ideas, which is a concept central to all democratic societies.

ABOUT WRITING RIGHT

The advantage of having a central clearing house for the sake of establishing accuracy of published information—at least in theory--is that anyone running a search for a response to a question could be sure of receiving only accurate answers. *In theory.* And, facts—not fallacies—are the fuel that feed intellect, knowledge, and the future. Medicine, science, the performing arts, and even writing require facts to thrive; without them, they would wither and die on the vine like an overripe tomato.

In a way, we do have a "central clearing house" of sorts on the Internet. In fact, we have several. Wikipedia comes to mind, as do other sites that employ impartial editors to research and approve the information shared by other writers and researchers on the sites. While not perfect, these "wikis" do a remarkably good job of separating the correct from the incorrect and promoting care in posting information. Make the wrong claims or inaccurate conclusions, and your "facts" will be targeted as incorrect or, at least, open to challenge and debate.

Unfortunately, the vast majority of answers on the Internet come not from various contributing editor-controlled wikis and similar sites but from simple Web searches, and that's where most inaccurate information lives and procreates.

Now, what's so important about accuracy when it comes to our daily lives? Not much if you dial up a weather report that says partly sunny and warm Tuesday and it turns out to be mostly cloudy and cool. Unless you're a farmer planning on planting or harvesting under certain conditions, such discrepancies don't matter all that much. But if you're a surgeon or a NASA engineer, they could be costly.

In fact, there's not a line of work anywhere that benefits from inaccurate information obtained in the belief that it is correct. Life revolves around facts and would flounder without them.

And, so it is with writers.

I have been teaching, researching, evaluating, and analyzing various pieces of information all my life. I have been writing about my conclusions for nearly that long. In that respect, I'm something of an enigma. I don't exist much anymore, and at times I feel more than a little antiquated, like a *Tyrannosaurus Rex* on his last stroll around the universe. Still, that's a small enough burden to carry when I think back over the years I've been answering questions about writing, publishing, acquiring a literary agent, avoiding copyright infringement, self-publishing, marketing, and more. In that time, I have corrected more misbeliefs and straightened out more misguided "facts" than I care to admit. The reason for this is twofold.

First, I'm pretty good at what I do. My longevity in this crazy business we call writing attests to that. I wouldn't have survived my first year as a full-time freelancer otherwise. Nor would I have lived through my periodic stints as a writing instructor, fact-checker, researcher, and editor for magazines, newspapers, and book publishers only to return once again to writing.

Second, inaccurate information proliferates. It seems that, as more people learn how to navigate the Web, more find ways to post information. Not *accurate* information. Just information. The result: a growing amount of inaccurate jargon littering the universe. Sometimes, that happens via people who really don't know the truth but assume they do. Just as often, however, the obvious is true: People who know better *deliberately distort facts* or present outright lies as truth in order to gain financially, socially, or politically. Or all three.

"What's that?" you ask. You're shocked?

Uh-huh.

What *should* shock you, though, is the realization that every inaccurate belief that freelance writers harbor about the writing and publishing industry costs them. Sometimes it costs them time, sometimes money, and sometimes both. Occasionally, it costs them their very careers.

I face that enigma every single day—and not only on the Internet. I also find absurdly wild "facts" in the printed word as well as on radio and television. That shouldn't be surprising, considering that the social-media giants, including Facebook and Twitter and other social-media sites, boast more than *billions* of combined, unique monthly visitors. The result is a "too-big-to-fail" mentality leading to a plethora of inaccurate information that hovers at an all-time high.

The negative pattern of inane questions and incongruous responses has gotten worse since the number of people working at home continues to rise. Many of these people want to know about the general field of writing as a worthy avocation, a spark-generating creative outlet, or a potential life-changing career move. As Amazon's

ABOUT WRITING RIGHT

KDP, IngramSpark, and others push to gain market share in the field of Print on Demand (POD) publishing, the need for accurate and informed information has never been greater.

Despite that need, a growing dearth of information exists--honest, accurate, educated, and complete answers to questions related to all areas of writing and publishing. These range from how to get motivated to write and how to compose a dynamite first line for that new book you've been planning for years to how to become a published author (conventional vs. self), how to market your work, how to find a reliable agent, and how to pitch a book or script to Hollywood.

I consider myself fortunate to have cut as broad a swatch through the publishing industry as I have. As a result, I bring a unique and wide-ranging set of experiences to the table. Having written my first book at the age of fourteen and worked as a book, magazine, and newspaper editor on numerous occasions, I have also been fortunate enough to have taught everything from analytic grammar to Creative Writing Workshop. I have also served time as an editor, ghostwriter, and book doctor for other writers who have become successful authors. Having written and published more than 90 conventionally published books of my own, I come across few questions to which I don't have authoritative answers. And, in those rare instances where even *I'm* stumped, my experience as a factfinder and a researcher has helped me gain insight into the truth.

So, with that in mind, here are my answers to my selections for some of the best, most frequently asked, most pressing questions plaguing the minds of writers throughout the country and the world. Culled from numerous Internet and other sources over the past four decades, they are both illuminating and revealing. I hope you enjoy reading what your compatriots are thinking, saying, and pondering, and I hope that, if you have a question to which you've been unable to find a reliable response, you'll give me a shout. I'm here to help guide you and every other writer who has ever struggled to become a published author and fought his way through the mass of rhetoric, red tape, and roadblocks in your path.

Ladies and gentlemen, start your engines!

ONE: The Mechanics of Writing

When I began laying out the chapters for this book, I found myself confronted by a single question: Why worry about the mechanics of writing? After all, writing is writing, right? But that's not necessarily writing *right*. So, to whom should that matter? I mean, writing right or writing wrong. Should it matter to you? Should it matter to me?

Does it matter to the casual reader or only to the professional scribe, striving to make a living from his writing? Does it matter to the businessman looking to increase the value of his corporate portfolio or to a salesman seeking to land a new client? Does it matter to the high-school or college-age student who has so many other things on his plate (like girls and guys, for instance)? Or to the medical doctor more concerned about communicating orally than in writing?

In short, who really *cares* about the mechanics of writing and whether or not that writing is perfect, pretty good, or outright horrible?

The answer came to me shortly after I asked the question. *Everybody* cares about the mechanics. Or, at least, everybody *should*. Here's why.

We are a nation—a world, a species, a genus—of social beings. In order to relate to one another, we need to communicate. One of the most frequent ways in which we do so is by writing.

We subliminally break down every form of communication our brains take in. Each communique is excellent, good, bad, or horrible. Or somewhere in between.

The next question is: So what? Does it really matter? Or are we merely playing mind games with ourselves?

The answer to that is, yes, it really matters. Here's why.

ABOUT WRITING RIGHT

We judge one another on our mutual ability to communicate. Universally acceptable forms of communication—that is, good or effective communication that is clear, concise, and *understandable*—are easier to assimilate than poor or ineffective forms of communication. The people with whom we communicate most often are the ones who understand us and vice-versa. On the other hand, bad forms of communication—or poor, ineffective communication—are the most difficult to assimilate. If we listen to someone talk or read what someone has written and can't understand exactly and *precisely* what that person is saying, our minds wander. Our ability to focus on what the other person is saying diminishes. Our successful interrelationship with that person eventually disappears as we shy away from future attempts to communicate with him or her. Instead, we instinctively look to find others with whom we can communicate more amicably and effectively.

Effective communication might not have made a world of difference in Cro-Magnon days (or it might have made a world of difference when being chased by a *Tyrannosaurus rex*), but it certainly matters today when we go to exchange critical information: the stock-market prices, medical advice, food costs, tax information, the cost of living, social-security benefits, safety concerns. An efficient exchange of that information may well benefit us; a failure to communicate simply wastes our time, places us at risk, and leaves us in the lurch.

So the question arises: How do we communicate efficiently? One might also ask how one wires a house for electricity or builds a bridge or lays a road. The answer to all those questions is simple: By following the rules.

In the case of construction, the rules are well defined and often delineated by government-enforced dictums called building codes. In the case of linguistics (speaking or writing), we have no codes, but we still have dictums. They're called grammatical rules, and they're understood and followed by those who pursue the knowledge of them while being ignored by others.

Now, a good road-building contractor who knows the building codes and how to build roads efficiently can make two or three hundred thousand dollars a year in income and potentially much more. A laborer who doesn't have a clue about code and couldn't build a road if his life depended upon it might make $18 an hour. Do you see what I'm getting at here?

Know the rules, and you rule the roads. Travel through life ignorant of the rules, and you rule nothing.

With that in mind, then, it's obvious that the mechanics of writing are everything. They are the beginning, the middle, and the end of efficient and successful writing—or *communication*. And, while many of our vaunted English grammar teachers throughout our school days made their subjects tediously boring and endlessly mysterious, the rules of grammar and syntax are actually quite simple to master. Do this here. Do that there. Think a little bit in between, and you'll get it.

With all this in mind, then, here are the Rules of the Road for writing. Here are the Mechanics of Writing. Here are the keys to success and your future. Learn them well, and use them always because your future may well depend upon them.

The envelope, please.

How important is using the proper subject and verb agreement when writing?

Actually, subject-verb agreement isn't important at all ... until you write something for someone who understands the rule and believes in following it. At that point, ignorance of the rules becomes painfully damaging to the practitioner. (*You!*)

In English grammar, subject-verb agreement requires matching the subject and the verb in *number* (that is, singular or plural). Also occasionally called subject-verb *concord*, here's an example:

The car is red (the word "car" is a singular subject, and "is" is a singular verb, so both subject and verb work properly together).

The cars are red (the word "cars" is a plural subject, and "are" is a plural verb, so they also work properly together).

Often, determining the number agreement of subject and verb is relatively easy, but it can get tougher when you introduce a prepositional phrase that "masks" the true subject, making it appear that the subject is singular when it's plural and vice-versa. For example:

Incorrect: *High levels of mercury occurs in some fish.*
Correct: *High levels of mercury occur in some fish.*

ABOUT WRITING RIGHT

In both sentences, the subject is "levels" (which is plural) and not "mercury" (which is singular). On a quick read-through, though, one might assume the subject is "mercury" except that it's the object of the preposition "of" and therefore can't also be the subject. So, the correct version of the sentence is this:

High levels [plural subject] *of mercury occur* [plural verb] *in some fish.*

The reason is that levels is plural and occur is plural. If you strip away all but the subject and verb, it's easier to understand: *Levels occur*.

Of course, if the original sentence sounds stilted to you when written correctly, you can always change the word order and rewrite the sentence so that the singular subject becomes "mercury" and the singular verb becomes "occurs." For example:

Mercury occurs in some fish in high levels.

By merely inverting the word order and making "Mercury" the singular subject, we can use the singular verb "occurs" for better clarity and readability.

Confusing? Not once you get used to looking for the real subject of a sentence. Remember that, if the noun you think may be the subject follows a preposition, it is always the object of the preposition and thus can't be the subject, which must be some other noun. To find the true subject, cross that object of the preposition off your short list and dig a little deeper into the sentence. Then, match the number of the verb with the real subject, and you're writing like the Big Boys write. And girls!

Are there rules or guidelines about avoiding the use of adverbs in your own writing and, if so, with what do you replace them?

Rules or guidelines? In writing? There are none. And there are *plenty*. It all depends upon semantics and your use of the words, rules and guidelines. Rules and guidelines are different than laws. Can you have rules and guidelines in writing, break them, and avoid going to prison? I'm betting you can. Here's the bottom line.

Tips for better writing (how's that for skirting the semantics' issue) are many and varied. One of them is, indeed, to avoid adverbs. Not always, but whenever possible. As a writer of nearly half a century, I can guarantee you that there are times when the use of some adverbs is absolutely necessary to create the strongest possible image in your readers' minds. I can also guarantee you that there are far more times when the use of adverbs is a quick-and-easy escape from the rigors involved in good writing, and their use in such cases only weakens and dilutes your imagery. That's why the "rule" about adverbs came about: It's easier to exhort inexperienced writers to avoid adverbs at all times (even though that's not possible) than it is to teach them when to use them and when not.

I noticed in a previous commentator's response a reference to Strunk and White's *The Elements of Style* as a good source to read, study, and consult in your day-to-day approach to writing. It's a classic, and I also recommend it. At one point in time (back in the days of dinosaurs and dragons, princes and toads awaiting divination), the book was mandatory reading for all cub newspaper reporters. If you didn't own it, read it, and follow its recommendations, you didn't hold your job for long. It was that simple.

Today, alas, journalism as it once existed is dead, and, at many "publications," from print to Internet, anything goes. Including poor writing.

So, it all boils down to this: Are you a quick, sloppy, and lazy writer? If so, ignore the "rules or guidelines" of writing, and you'll receive your just reward. If you want to be the best writer you can be, listen to the masters, to those who have been there, analyzed writing both good and bad, put in their time, and come out on top. And then bust your butt to join them.

Doing so will pay dividends in the end.

What are some common errors that writers make when writing a book?

Do you want to know the most *basic* errors people make when writing a book? Or would you settle for the number of stars above?

Seriously, writing well isn't a matter of luck or desire. It's a matter of studying, learning, and practicing—just as with any profession. I'm going to bet that, if someone removed your appendix without ever having taken a single medical course or observed a solitary operation, you wouldn't be very happy with the results. The same is true for every profession, including writing. Here are only a few of the pits into which novice writers tumble.

ABOUT WRITING RIGHT

Failing to outline. If you don't create a synopsis followed by a chapter-by-chapter breakdown of your book (fiction or nonfiction), you'll find yourself winging it until you flat run out of gas or trip over your thoughts. When that happens, getting your writing back on track becomes far more of a chore and less of a joy than it should be.

Using passive voice. If it can be written in passive voice, it can be rewritten in *active* voice, which reads *so* much stronger. So, get in the habit of learning the difference between the two and concentrating on powering up your choice of verbs. Instead of this: *He was being hit by John*, write this: *John hit him* or *John began hitting him* or *John beat the living daylights out of him.* In the passive case, the subject, "John," is *receiving* the action. In the active cases, John is *producing* the action. That's one difference between weak and strong writing.

Using adverbs. Nine times out of ten, an adverb merely succeeds in greatly weakening (see what I mean?) a sentence. Better: *Nine times out of ten, an adverb ruins a sentence.*

Saying it instead of showing it. You should *see* the scene in your mind, evaluate it, play with it, and explore it before committing it to paper. Ask yourself what you see, what images are projected in your imagination. Explore the sensory triggers such as taste, feel, and smell. If you don't do that, you're merely stringing empty words together. Words don't create thoughts in people's minds; images do. Instead of this: *The sun rose in the sky*, try this: *The sun erupted over the city.* Same thought, different results. One enables the reader to see absolutely nothing; the other paints a mental image he may well remember for days, weeks, or even years to come.

Failing to revise. Revisions to most writers are a waste of time. Beginning writers, especially, want to keep charging forward. Unfortunately, a single look into the rear-view mirror would show them a world of inadequacies. Every writer must take time to re-read, revise, and refine. That's called "editing." If you don't know how to edit (it's not a God-given, inalienable talent), take some courses, read some books, or go to work for someone who does. Like your weekly newspaper publisher or a local blogger in need of clean copy.

Not realizing there's more than one way to filet a trout. If the way you write something sounds "funny," take the same thought and rewrite it. Use a different word order, or create the same thought using different words that mean roughly the same thing. Writing isn't about putting words "out there" and walking away from them. It's about combining words into phrases, clauses, sentences, and paragraphs to create strong imagery and then honing that imagery to near perfection before trying to make it even stronger.

Failing to read out loud. That's right. *Out loud.* Effective writing for inspiring reading requires a strong literary voice. You'll never develop one if you don't read your material out loud so that your ears can actually "hear" the cadence and rhythm of your words, the alliteration, the poetic meter—all those things that happen when a writer puts words together. If your literary voice is weak, you'll never know it by reading to yourself from a typewritten piece of paper or, worse yet, a computer monitor. Instead, lock yourself in a room somewhere, and read your work aloud, noting weak spots that need revising. If anyone overhears you and questions your sanity, refer them to me. Believe this: If you ever want to be a great writer (forget merely "good"), you'll need to develop a powerful literary voice—just as you need a robust spoken voice to become a great speaker. So, read your work out loud, and hone in on the "real" you. End of subject.

Writing differently than you speak. Going hand-in-hand with finding your literary voice, beginning writers often turn to "Writerese" when they sit down in front of a typewriter or keyboard. Writing to them suddenly becomes an exercise in displaying their innate brilliance. Believe me, whether or not you are brilliant, no one will know it if you write in a stilted, unnatural voice. Leave the Writerese at home, and "dance with the one what brung you." That is, use your *true* voice, whether speaking or writing.

Relying upon the advice of amateurs. Yes, that includes most writing group members, literary reviewers, self-anointed "critics," and even many writing "instructors" or coaches. The best writers write. If you happen to find one who also teaches, count your blessings. Otherwise, taking advice from an untrained, unqualified, unskilled writer is like deciding what pill to take based upon your plumber's recommendation. You may get lucky now and again, but I wouldn't bet my life on it.

Not writing. By this I mean not writing *regularly*. I don't believe in regulating the number of hours you write in a day or a week or a lifetime or whatever unless you absolutely need to do so to become more disciplined. I do believe in writing everything you can, in all different genres and for all different style readers and educational levels, as often as you possibly can. Easy enough for me to say: I write for a living. When I sit down at my desk every morning, I have two things to do. Check my e-mail and write. I understand from a previous life, though, that not everyone has the luxury of concentrating on writing. But, everyone has the luxury of writing as often as circumstances allow, and that's all anyone can ask of you.

There you have it. My top ten tips for becoming a better writer and avoiding those mistakes that beginning writers often make. These, as I said, are only the tip of the iceberg. But learning from them will take you a long way toward becoming a better, more consistent, more successful writer. So, what are you waiting for?

What are some tips for writing popular nonfiction?

Writing "popular nonfiction" is simple. Devote 10 percent of your time to inspiration and 90 percent to perspiration. And *never* assume you have to "write what you know." *Bad* advice. *Huge* mistake. If you did that, you'd run out of topics within your first three weeks. Not to mention the fact that we'd have no newspapers, radio and television coverage, or Internet content. Instead of writing "what you know," write "what you want to learn."

By this I mean be willing to dig down into a subject, research it to death, and then tell what you've learned about it so that your reader (who you have to assume is a complete idiot for this to make sense) can understand what you're talking about. Whether you're writing on the molecular structure of cataclysmic particles in space or why grass is green, nail it.

Also, be sure to include a human element whenever possible to make your story more easily identifiable. That may necessitate inserting yourself or others into the story. Instead of writing: "People don't understand scientific jargon," write: "I never quite understood scientific jargon—at least not until I learned these three rules."

Suddenly, you've set up a human-interest element for the reader with whom to identify. Instead of saying "Rarotonga is a round-shaped island in the South Pacific," write: "I peered out the window as our plane approached a nugget-shaped shard of sand and palm trees: Welcome to Rarotonga!"

In short, two significant elements are at work in writing compelling nonfiction. The first is "research." You must do far more than you'll ever need to complete your work. You have to become an expert on your subject, which in today's world of Internet accessibility is relatively simple to do. Research is what has made me an "expert" on everything from auto racing and bicycle touring to growing plants indoors and raising a healthy baby. And, yes, I've written books on them all. You know—an "expert."

The second element is "approachability." You have to make yourself, the expert in the field, seem approachable. You can't be some encyclopedic entry sitting off in the corner somewhere, or no one will like you. And if no one likes you, no one will read you. Instead, be one with your reader. Don't preach to him; share with him. Place yourself on an equal footing. *Never show off or talk down to your readers.*

One caveat before we leave this subject. Don't ever feel a need to write about every single thing you learn. Prioritize your findings. And then build a narrative arc, just the way you would in writing a novel. Begin with a hypothesis, start laying out your case for your writing, and finish with your conclusion. In that way, your work should be as appealing as it is informative.

Can a writer create a mystery without a sleuth or must he do it the conventional way?

I think what we have here is a failure to communicate. Can a mystery without a sleuth still be a mystery? Can such a book be written at all?

Naturally, a lot depends upon the question of just what constitutes being a "sleuth." In its broadest definition, a sleuth could be defined as someone intent upon solving an act known as the "mystery," which similarly can be defined as some action for which the rationale is unknown (Professor Plum in the library with a candlestick, for example). The sleuth can be someone intimately involved with the act and intent upon discovering the identity of the perpetrator. The sleuth can also be someone called in from outside the pages of the story and, thus, unacquainted with the act, the mystery surrounding it, or any of the real-time "players."

ABOUT WRITING RIGHT

But what, you ask with amazing alacrity and deviousness of mind, if no such sleuth is introduced into the story but, rather, the facts unfold as the author chooses to release them for the reader to act upon on his own accord?

"This happened."
"Oh?"
"And then, this."
"Yes?"
"And this."
"I see."

Well, then, you would have not one sleuth but two, wouldn't you? One would be the author in his unannounced role as sleuth as he lays out the mystery for the reader to solve on his own, and the other would be the reader, himself, placed by the author into a position of sleuthing, or discovery.

Obviously, there are mysteries, and there are mysteries. Contrast some of the works of Arthur Conan Doyle with those of Edgar Allen Poe. Both involve mysteries and entail people employed as "sleuths"— one more traditionally than the other. Taking those author examples to the next degree, how about Dostoevsky or Tolstoy and their stream of consciousness as they struggle (sometimes in vain) to learn the identity of the perpetrator of some nasty deed? Could the sleuth not be the author, himself, perhaps while acting as narrator?

To make a long, belabored point less painful, if there's no sleuth, there's no mystery. As soon as someone begins asking questions (whether as the author or one of his characters or even the reader himself), we suddenly realize something is unknown, and we want to correct that fact. We want to uncover the truth. The "sleuth" can take many different forms over the course of the story, and he's not always the most obvious of candidates.

Should I plot my complete NaNoWriMo project or just play it by ear?

I suggest you plot out everything you write that's longer than your average cursory e-mail. As a writer, "winging it," or writing as you go, sounds romantic. In reality, it's likely to result in a horrible book. It's difficult enough to keep storylines, characters, personalities, plots, subplots, descriptions, and other elements of a book straight in an outline. It's virtually impossible to do so without one.

As a bonus, working from an outline allows you to take the skeleton of the book and "flesh it out" as you write, adding bits and pieces, little chunks of meat here and there, in a manageable manner that writing off the top of your head simply can't allow you to do.

Just my two cents-worth in what works best for me and for other writers whom I've mentored over the years.

When you begin a new book, do you structure the complete outline or just come up with headers? In other words, do you outline the structure and flow of every chapter?

Okay, to begin with, I've conventionally published more than eighty or ninety books and written another couple dozen that will likely never see the light of publication. That's a lot of books. And I've tried everything in preparation for writing—from no outline (totally "winging it") to detailed chapter-by-chapter outline and everything in between. Here's what works for me and will probably be best for the vast majority of writers at any stage of their career.

First, get a clear view of your book in your mind. Beginning, middle, and end. Just the highlights, please. At this point, you don't want or need to waste time on the details.

Second, put it all down on paper. It shouldn't be too long, perhaps as short as a paragraph or two. Perhaps twenty pages. It all depends upon how fertile your mind is and how long you've been mulling this story over.

Third, break down the outline (really more like a synopsis at this stage of development) into manageable chunks that you'll eventually refer to as chapters. Look for natural stopping and starting points, and make your breaks there.

Fourth, go through these "chapters" one by one, fleshing them out according to the vision you have in your brain combined with whatever new material seems to make sense as you go. Once you've finished fleshing out the first chapter, move on to the second and so forth.

Fifth, review your completed chapter outline and make whatever corrections, revisions, or additions are necessary to advance the story and plotline while still making sense. If it reads a little slow, now is the

ABOUT WRITING RIGHT

time to insert some action into one or more chapters. Or perhaps insert a sub-plot (a smaller plot within the main plot) with its own beginning, middle, and end. If it reads like a runaway locomotive, insert some dialogue or descriptive passages to slow things down and allow the reader to stop, catch up with you, and smell the roses.

Sixth, review your chapter outline again—it will be considerably longer than your original version because of all the added details—this time with an eye on character development. Do you have some fragile characters that need strengthening? Some "good guys" who don't come across as good enough and vice-versa? If a particular vocal exchange between two or more characters pops into your head, feel free to write it out. Now is the time to add all the material you can think of to advance the story, plot, and character development.

Seventh, review your fleshed-out chapter outline one last time, this time with an eye on *deleting* things that aren't necessary and may detract from the story or your reader's attention. In short, this is where you admit you're only human, and some of the material you just added is unnecessary and should be cut. Be brutal. If in doubt, cut it out. If you make a mistake by eliminating something that you discover you need, you can always go back and restore it later.

Finally, begin writing. Take each chapter in order, one at a time, and begin re-telling the story, this time not as a series of points to include but rather as a complete tale from the first chapter to the last. By the time you finish, you'll have the first draft of your completed book. Put it aside for a few days or more, and then go back and review it to tighten, expand, cut, and do whatever else works to perfection.

Easy-peasy. Much simpler than trying to recall everything and pulling in material off the top of your head! As you roll through your outline, you'll find the story literally jumps out of you and onto the page.

Note that, while this advice is designed for fiction, it also works pretty well for nonfiction. The key to success no matter what you're writing is to outline, organize, think, revise, and outline some more—all before sitting down to write that first great opening line:

"It was a dark and rainy evening."

Do most mystery writers know how their stories will end before they begin writing, or do they just grit their teeth and "wing it"?

D. J. Herda

I'm not sure if most mystery writers know the end of their stories, but I know that *all* of them *should*. Let's face it; if you want to end up with a chocolate cake, you don't start by blending Bing cherries, graham cracker flour, condensed milk, and pickles and hope for the best! Your cake recipe should reflect your desired goal: chocolate cake.

A mystery novel is no different. Your outline (or recipe) will tell you how to reach your goal, which is the ending of your story (or cake). No ending, no need for an outline. You can just wing everything and hope, as with our chocolate cake example above, that all somehow turns out for the best.

I'm not certain about this assumption, but I'm pretty sure that most writers (and that includes me) know where their story is headed and how it will end long before they figure out how they're going to get there. Often, a basic story structure appears in a writer's mind: beginning, something of a vague middle, and end. It's filling in between the "beginning" and the "end" that makes for a great read. Or it *should*.

The fun is in playing with various options along the way. There must be a billion different combinations of characters, settings, and actions that will work. Choosing precisely the best ones is where the fun—and possibly the frustration and aggravation—begins. *And* the reward. And it all starts with the outline.

Create it, modify it, put it aside for a while, modify it again, put it aside again, and modify it once more. Think about it in between your modifications, and write down any pertinent notes you might want to consider incorporating. Finally, when the outline is as good as you think it can possibly be, begin fleshing it out. Chapter one. Chapter two. And so forth.

Along the way, you'll have a couple of hundred literary distractions calling you aside. Consider every one of them seriously before dismissing those that don't add to the overall effect you want for your mystery and accepting those that do. Then, adjust your outline as necessary to keep you on track.

In time, this living, organic approach to mystery writing will seem like second nature to you. But you won't ever feel as if it's "old hat." *Guaranteed*!

ABOUT WRITING RIGHT

How often do mystery writers change their endings as they write?

I don't think there's any single answer to this question any more than there's only one approach to writing. A well-written, rewritten, and re-rewritten outline (take that to the Nth degree if you will) will generally hold up to a writer's most fanciful and intentional mid-story changes. Sure, you may need to tweak the book toward the end or even along the way to make those changes work, but by and large, the basic story/conclusion should remain true.

With that said, there's probably *never* been an outline so meticulously thought out that, upon fleshing out the story, the writer never varies from the preconceived ending. And sometimes tosses out the original ending and substitute a completely new one!

I don't think I've ever written a mystery—from short story to novel—in which the ending has held up to any and all changes I've made along the way. In fact, I think that's a big part of the allure of writing mysteries—or any other genre for that matter. The human mind is capable of conceiving things from day to day or even moment to moment that could never have been anticipated originally. People like to organize their thoughts; the mind prefers to wing it. That's part of the challenge of creating literature.

Don't get me wrong. I'm not advocating eliminating the outline *before* you sit down to flesh out the story—nor even to minimize the time you spend working on it beforehand. That almost always leads to disaster. A good outline is like a roadmap of where you want to go and how you want to get there. You wouldn't set out on a trip from Detroit to San Diego without consulting a map or GPS, would you? Of course not. But, that doesn't mean that you can't stop off at a Dairy Queen in Oklahoma City for a burger and some fries or swing by Zion's National Park for a day-long side trip of hiking and sightseeing. And it doesn't mean you won't take all the facets of your journey into consideration from day-to-day and change your route mid-stream as you think best. If you find out that 300 miles of Interstate ahead of you is closed down to one lane for construction, I'm betting you'll alter your plans and drive around the headaches. The important thing is that you end up in San Diego and not in San Francisco. For many reasons.

So, spend as much time as possible working up the strongest outline you can, modifying it as you think of new things or as your book emerges with a life all its own. Beyond that, enjoy the writing process. That's where the fun *really* begins.

Where can I find respectable resources for learning how to write better?

First, get the help you need from your mind. Get inside yourself. Become a psychoanalyst. Think about the story. Feel it. *See* the characters (whether or not it's fiction). Recognize their hardships. Understand their motivations. Question their actions and why they did what they did. Explore their fears and their passions. Paint a vivid picture *in your mind* first, and then struggle with the hard part, which is putting that picture into words that will trigger in others the same mental imagery it triggered in you. That's what being a writer is all about—creating compelling *imagery* that allows others to see what's in your mind, to see what you "see." For example:

"He felt vexed" is pretty lame. "The demons swallowed him whole" says the same thing in far more vivid terms. Whereas the first clause *says* it, the second one *shows* it.

Beyond that, a good word processor will have a synonym dictionary that may come in handy. And a style book such as *The Chicago Manual of Style* can help with the everyday quirks of style, punctuation, common usage, and grammar.

But don't let any external books or other people's interpretations of what you should be doing and how you should be doing it come between you and your "baby." Create it the way you want it first, and then look around for outside help if necessary to fine-tune it for pitching to the marketplace.

Remember: Great books aren't created in a test tube or in a laboratory; they're created in the mind.

How do I finish writing a book I'm really enjoying?

First, outline your book, something I suspect you didn't do when you started, or you wouldn't be asking this question now. Go back to the introduction or the first chapter (wherever you began your book), read it, and write a chapter outline for it. Short and to the point. Cover only the main events. It may take one sentence, or it may take ten. The

ABOUT WRITING RIGHT

point is to summarize each chapter right up until the point in the book where you stopped writing, like this:

Margot found out from a neighbor that she'd been adopted. Devastated, she confronted her "parents" who explained they thought they were doing the right thing. Margot decided to run away, but to where? And how?

Next, think through the unwritten chapters, and write a summary of each of them. Again, keep each chapter summary short, covering only the major points, as in the example above. Continue in that manner until you have the entire book blocked out from beginning to end.

After that, go back and start writing, filling in the blanks of the unwritten chapters and expanding their summaries until you're comfortable that you've said all you want or need to say within each chapter. Add dialogue, narrative, description, and whatever else is required to turn a summary into a chapter, to "fine tune" it into literature. Repeat the process with the remaining blocked-out summaries until you've finished each of the chapters in the book.

Finally, print the book out on paper—very important. Then, lock yourself away somewhere for privacy, go to the beginning of the book, and begin reading each page *out loud*, making brief notations in the margins where something doesn't sound "right." Even a check mark or an "X" will work at this point. You want to do this while reading out loud because the ear hears far more accurately than the eye-brain combo does when you read silently. You'll find some weak spots that need changing and others that need fleshing out. You may even find a few repetitive areas that need cutting out entirely.

Once you've read the entire book aloud and made your notations, go back and rework whatever needs changing. Then, put the edited manuscript aside for a day or two before going back to the beginning and re-reading the book—out loud again—to make sure all of the latest edits you made work. (You may find printing the book out a second time helpful if you made a lot of changes to the original printed version.)

When you're satisfied that the book is just the way you want it, congratulate yourself. You have just completed a book of which you can be proud to place your by-line.

What should you know about writing before starting a book?

D. J. Herda

There are as many different ways of preparing yourself to write a book as there are writers doing so! After ninety-some conventionally published books, I've found the best way for me is to work out in my head the rough storyline from start to finish. Then I set about transferring the synopsis to paper. It needn't be long at this point—perhaps only a page total; the story will dictate the length. I'll do the fleshing out later.

I set that synopsis aside for a few days, continuing to think about it while I go about other business. If I come up with some new elements worth including or some new directions or characters to introduce, I'll go back and add them to the synopsis before I forget them. Finally, when I'm convinced the story is pretty much the way I want to write it (that will change along the way, but for now at least it should be pretty close to finalized), I find the logical starting/stopping points in the synopsis and turn them into chapters. The first incident in the synopsis might be my main character's background (perhaps comprising only a single sentence in the synopsis), so I label that sentence Chapter One. That might be followed in the synopsis by the night everything turned sour and how that involved my character (another two or three synopsis sentences), so I label those sentences Chapter Two and so on.

Once I've finished turning the synopsis into sequentially numbered chapters, I go back and start filling in as many details to each chapter as possible. My hope is to have several pages of details for each of the chapters I've roughed in. A ten-chapter book, then, might have three or four pages per chapter or thirty to forty total pages of fleshed-out material. Include as many important details and those "trigger points" that will need revisiting in later chapters as possible. This new-and-expanded material will be my finished Chapter Outline and will from then on be my book-writing "Blueprint."

Finally, once I'm convinced I've fleshed out the chapters as much as possible, I sit down and begin writing out the story in my own literary voice, telling it the way I normally speak, incident by incident, chapter by chapter, as if relaying the story to a good friend over a couple of beers. I repeat that process until I've written the entire book. As I write each chapter, I'll find areas I hadn't thought about before and add those to the chapter, and that's fine. The chapter outline isn't written in stone! Of course, that might mean I'll have to adjust some elements of earlier or later chapters in order to fit in with the additional new material and still make sense, but that's no big deal.

When the book is finally finished, I set it aside for several days to a week or longer before going back and "editing" it, which sometimes involves polishing and sometimes means rewriting entire sections that I see—after some distance from the book—don't work. In the end, I'll know when I've gone through it, both editing and fine-tuning, enough.

Next, I lock myself in a room so no one else in the house thinks I'm crazy, and I read through the book out loud, start to finish, to "hear" with my ears what I've been "hearing" with my eyes and mind while I was writing. As I read out loud, I mark for change anything that doesn't sound right. Then, I go back and make the appropriate changes later. When I'm convinced it's the best it can be, I send the book off to my agent to begin pitching to publishers.

Again, this is my approach, and after nearly fifty years of writing books, using all different preparatory approaches imaginable, I've found this blueprint the best, easiest, least painful, and most effective way of getting the job done for me. Hopefully it, or some derivative process, will work for you, too.

Do you advise a scriptwriter to work from an outline or just write the script from scratch? I have an idea of what I want to write.

Outline, outline, outline, outline, outline, outline, outline.

Or not.

Actually, unless you have the best memory and most organized brain on the planet, an outline will keep you moving in the right direction, prevent you from going astray, and guide you to the finish line with your script.

Of course, outlining isn't the only way to go. You can also wing it. A lot of writers prefer working that way. I used to be one of them, although I don't advocate doing so anymore. In fact, I'd guess that probably 98 percent of everyone sitting down to memorialize a story longer than a dozen pages works from an outline. Or *should*. I've seen outlines come in handy when writing a short script or story, too. Have you ever heard of storyboarding? That's just an outline with pictures. In fact, outlines are even valuable when writing nonfiction articles—

just to keep track of all the points, issues, sources, and quoted material as you put all the pieces together.

What happens if you decide not to "waste your time" by outlining a story you're sure you can tell from start to finish without organizational help? Either not much (you forget where you're headed or, more often, how to get there as you become overwhelmed by details) or too much (you begin wandering all over the place with auxiliary information and never do make it to the goal line in one piece).

For those writers who are concerned that an outline will stifle their spontaneity, nonsense. Outlines, like dishes, are made to be broken. If your mind or your gut tells you to add some material that you hadn't included in your outline, do it. Adjust the outline to show what you've added and keep future events on track. Conversely, if you think the outline needs some cutting here or there (say, a passage you wrote just doesn't "flow," or you no longer think it's necessary to the story), cut it from your book and adjust the outline accordingly.

That's one of the beauties of outlines. You can adjust a few words, cut or add whatever you want, rearrange to better advance the timeline or story, and you'll spend a lot less energy than if you had to do that to the main body of the work. See what I mean?

Do I outline when I write? Absolutely. Always? Absolutely. Well, not absolutely. Sometimes I'm in such a hurry to dig into the meat of a story that I charge ahead, thinking that I can always come back and create an outline later. And, you know what? I always do. Usually when I'm around page 87 and can't remember what I've written to that point and can't figure out how to keep things moving or where to go from there or whether or not I'd already introduced a minor character. So, I go back and create an outline, half in retrospect and half the way I should have done it in the first place. And, FYI, doing it later is always more difficult than doing it at the start.

Another benefit of outlining is that producers and directors, not to mention editors and publishers, nearly always want to see an outline of the story at some point down the line. So, if you're going to have to create an outline anyway before you collect that big paycheck, why not do it upfront and make your work that much easier, more efficient, and more productive? It's your decision, of course. You know where I stand on the subject. I've seen far too many stories over the years run amok because the writer lost control of his own work—particularly young, inexperienced writers. That's something that's far less likely to happen when working from an outline.

Your call.

I've just finished my novel's first draft. What's the typical process for editing it?

First, I have read good suggestions from several writers on this topic over the years. I've also read some really ridiculous ones.

Second, keep in mind that what works for one or two or ten thousand writers won't necessarily work for you.

Third, if your writing contains phrases such as "I and my co-author," as one of the commentators' suggestions did, plan on hiring a first-rate, experienced editor who also has written numerous books of his own, gotten published, and received rave reviews. One who ideally has worked professionally as an editor. If you're not a professionally trained editor, the chances of you producing a book clean enough to submit to publishers are low. Remember: Everyone can write a book; not everyone can write a technically perfect book (or come even close to it). And certainly not everyone is capable of self-editing it.

Fourth, contrary to popular opinion, writing the first draft is *not* the most demanding part of writing. In fact, it's one of the easiest. Honing that first draft to perfection, pitching it so that it piques the interest of an editor, and seeing it through to publication are far more demanding tasks than sitting down and spilling out your soul. Not necessarily more creative, but definitely more demanding.

Now, as to a process for editing, those commentators who advocate starting each day's writing by first re-reading the previous day's work would be "right on" if that's what you had asked. That technique is great for eliminating the possibility of "writer's block" or even avoiding stumbling into a chapter without having set the stage for it in your previous chapters. Since you have already finished the book, though, that advice won't help you here.

But you can use a variation of that process in editing, assuming once again that you're qualified to edit your own work, which means that you're knowledgeable, receptive to making changes in your work, and objective. I suggest you edit the first chapter or X number of pages, stop, put the book aside for a day or more before continuing. Then, review what you edited the day before prior to moving forward. Resting in between editing sessions gives your brain a short vacation so that it approaches the project with a clean slate. Reviewing your previous edits gives you a second chance to correct things while getting you "up to speed" from where you left off.

Follow the same process with the subsequent edits you make, always beginning that day's editing by first reviewing what you edited the day before.

Finally, when you've finished editing each chapter twice in succession, put the book aside for a week or two or a month or more. I'm not kidding. Then print out the edited version, and read it out loud without any interruptions. (This assumes that you don't have kids, a wife, a girlfriend, a roommate, or a cat, not necessarily in that order.) As you read, make notes of things that don't "sound" right to your ears. A pencil mark in the margin may be all that's necessary at this point.

When you've finished reading as much out loud as you wish during that session, go back and re-read those marked areas and make whatever changes you think will help correct the problems you found there.

When you've finished your last out-loud editing pass, assuming again that you're a qualified editor, you can be pretty sure the book is very close to going public. If you're still not certain, hire a professional editor to give it a quick once-through and let you know what you may have missed. A cursory edit with a paragraph or two of generalized comments shouldn't cost more than a few hundred dollars. If you've done your job, there shouldn't be much for the editor to point out.

All this rigmarole begs the question: Is this a lot of work to do after you've completed writing your first draft? Of course, it is. Is it as difficult and time-consuming as it sounds? Absolutely. After all, if this were an easy process, everyone would be a writer, and no one would be left to read other people's works.

With all that said, I do offer you congrats on what you've accomplished so far. Just remember that you have a good way further to go before your book is really finished and you're home free!

In writing, what's the difference between a scene and a chapter?

ABOUT WRITING RIGHT

Actually, contrary to some common responses I've seen to this question over the years, one scene in a book (as differentiated from one in a play—the two are completely different) may comprise an entire chapter. Usually, though, several scenes are included in a chapter. A scene is a tightly connected series of events, usually containing a beginning, a middle, and an end. It varies in length and should be conclusive:

John meets Marsha in the parking lot, and the two reminisce before agreeing to go to dinner together.

A chapter is often two or more scenes that that are somehow tied together. Chapters, like scenes, have an arbitrary starting and stopping point in the story. They're arbitrary because determining their lengths and where they start and stop is up to the author. For a chapter to stand on its own, it, too, usually has some sort of beginning, middle, and end—even if the conclusion is a cliffhanger designed to get the reader to turn the page to begin the following chapter to discover what that end might be.

So, it's up to the author as to how many scenes, or mini-stories or vignettes or images or whatever you want to call them, fall within a single chapter. I have written chapters of forty pages with five or six different scenes or more. I have also written some chapters with a single short scene of only a page or a page-and-a-half, usually for dramatic effect to *shock* the reader into continuing. (And, by the way, it often works.)

Most readers, though, feel comfortable with chapters that include a number of scenes that interrelate (or will eventually) to one another—usually via some relatively connected timeline. When two consecutive scenes are dramatically and unmistakably different from one another or separated by a noticeable passage of time or by different locations, the author should consider beginning a new chapter.

This is a basic simplification, of course, but it holds true for most literature, depending upon the scope, vision, and expertise of the author.

Is a 50,000-word manuscript a novel?

If you're self-publishing, you can call it anything you want—a novel, a novella, or even a really long paragraph. Your readers most likely won't know and even more likely won't care. You might get a couple of wayward glances when you get together at your next writing workshop from fellow scribes who have self-published their own novels of 60 or 70 thousand words or more, but, hey, nobody ever said being an author was easy.

What really matters, far more than the opinions you can solicit on the Internet or virtually anywhere else, is what conventional publishers think. Again, only *if* you hope to entice a publisher into issuing you a contract. I recall vividly one author who submitted a "novel" of 45,000 words to a conventional publisher only to have the editor reply, "This isn't a novel, it's a pamphlet!"

Publishers understand better than anyone else that consumers won't drop $25 on a hardcover book no thicker than a *Sports Illustrated* magazine. Readers want *value* for their buck. Value means good writing, a good storyline, and plenty of it. If a reader gets the impression that a particular publisher is short-changing him out of the value of his dollar, he'll quit buying books from that publisher *and* that author. Period.

Once again, things boil down to self-publishing vs. conventional publishing. Even if you self-publish and sell your 125-page "novel" for 95 cents, chance are you won't get any complaints. Sell it for 2 or 3 bucks, and you'll hear lots of squawking. If the reader doesn't feel he's gotten his money's worth, your name will very quickly turn to mud.

My advice then: Lengthen it to at least 60- to 70-thousand words. If you don't know how, learn. Only then can you say without equivocation that you've written a *novel*.

What's the best person to use in writing a novel in which you want to contrast two different characters with conflicting personalities and opinions?

The easiest way to present contrasting perceptions and opinions of multiple protagonists is, without a doubt, through the third-person omniscient point-of-view. In it, the narrator has complete control over the entire novel, including what he reveals to the reader and when. First person is a lot tougher to pull off for numerous reasons, and it's certainly not a serious consideration for an inexperienced novelist. It's also far tougher to change character perspectives in first person than it is in third, not to mention the fact that, in first person, each point-of-view can only reveal a limited amount of information to the reader at any given point in the novel, depending upon what each protagonist can be expected to know at that time. That often results in reader confusion, which, for a writer, is not a good thing to create. Trust me on that.

Some beginning scribes have the mistaken notion that, since they're "first-person people" who refer to themselves in the first person (I did this, I went there, I saw that), writing a novel in the first-person point-of-view is as natural as falling off a log. That may be so in a memoir or a diary but far from it in long fiction. You have enough to worry about when writing a novel in third person; why ask for more trouble by trying to force your point-of-view into first?

If adverbs are bad, why do they appear in best-selling novels?

Best-selling is *not* the same as critically acclaimed. In fact, they are often diametrically opposed. As for adverbs, their use is considered a sign of sloppy writing. Want it down and dirty? Use a weak verb, and rely on an adverb to help pull you across the finish line. That's where most sloppy writers fall. Instead of saying, for example, "He sings badly," why not say, "His singing bombed." Same meaning written in much stronger terms (or, falling back on the adverbial perspective, same meaning written more *strongly*).

The truth is that, if you select the right verb, you won't have to use adverbs very often (adverbial translation: you'll *rarely* have to use adverbs). In short, there are always two roads to travel through life—the hard one and the easy one. Or, as pertains to writing, the thoughtful one and the careless one.

As for best-selling authors using adverbs in their books—again, I think you doth protest too much. No one ever said you can't use *any* adverbs. That would be virtually impossible in a book-length work. But most beginning writers, and even a frighteningly large number of experienced pros, rely on them far too often. Again, best-selling books aren't necessarily well-written books. They're best-selling books for one or more reasons.

I can't explain it any better than that. (Adverbial: I can't put it any more *clearly*.)

What is the rule for adding a space after an opening parenthesis mark?

There is no rule for a space after an open parenthesis mark, at least not in American English, because doing so is wrong. As for the varying rules of other countries, sorry. I can't help with those. I'm fortunate to understand those of my own country let alone those of any others!

How do you plan out a new book, particularly each chapter?

There is no doubt about it. Having used multiple methods of writing a book (or anything of any notable length, for that matter), creating an outline is the *only* way to work. An outline helps crystallize in your mind what you want the story to be, where it begins and ends, what's in the middle, and who the major and minor players are going to be. It also helps you to focus on smaller chunks (chapters) so that you can more easily identify any weak spots or areas that need pumping up.

With that said, an outline isn't a legal document: it's a guide. I start my outline with a single paragraph or two that defines the book from start to finish, like a shortened version of Cliff's Notes. Next, I identify the major sections of that outline (or synopsis, if you like) and give them chapter headings, from 1 to 10 or however many chapters the material seems to indicate are needed.

Next, I go through the different chapter outlines, expanding, tightening, and adding or eliminating elements and characters for each one as they come to mind and seem to make sense.

When I'm convinced the complete chapter outline includes everything I want in the finished book, I begin writing, using each chapter outline as a guide for writing that chapter. I fill in between the "blanks" and add dialogue, description, and other elements as necessary. That's where creativity comes in.

As you write, you're going to find that you think of things you hadn't thought of while writing the outline, and you'll want to put those things into the book. That means the order or scope of the outline may change. Timelines may be altered, new characters may be introduced, old characters may make no sense anymore and have to be eliminated, Chapter 3 may make more sense appearing later in the book as Chapter 7, etc. Reworking or tweaking each chapter as you write may also mean Chapter 1 may work better as two chapters, or it may mean there's no reason to break between chapters 1 and 2, so you end up combining the two of them into a single chapter.

Now, you may be thinking: With all this "winging it" going on, why bother with a chapter outline at all? The answer is that all writers use outlines, whether or not they realize it. Even writers who like to write by the seat of their pants have an outline in their heads. The only thing that separates them from other writers is that they don't like to take the time (or discipline) to write their outlines down. They'd rather rely on their memories, which seldom serve them as well as a written outline can.

So, the simplest, most effect, and most productive way to write a book, chapter-by-chapter, beginning to end, is to work from a chapter outline, keeping in mind that an outline is merely a guide to wherever it is you ultimately want to go with your book. Clear?

What qualifies a book as "Young Adult"?

"Young Adult" (YA) is a category written for readers from ages 12 to 18. Even though the genre applies to adolescent teens, nearly half of all YA readers are adults. Besides the age group of the readers the author is targeting, the work should also tie the age and experience of the protagonist to that of a young adult. In other words, the hero or heroine should be a young adult with young adult interests.

While different book publishers may have various age groups into which they slot their acquisitions, most adhere closely to this age range. That's for the benefit of their sales departments. Book marketers and salespeople need to know to which age group a book is geared in order to sell that book to a store or online outlet.

YA books aren't necessarily fiction or nonfiction but can be either. While the subject matter for YA books is mostly wide open, much of YA's appeal is to those areas in life that cause pre-adolescents and teens the most concern—areas such as sex, drugs, dating, alcohol, interracial relationships, and family life. Surprise!

Some of the category-bending attributes of a YA that might entice adult readers to jump on board include advanced subjects and the main character's advanced level of social awareness, experience, intellect, and activity. In other words, if she's a girl, she's Ramona Quimby on steroids. If your Young Adult protagonist is more advanced than most other kids her age, adults are more likely to pick up the book and identify with it. That's true even with the sappiest (oops, did I say that?) and most naive examples of tween-sex series such as Nancy Drew and Trixie Belden. Often, adults will read a YA book simply because it's easier to read than adult books, faster-paced, and shorter.

Oh, and did I mention "more fun"?

One special note of caution for developing writers in search of their first book sales: Contrary to popular opinion, YA's are *not* easier to write than adult books. A lower level of sophistication doesn't make writing a YA a walk through the park. Also, knowing what interests YA readers these days is not always easy for an adult to determine, and wording the book to a specific reading level can be trying.

Still, for YA writers who want to make a difference by influencing their reading audiences from a young age on, YA's are worth considering.

What's the best way for me to begin writing my first book?

"It was a dark and rainy night."

Seriously. Feel free to use that as your opening line. No credits necessary, free of charge.

Actually, I'd be amused at so many bad responses from various commentators who seem to like to evolve their personal habits into immutable laws except for the fact that these "experts" are doing harm to young writers. The unvarnished truth is that there is no "best way" to start writing your first book. But there *are* innumerable ways from which you can choose, the most common being:

1. *See the book in your mind.* Or, rather, see the *story* that will become your book. And, no, it doesn't matter if you call it a book or a draft or a toenail. What matters is that you understand the story, where it starts, and where it concludes. Every book has a beginning, a middle, and an end. That applies equally to novels as it does to how-to or self-help books. I already gave you the opening for your first book; now, all you have to do is envision your story from there. Once you can see that story from start to finish, you'll have an easier time committing it to paper. You'll be working from a "mental roadmap" of your story. Will you need to go back and edit, rewrite, revise, and invest more blood, sweat, and tears into your baby after you've finished your first draft? Of course. But that's an immutable part of the writing game, no matter how you begin your book.

2. *Create an outline.* Many writers start their books with an outline. Some create a general synopsis of the story from beginning to

end; others, a chapter-by-chapter, running account of what happens where and when. Some writers do both, creating a one- or two-page synopsis first and then breaking that down into individual chapters. *This happens in chapter one. This happens in chapter two,* and so on. Once again, the purpose of beginning with an outline is to make the transference to paper easier and less convoluted.

3. *Wing it.* Yes, that's what I said. Sit down, think of something of interest to you, and start writing. That's how I began my first novel, and I'd like to say it went flawlessly. But, of course, I can't. It was a disaster. Winging it may work for some writers (Jack Kerouac springs to mind), but it was a brutally demanding approach for me, leading to numerous stall-outs, side roads, and wasted time and energy, not to mention paper, typewriter ribbons, and frustration. For my second novel, I began with a chapter-by-chapter outline and expanded the story from there. The book practically wrote itself. Again, it required innumerable rewrites until it was precisely the way I wanted it (well, mostly), but so what? You have to *write* a book before you can *rewrite* a book! Get my point?

So, there you have three basic approaches that are commonly employed by writers starting out on their initial literary journey. Pick the one you think will work best for you, and stick to it. Unless you find it doesn't work all that well after all. In that case, you're on your own.

"It was a dark and rainy night."

How can you tell when to leave something out of your writing or put it in?

You can accomplish that in one of two ways. The first is by asking yourself questions: *Is this necessary? Is this something the reader can figure out for himself? Is this something the reader needs help in understanding? Is this something that will cause the reader confusion if I leave it out? Is this something that will anger or frustrate the reader if I leave it out?*

The second way is by placing yourself in the reader's skin. That's not always the easiest thing to do because you have to divorce yourself from … well, *you*. Become someone else. Forget that you're the author and the creator of what you're asking the reader to evaluate with every word he reads. If you can do that, you can tell when the author (that means *you*, silly goose!) is coddling you or underestimating your cognitive abilities or talking down to you. If, as the reader, you find any of that taking place, you, as the author, had better start making some cuts.

There's an old saying from Shakespeare or George Patton or Tucker Carlson or someone: *When in doubt, leave it out*. If you're ever unsure of whether or not to include some information that isn't necessary to reveal, give the reader the benefit of the doubt and leave it out. He'll thank you for not pandering to him and for assuming he has enough brains to figure things out for himself.

Why do writers have their male heroes fall in love with their female villains?

Just as "Boy Meets Girl/Boy Loses Girl/Boy Gets Girl" is a classic storyline for romance, "Boy Meets Girl/Girl Entices Boy/Boy Survives Girl" is a classic formula for both film noir and literature. And it's not a wish-fulfillment fantasy at all, as some people may believe; it's traditional Christian-Judaea development. Ever hear of Adam and Eve and the Garden of Eden? Tristan and Isolde? And a million other tales spun over the epochs?

The fact that a man is lured nearly to his death by a woman who starts out walking the straight and narrow and eventually goes bad and lures him to her side of the garbage heap needs a catalyst. That catalyst is love. That gives the woman an advantage over the man: "How could the woman who loves me do me wrong?"

Love, in the unlikely event that you've never been there, has a way of muddying the waters. It taints one's thinking ability and rationality. It clouds reality. For both men *and* women. What better (or easier, more effective, more engrossing, *better* grossing) mechanism to enable a woman to lure a man astray than through the blinding love he has for her?

Now, for all those socio-psychoanalytic critics out there preparing to castigate me for my chauvinistic attitudes: I didn't do it. I didn't make it. I just reported it.

If you want to alter the facts, go for it. If you want to change reality, good luck. If you want to influence Hollywood, stop spending your

ABOUT WRITING RIGHT

hard-earned money on film noir and start spending it on *Chainsaw Massacre 57: The Happy Years*. Otherwise, just go along for the ride, and enjoy the show.

In the end, believe me. I'm the quintessential witness for the defense, making me something of an expert. I've assembled several short stories and a novella into a volume entitled *Chi-Town Blues* that's loaded with classic noir plus one story of noir in reverse—where the guy tries to get the girl to join him in his illicit affair only to have her switch the table on him.

It may be formulaic and done to death, but it still seems wildly entertaining and rewarding, whether for readers or film-watchers. And, perhaps, just a little bit narcissistic. That may be the best reason of all that it remains such a popular theme.

How do I fill in between the beginning and the end of my book, which I already know? How can I write the rest so that it makes sense?

You've received a lot of answers to your question, most of which are unnecessarily convoluted while others are outright wrong.

You say you *know* what the ending to your story is. You don't say you have *written* it yet. Big difference. Now, how do you fill in what happens from where the story begins to where you picture it ending? Simple.

Ask yourself questions. You know the ending. You have a beginning (wherever you choose to start your story). Now, ask yourself, "What happens next?" Think logically, just as your character would. Then ask, "What happens after that" and then "How about after that?"

Then introduce some conflict. "What if this character shows up and does this?" And "what if this happens to my protagonist next?"

Keep adding elements leading to your desired ending. And *go back and read out loud*. If there's too great a jump between elements, fill it in with something exciting or meaningful or prophetic about the character, the challenges he or she must overcome, or a shifting storyline. Keep in mind where you want the story to end.

In short, *think*. And then *ask*. And then *think* some more and *ask* some more. Put on your prosecuting attorney's hat and place yourself in a court of law. Do whatever it takes to keep those questions coming.

Retain the best answers and write them into the story. Discard the rest. Adjust the ending you have in your mind, if necessary, only to produce a more logical storyline as you move toward the conclusion. But do so only *if necessary*.

Before long, you'll be at the top of the hill, looking back at the long climb you've just made.

By the way, all writers struggle with how to get from Point A to Point B, what to include along the journey, and what to eliminate. It's part of the fun of writing. Remember what I just said: *It's part of the fun of writing.*

"What if, what if, what if?"

Ask, as the adage goes, and ye shall receive. In this case, beneficial answers that lead to your (possibly revised) story's conclusion.

What's the best way for one male character to strangle another in my book?

To death.

Seriously, if you have to ask a question such as this, you're not ready to tackle writing a novel. Stories should evolve in your head *long* before you sit down to commit them to writing. The fact that you don't yet know how one man is going to strangle another tells me you haven't thought this thing through. That means the method of strangulation is the least of your problems. Until you have worked out the entire story in your mind (minus those surprises that pop up and bite even the most diligent, meticulous, and anal author in the butt), you're going to run into one problem after another before finally throwing in the towel and giving up in frustration.

The answer to your question? *You* decide! *You* think it through. *You* consider all the different options available to you, both reasonable and otherwise. Once you've done that and worked out the rest of the plot or storyline in your head, you'll find you won't need to ask someone else to step in and help you write your book. You'll be primed and ready to sit down and tackle it yourself. And far more likely to do a better job than if you were flying by the seat of your pants!

Or letting someone else take the yoke and do it for you.

I read that every good novel has "flat" characters, but what are they, and how are they used in creative fiction?

ABOUT WRITING RIGHT

Let's step back for a moment and think about *characterization* in general. The word, itself, strikes fear into the hearts of trembling young novelists. What I'd like to know is ... *why*?

The characters in your fiction make the whole thing work. It doesn't matter how brilliant a plot you construct or how lively the action. It doesn't mean a thing if you paint the most glowing descriptive passages ever. The whole book isn't worth a tinker's damn if your characterization is flawed. Here's why.

People care about people. Or, at least, they *want* to. They may love them; they may hate them. But the bottom line is they're empathetic toward them. Even books that have non-people as their characters (remember Stephen King's *Christine*?) imbed those non-humans with human-like characteristics, making them, in effect, *people*.

So, what are some of the things your readers want to know about the characters in a book?

1.) *Physical appearance*. Readers like to be able to "see" the characters in their minds. That's where descriptive writing comes in. Take this description, for example:

Studley was small in size, 5-foot-nothing, with saucer-sized eyes that never seemed to close even when he slept. His nose was larger than normal, shaped like a walnut before it's husked, and his mouth turned down at one corner, down even farther at the other. His skin showed the color of concrete before water is added--ashen, dry, powdery, mildewed, with small blue and green flecks in it, like a piece of aged Stilton pocked with mold. He bore none of the features that could normally be called "striking." Yet, he held a twinkle in those saucer-eyes, a glow that displayed a love for life unlike any anyone had ever seen before.

Contrast that with this:

Studley was the kind of guy who was unique; you'd never call him your average Joe.

Do you get a better understanding of what Studley looks like from the first or from the second example? Let me hazard a rough guess.

It's called imagery, and that's what makes fiction work. Words don't relay a picture to a reader; images do. Images such as "saucer-sized eyes" and "a walnut before it's husked" and "the color of concrete before water is added" and "aged Stilton pocked with mold."

Paint your characters' descriptions with images, and you'll have your readers panting for more.

2.) *Internal makeup.* This is the stuff that powers a character, that makes him go. It's what's inside, a character's character, and it can be a strong motivational tool. Check this out:

Sean had the kind of fire burning in his belly that you read about. On days when everything went well, he was all fired up, burning, yearning for some action. On those other days, those days when everything turned to shit no matter how hard you tried to prevent it, he was worse. He carried the thought of revenge like a carpenter carries a tool belt, from one day to the next, from hour to hour, minute to minute. He was obsessed with the stuff. He never ate, drank, or slept without feeling the need for revenge gnawing inside of him, trying to escape, like a rat chewing its way to freedom from inside a barn ... one angry, determined bite after another.

And now this:

Angelica was always upset. Nothing ever seemed to calm her down.

Do you get a stronger sense of a character's motivation from the first or the second example? Once again, the key is imagery—creating it in such a way as to reveal what makes the character tick.

3.) *Personal history.* This is what your characters have experienced before the reader ever had a chance to meet them. It's what determines their internal makeup (and sometimes, even their physical appearance). For example:

Bartell's face lit up from within, not with a pleasant, warm, loving kind of glow, but with a maniacal fanaticism that threatened to devour him. In fact, it almost had. When he was just a kid loading hay in the mow, one of his brothers thought it would be fun to scare him. Bartell had always been afraid of fire. So, three days later, still wrapped in the nebulous protection of Intensive Care, the first of the bandages came off ... and eight months after that, after four attempts at covering the damage through plastic surgery, the last. There was little difference between the two unveilings. But there was a world of difference in Bartell. Staring at his grotesque, misshapen form in the mirror, he vowed not to get even. No, that would be too easy, too predictable. He vowed, instead, to remove the plague that had haunted him for most of his life. He vowed to share his misfortunes with his brother the best way he knew how. He vowed retribution.

And this:

Margo's life had been wrapped in sorrow ever since the accident. She walked with a limp still. And the anger she felt because of it followed her.

What's it all about, you ask? And what does all this have to do with "flat" characters? I'm glad you asked.

In each instance above, the longer, more elaborate descriptive detailing of the characters creates what's called a "rounded" character. It is someone the writer intentionally fleshes out. It is someone the author wants to expose to the reader because that character is going to be pivotal within the story. He's there to make a difference. That character *needs* to be known and understood--pitied or admired, shunned or respected. Upon that character (and usually other nearly equally rounded characters within the story) lies the success of the writing.

But imagine what that writing would be like if *every* character that passed through your pages received the same rounded development. The bellboy who shows the young couple to their room before disappearing from the story completely ... the gas-station attendant who makes a four-paragraph appearance never to be seen again ... the priest saying mass one Sunday and never popping up again. What a slow, boring, agonizingly distracting read *that* would be!

That's where "flat" characters come in. Not only do flat characters receive less development than their rounded brethren, but also they *deserve* less. Think of them as foils, human bridges to get from one scene or set of occurrences to the next. Then, you'll see how ineffective giving them too much "roundness" would be to the overall flow of the story.

Flat characters serve to connect the dots in a work of fiction, but they also tend to revitalize the *rounded* characters by their very comparison. As the writer, you throw together a flat character; you spend tons of time developing a rounded character (not necessarily all at once, of course, but throughout the entire work). But in so doing, you automatically and instinctively trigger in the reader a feeling of which characters are most important (and, therefore, to which they need to pay the most attention) and which are little more than window dressing or stage props.

Make sense?

So, the next time you sit down to write a work of fiction, take the time to identify those characters that are rounded versus those that are flat. Understand the difference between the two, and spend more time developing the first than the second. You'll find that characterization becomes much more manageable... when you're not trying to make too much out of too little.

I understand the need for "rounded" characters in a story, but I'm not sure how to create them or why it matters.

Think about one of your favorite classic stories in fiction. Something you enjoyed reading more than anything else as a child. Something you read over and over again. Was it *Alice in Wonderland*? *Treasure Island*? *Black Beauty*? *Harry Potter*?

Now, ask yourself why you enjoyed reading that story so much.

ABOUT WRITING RIGHT

The answer is nearly always the same. The main character. The protagonist. The person around whom the story centered.

Characters are what the reader identifies and empathizes with; they are what the reader loves to love ... or hate. Many great stories with weak plots, shoddy descriptive passages, and marginal dialogue have relied for their greatness solely on characterization. If you don't believe me, go back and read Hemingway's *The Sun Also Rises* or *The Old Man and the Sea*. Papa's works are notoriously weak on storyline and only marginal on descriptive passages and dialogue. Where Hemingway works his magic is through his characters. When he writes about Ezra Pound or Gertrude Stein or even F. Scott Fitzgerald, we develop a love-hate relationship with those characters that is strong enough to keep us coming back, looking for more pages to turn.

So, how do you get from here to there? How do you take a blank screen and fill it with lovable (or at least empathetic) characters? Let's take a look at some of the things that have always worked for me.

See Them! First and foremost, you need to take time to visualize your characters, one by one. See them in your mind. Ask yourself what it is about their looks that makes them stand out, that makes you notice them in a crowd. Come up with some mental images of each character. How does he look dressed casually, formally, and ready for bed? How does he look not dressed at all?

How do his eyes move? Do they dart around quickly, like those of an anxious ferret, or are they slow to move, cautious, hesitant to be seen in the eyes of others? How does he stand? How does he hold his hands? What does his mouth look like? Can you equate that mouth with something non-human (a "gaping hole" is a bit trite; how about a "great stone cavern")? Often, equating a human physical trait with a non-human feature enables the reader to conjure up a whole boatload of visual images in just a few words.

Show Them! Once you've painted a mental image of your character's physical appearance in your mind, set about sketching him out in a few short paragraphs of descriptive passage that match your own internal vision. Here's an example from *Solid Stiehl--The Death and Life of Hymie Stiehl*:

I quickly surveyed his large, bulging eyes, puffed out and encircled by several rings of time, then let my gaze drift across his thick, meaty face to his nose—a great bulbous affair that shone bluish-grey in the cast of a long bank of fluorescent lights stretched out overhead. Running from one side of his nose to the other were scores of tiny blue-green lines—ribbons of highway seen from a jetliner, at first barely visible from high above the city, then growing ever larger and more prominent with each passing second until they threatened to explode into a billion shards of concrete and shattered steel.

His mouth was the only thing about him that did not seem too large for his overall carriage. Not his mouth, exactly, but his lips. Two thin lines that, later when I got to know him, I would see purse out in an effort to expand their size, as though he knew these mere slivers of pastel were the one feature out of keeping with his greatness and set about to change them.

These two short grafs say as much about the physical appearance of the man as anything; yet, in doing so, they also reveal something about his character and internal motivation. Just a touch of vanity appears to reside in this character, which we learn when he tries to expand the insignificant slivers of his lips to make himself look more the role of personified greatness.

Notice, though, that while the paragraphs are revealing, they're not overwhelming. The reader doesn't need to know every physical aspect of the character all at once--and, in fact, he doesn't *want* to know everything. Just as we come to observe through time things about the real people around us, so, too, must the writer reveal those things about his characters at a staggered pace, a little at a time. Dumping seventeen pages of physical description on the reader at once not only places an unbearable burden on the reader's retentive powers but also bogs down the flow of the story.

Here's more from the same book:

"You know him?" one of my students asked casually as we stood in the hall, talking of literary greatness and how best to achieve it.

"Who?" I asked foolishly, following the gaze of a pimply faced young literary radical down the corridor to a stoop-shouldered old goat with pock-marked skin and dead stogie dangling from a pale and puckered mouth. "Him?" I'd known of Hyman Stiehl, the great and famous poet laureate, for years. But who was this? I turned to

my student and shrugged, then glanced again at the old man. His steel-blue eyes met mine briefly before darting away, speeding off down the hall where they came to rest on the sylvan form of a young maiden in a tight-fitting green knit dress."

Now we know a little more about the looks of this character. As a bonus, we also know a bit about the physical appearance of the student to whom the narrator is talking, as well as about some of the habits of our main character. In particular, he smokes a cigar, has quick-moving eyes, and lusts after young girls in tight dresses.

Be Them! Finally, once you've envisioned your character's physical traits and written them down to share with your reader, try to *become* that character. Put yourself in his place. Step into his shoes. Learn what motivates him, how he reacts to certain stimuli around him. After all, if a character were developed simply by describing his physical attributes, writing would be damned easy stuff.

No, much as an actor onstage would do, we writers must become actors offstage. So let's act! Here's more:

"Yeah," the student replied as the old man turned and took several sure steps toward us. "Hymie Stiehl. You know him? We have coffee together at Francie's in the mornings."

"You? You and ..." My mouth fell open as I looked from one face to the other.

"Hey-yeah. Pleased to meetcha," the two thin lips said, quivering lightly as he held out his hand. "What's your name again?"

"This is D.J.," the student responded. "You know, the guy I told you about. The writing instructor?"

"Oh, yeah, yeah, sure," he said. His eyes glowed suddenly brighter and his brows—already sprouting in every conceivable direction—seemed to rise and swell to twice their previous size. "Oh, so you're D. J. Yeah. I've read your stuff. Some of it. A little. In the papers. Or the magazines. Very nice."

He held out his hand, and I grasped it firmly, surprised at how weak it felt, how light the grip, delicate, effeminate practically.

Now the reader learns that the character is more complex than originally revealed. And, perhaps, just a tad superficial ("What's your name again?"). He's also not above laying out a little trash, as when he claims to have read the instructor's *stuff*, and then he quickly adds "Some of it" without being able to recall what or where. Notice that, even though you may have laid out the main elements of physical description earlier in the book, new bits and pieces are continually emerging to keep adding to the overall portrait.

At last, we have some real character development taking place! Now the reader knows for sure what he has so long suspected: Hymie is a stitch! A round, full, surprising, likable *stitch*. These grafs also speak worlds about Hymie's character through the words he chooses to use. *Meetcha* instead of *meet you*. Within the relatively short space of a few pages, the reader learns that Hymie is crude, boorish, educated, selfish, vulgar, opinionated, self-confident, lustful, rough, gruff, and yet somehow likable. From here on out, the reader is hooked. Hymie is reason enough to continue turning the pages if for no other purpose than to find out what extraordinary things he's going to do--or say--next.

And that's precisely what a round character in a work of fiction is supposed to make us do.

Round characters. They make the world go ... Well, you get my point. Take your time in creating them, seeing them, and describing them, and your reader will be forever grateful to you.

How do you create a really good, classic mystery novel?

Everybody knows what mystery is; hardly anybody can explain how to create it. And for good reason. Teaching a writer how to craft a mystery is about as simple as teaching a hydrophobic how to swim. But that won't stop me. *Uh-uh*, no, sir. This long-time aficionado of Edgar Allen Poe and Arthur Conan Doyle is going to go even a step further. *Yup*. I'm not only going to teach you how to *create* a mystery ... I'm going to teach you how to do it with *style*.

First: a definition. *Mystery is the unknown.* We don't necessarily care at this point just what that unknown *is*. For now, let's just keep it simple.

Second: a given. A writer creates mystery when he deliberately prevents his reader from knowing the truth. Take a look at this:

A car roars by a fast-food restaurant. An Arabic suicide bomber leaps out the back door and goes tumbling through the crowd. Dazed and barely conscious, he comes to rest in a pool of blood by

ABOUT WRITING RIGHT

the entranceway as several people cluster around, anxious to help. Suddenly a bomb hidden beneath his coat explodes, sending tables and chairs, shards of glass and human flesh flying everywhere.

There is no mystery here. The writer has explained it all--except, of course, why it happened. But once you know *what* happened, the "why," except in psychological thrillers, is rarely more than an also-ran. Now check this out:

A car roars by a fast-food restaurant. It slows for a brief second as the back door flies open. Perched halfway out of the car is a man wearing a long coat, despite the grueling mid-August heat. As the driver hits the accelerator, the man flies out of the car, tumbling through the crowd until his body slams up against the brick facade of the building, where he lay for several minutes in a swelling pool of blood.

Now, all of a sudden, we have a *ton* of mystery. Who are these people? Why did the driver slow down? What made the car door open? Why was the man perched at the edge of the door? Why was he wearing a long coat in the middle of summer? Why did the driver suddenly hit the accelerator? What sent the man flying from the car--did he leap, or was he shoved? Who is the man? Is he dead or alive? What happened to create all that blood? What's going to happen next?

Mystery. So much *mystery*. And all because the writer of the second passage chose to hold back some very pertinent information from his reader.

Holding back information is the lifeline of all mystery writers. Doing so accomplishes two things. First, it keeps the reader in the dark. He doesn't know what happened or why, so he's forced to guess (everyone wants to know if his "hunch" is right almost as much as he loves to solve puzzles). That creates tension and intrigue within the reader and keeps him turning the pages, keeps him coming back for more.

Second, holding back information creates multiple avenues of action and motivation for the writer. Even when working from the most complete outline imaginable, as a writer unfolds a mystery, new possibilities and new wrinkles invariably strike him. Changing an outline on-the-fly to incorporate these new concepts is often one of the most enjoyable things about writing a mystery. Not only has the writer figured out the mystery in advance of starting the book, but also he gets numerous opportunities to alter it along the way to its completion. Talk about *fun*!

But where--I know you're getting ready to ask--does the element of "style" come in? Mystery is mystery, isn't it? Withholding information is withholding information, no matter how it's done.

Well, that's true, but only to a point. Style, as I define it within the realm of creating mystery, is an unmistakable uniqueness to a character or a situation. Here's an example of mystery with very little "style" in the opening graf of a mystery novel:

John watched as the young woman got onto the bus and slipped into a seat across the aisle. As she opened her purse to reach for a tissue, he saw the unmistakable glint of hardened metal--blued metal--the kind of metal you find nowhere else but on the barrel of a gun. "Now, what the hell would she be doing with a gun," he mumbled to himself.

That's an example of what I call a generic mystery scene. It works. It creates suspense in that it asks a question, but it carries little, if any, style. Now listen to this version of the same scene:

John settled into his seat, his knees squashed against the metal frame of the seat before him. His eyes, twin narrow slits in an otherwise placid face, scanned the bobbing heads of the passengers ahead of him. "I hate buses," he thought before settling on the sylvan shape of a young lady picking her way slowly down the aisle. She stumbled awkwardly to one side as the bus weaved and veered its way through late-night traffic. Grabbing the polished metal frame of the seat just across the aisle and in front of John, she slid down into the time-worn vinyl. She shifted her hat and tilted her head. John ran the narrow slits down the side of her body, the red chintz of her dress, to her heels--black with no straps--and then back up again in time to see her open her purse and reach one hand inside for a tissue. The slits suddenly widened. Peeking out at him from the corner of the bag was the gaping muzzle of a snub-nosed revolver--its time-dulled, steel-grey complexion in marked contrast to the honey-blonde hair dancing only inches above it.

ABOUT WRITING RIGHT

Notice how the second passage relays the same sense of mystery as the first one: the reader knows that John saw a gun in the woman's purse and that he wondered what it was doing there.

But the second passage goes on to spread a thin layer of jam across the bread. Its sweet, sticky, tasty *thereness* draws the reader in more deeply, gives him a sense of what the characters are all about ... and maybe what the tone of the story is about, too--something the first passage fails to do.

It accomplishes all of this and more, of course, through description. Not just general descriptive banter, but description that adds to the sense of mystery, of the *hush-hushedness*, of something going on that the reader simply can't fathom. In the second passage, the woman suddenly becomes a *lady*. John's eyes are *narrow slits*. Her form is *sylvan*. She wears a *hat* and tilts her head *forward*. Her dress is *red chintz*; her heels, *black strapless*. The gun is a *snub-nosed revolver*. Its coloring is *time-dulled steel grey*, while her hair is *honey blonde*.

All of these descriptive adjectives and phrases feed into the reader's sense of heightened mystery. By the time this paragraph is history, the reader is convinced that something extraordinary, something awful, something sinister and unpredictable is going to take place here. And, chances are, the reader is right. The author has succeeded.

So, you want *mystery*? Plan in advance. Work carefully. Give the reader enough information to make sense but not enough to make *too* much sense. Never, *ever* give him enough to allow him to figure out who did what and why until you're ready to reveal all.

You want mystery with *style*? Give the reader precisely the same thing and *then* some ... but still leave him wondering--and *wanting*--more.

What is style, and in what style do you normally write?

At first glance, one might expect the word, "style," to be difficult to define. But, like so many things taken at first glance, that's simply not the case. Take this definition of style from no less a revered authority than *The Chicago Manual of Style* itself.

"The word style means two things to an editor. The first meaning is that implied in the title *A Manual of Style*. Publishers refer to style in this sense as *house style* or *press style*--rules regarding the mechanics of written communication ... Authors more often think of style in its other sense, as a way of writing, of literary expression. Editors are, of course, also aware of this meaning of style when they undertake the second, non-mechanical, process of editing."

Got that? In other words, Editors most often think of style as how to make all of the copy they're preparing for publication conform to certain in-house standardized formatting rules; i.e., how to abbreviate the 50 states ("Neb." versus "NB") when to hyphenate and when to combine two words into one ("free-lance" versus "freelance"), when to use numerals and when to spell out numbers ("12" versus "twelve"), and so forth. A good example is in the word "non-mechanical," used in the paragraph above. While *The Chicago Manual of Style* chooses to make the word non-hyphenated, the Microsoft spelling checker used to check this very answer to your question rejects that interpretation in favor of the hyphenated style of the word "non-mechanical."

While that's certainly something for an author to keep in mind when writing for a specific publication (editors are not likely to look kindly on a manuscript in which every other word needs a style change to conform to their in-house guidelines), we're concerned here with the more subjective use of the word, *style*; i.e., *expression*.

In that sense, I define style as something like this: "The way in which an author chooses to put words together in order to depict an idea or concept or to evoke a feeling or response."

Take a look at these two very different literary styles. First:

"Jack, upset with himself for not having stood up to the bully who had been goading him into a fight, chose to back down."

Second:

"Jack was upset for not having had the tenacity to stand up to his adversary. Bullies, he knew all too well, needed to be met with the type of response that they understood best--brute force. Only by meeting force with force (and all bullies, he realized, used force to instill fear into the hearts of their quivering quarries) could he ever hope to prevail. Yet, for one reason or another, he wasn't up to the task, wasn't willing to respond in kind. Or, perhaps, he had learned another way."

The first example of literary style is terse and to-the-point. There are few wasted words. The second example is more flowery, introspective, "literary." (Hey, use literary alliteration such as "the hearts of their quivering quarries," and we're talking literary!) See the difference? Now to a point more in keeping with my question of you: what is *your* style?

Do you usually write short, sweet, and to-the-point? Or are you more likely to expand upon a concept, spilling out everything in your heart and soul into your passages? Admittedly, there are more literary styles around than fishes in the sea. Remember our definition ... *The way in which an author chooses to put words together in order to depict an idea or a concept or to evoke a feeling or response.* Since no two people think alike, no two people write alike (although they might write similarly).

It's important to know what your primary literary style is so that you can project beforehand whether or not that style will be suitable for a particular audience (most notably, book, newspaper, Internet, or magazine readers and editors). If you know in advance that your literary style is not suited to a particular market, you'll either have to pass on trying to sell anything to that market or change your style for that particular piece (everyone is capable of writing in different styles.

Most writers breaking into print haven't yet developed a specific style, so they emulate the style of another, more successful writer ... it's only human nature. We want to be successful; we admire X Writer; so, we copy X Writer's style. The more to which we expose ourselves, the more literary styles we come to admire, and the more we tend to emulate and adapt. Finally, after copying the styles of two or ten or fifty or five hundred authors, we evolve our literary styles into something unique to ourselves. Still, when analyzing styles, we can see that they break down into several very basic categories. Our primary style is either:

- Terse (short and to-the-point)
- Flowery (embellished with often large passages of descriptive prose)
- Poetic (tending to include a great deal of rhyme and alliteration)
- Stream-of-consciousness (mirroring in writing what the brain is thinking)
- Journalistic (just the facts, ma'am--*Who, What, When, Where,* and *Why*)

D. J. Herda

As writers grow in literary proficiency, they often combine different literary styles within a single work. They may do so to keep their readers on their toes ("Hey, this guy is deeper than I *thought!*"). Or they may only be mirroring the vast diversity of the different characters in their work. One character may speak in dialogue that is terse and tinted with scientific techno-babble while another may soliloquy poetic. And that's another good reason for understanding--and being able to write in--different literary styles. Adaptability to various characters.

For example: Your hard-nosed editor/reporter character shouldn't talk in the same style as the retired school teacher of 53 years. Your rebel-without-a-cause protestor shouldn't speak in the same style as the career politician.

Just how do you decide what *your* primary literary style is? Take a couple of pages of your "most-you" writing, sit down, and analyze it with the list above in mind. Go paragraph-by-paragraph, if need be, and define each one, jotting its label down in the margin. Is it terse, flowery, poetic, stream-of-consciousness, or journalistic? Then tally up the numbers. Or ask a trusted friend to read something of yours and tell you which of the above styles he thinks you fit into.

And remember: Once you know what your primary literary style is, and once you learn to write in other styles, you're well on your way to being able to write anything ... for *anyone*!

How important is using realistic dialogue in a novel, and what exactly distinguishes "good dialogue," anyway?

The use of dialogue in fiction, to misquote Mark Twain, is greatly exaggerated. It's desirable and even necessary to most stories, sure. But not all dialogue is created equal, and setting it up in the wrong format can take a devastating toll on the reader. Take this example:

"I wanted to tell him that I needed him," Mary told John's mother. "I wanted him to know that I still cared. He's the father of my child." She stifled the urge to cry. "And even if I can't be with him for the rest of my life, I wanted to tell him that, for my sake and for the sake of little Max, he would always be welcome in our home. But when he began running around with that other woman, when he began using drugs and staying away for days and sometimes weeks

ABOUT WRITING RIGHT

on end..." Mary felt the anger welling within her. *"I felt I had to draw the line. So I did."*

Now, that's quite a bit of quoted dialogue to throw at a reader. It's so much, in fact, that it ends up sounding rambling, disjointed, and unnatural. Also, interspersing various expository sentences for clarity creates a sense of confusion within the reader. *Is this part of what Mary is saying, or is it something the author added?* To find out, the reader often has to backtrack and search for the quotation marks, which throws the story's timing off and acts to frustrate the reader.

Sure, readers want dialogue. They crave to know what a character says in that character's own words. But there's a better way of using long blocks of dialogue effectively. One way is to break up those blocks into shorter, more easily assimilated sections, such as in this example:

"I wanted to tell him that I needed him," Mary told John's mother. *His mother glanced up at her from her knitting.*
"Oh?"
"I did. I wanted him to know that I still care."
"And why would you still care after all he has done to you?"
"I care because he's the father of my child."
John's mother shrugged, started to speak, and stopped.

Do you get the point? By breaking up a long, rambling block of dialogue, you can make the scene move along more quickly and more naturally. That's often accomplished most easily by splitting the dialogue among two different characters instead of piling it all onto one's character's shoulders.

But what of those times when you don't *want* to break the dialogue down, when you don't *want* to add various asides and responses from another person? Or, maybe you have too much dialogue in your work already and hesitate adding more. You still need to relay information from one of your characters to your reader, though. Oh, what on earth can you possibly do?

Here's an idea. Why not use thoughts, called *internal dialogue*, in place of spoken material? You can accomplish that most simply by using italics and switching the thought to first person and present tense—just the way we all think--as in this example:

D. J. Herda

Should I tell her about her son? Or does she already know? I want to tell him that I still need him. I want to say I still care. He's the father of our child. And even if I can't be with him for the rest of my life, he'll always be welcome in our home. My home. But if he keeps running around with those people, getting arrested and thrown in jail, I don't know what I'll do. I'll have to do something. Something to protect our daughter. But what?

By converting a potentially long, rambling, and confusing block of information from dialogue into thoughts, you accomplish the same thing as you would have with quotes: You allow the reader to know what Mary is thinking. Only you did it without using confusing quotation marks, without starting and stopping direct quotes, and without the need for interspersing a number of unquoted elements to break up the quote. The result is that the reader gets to look inside Mary's mind, hear what Mary is thinking, and form something of a bond with her. As a bonus, internal dialogue is often easier to read and less confusing for the reader to follow.

Dialogue? It's mighty tasty stuff in nearly *any* work of fiction. But knowing when and how to use it so that the reader finds it a helpful tool--and not a major stumbling block to the story's flow--can make all the difference in the world.

What makes some novels' characters more memorable than others?

Good question. See if this works as an answer:

If you were to think back over all of the stories you've read over the years, I'm betting you'd be hard pressed to come up with more than a handful of truly memorable characters. That's because most writers don't take the time or the energy to create living, breathing, multi-dimensional people to populate their books. And that includes most successful writers. And that's a bad thing.

But if you were to think back over all of the real-life people you've met in your lifetime, you'd remember more than a few doozies! The reason is simple: memorable people are memorable because they are real characters. They stand out in a crowd. They break from the mold. They can literally knock your socks off. And that can only be a good thing.

ABOUT WRITING RIGHT

The reason I bring this up is simple. By introducing a memorable character early in a book, you can literally snag your reader for life. Better still, you can snag that overworked, jaded editor into wanting to read more--you know, catch him just long enough to get him interested in your story so that he keeps reading far enough into the book to discover the unique plot and your effervescent literary style.

Hook 'em, book 'em, and cook 'em. That's what it's all about, after all.

But what marks the difference between a truly memorable character and a ho-hum creation in your own writing? It's something I call the "quirk factor."

Remember Holden Caulfield in J. D. Salinger's *The Catcher in the Rye*? He's a morass of quirkiness, a cauldron of contradictions. Once you read some of his early reflections, chances are you're not going to want to stop reading until you find out just what happens to the guy. For example:

> *"If you really want to hear about it, the first thing you'll probably want to know is where I was born, and what my lousy childhood was like, and how my parents were occupied and all before they had me, and all that David Copperfield kind of crap, but I don't feel like going into it, if you want to know the truth."*

Let's be honest here. There's something awfully intriguing about a narrator who begins telling his life's story by saying he doesn't feel like telling his life's story. That unexpected vignette makes us more determined than ever to follow up on him, to learn what makes him tick, and to pick his brain for more details. Of course, when we do, we discover even more quirkiness.

> *"I'm the most terrific liar you ever saw in your life. It's awful. If I'm on my way to the store to buy a magazine, even, and somebody asks me where I'm going, I'm liable to say I'm going to the opera."*

Of course, we've all known liars in our lives. But liars, as pathetic as they may be in society, are still as interesting as hell. That's yet another reason we're anxious to learn more about this guy. He's a liar, and he says so outright--the paradox of the ages! But that's not all.

> *"Anyway, I'm sort of glad they've got the atomic bomb invented. If there's ever another war I'm going to sit right the hell on top of it. I'll volunteer for it, I swear to God I will."*

D. J. Herda

I think you're beginning to get the message. Characters who are lazy or crazy or loons or toons are simply more interesting, more intriguing, and more memorable than your run-of-the-mill guy next door. Writers who realize this get in on the action early. They're the ones who produce books such as *One Flew over the Cuckoo's Nest, The Caine Mutiny, The Maltese Falcon,* and even *Moby Dick.* Can anyone honestly say after reading that classic written 200 years ago that Captain Ahab was just your average Joe?

Of course, not all memorable characters are memorable for what they have to say. Some are memorable for other reasons, as in the case of the main character in *Solid Stiehl—The Death and Life of Hymie Stiehl.* In it, the narrator describes his first encounter with the venerable older writer:

"I quickly surveyed his large, bulging eyes, puffed out and encircled by several rings of time, then let my gaze drift across his thick, meaty face to his nose--a great bulbous affair that shone bluish-gray in the cast of a long bank of fluorescent lights stretched out overhead. Running from one side of his nose to the other were scores of tiny blue-green lines--ribbons of highway seen from a jetliner, at first barely visible from high above the city, then growing ever larger and more prominent with each passing second until they threatened to explode into a billion shards of concrete and steel.

His mouth was the only thing about him that did not seem too large for his overall carriage. Not his mouth, exactly, but his lips. Two thin lines that, later when I got to know him, I would see purse out in an effort to expand their size, as though he knew that these mere slivers of pastel were the one feature out of keeping with his greatness and set about to change them.

Without so much as uttering a word, Hymie Stiehl marks his debut as a genuine character, an intriguing personality with strange quirks and bizarre features out-of-keeping with most other characters we encounter in our daily sojourn through life. Of course, later in the book, he confirms that notion with his unique way of expressing himself:

"Hey, kid. You're all right. Got your head up your ass sometimes, but, basically, you're okay."

ABOUT WRITING RIGHT

So, writers reveal their characters' quirky personalities via their dialogue and their characters' descriptive features. That gives a writer two opportunities to wax chaotic, although there's a third more subtle but equally effective means: by noting the character's off-beat actions, as in this scene where Stiehl prods a taxicab driver into taking him to Chicago's Comiskey Park.

"Hymie leaned forward and rapped his knuckles against the driver's back as if he were knocking on a door. "Hey, Hor-hey," he growled contemptuously. "I said Thirty-fifth and Shields, not Forty-fifth and Michigan, comprende? *Where the hell you takin' us, anyway? Come on, wetback. There's fifty cents American in it for you if you get us there alive."*

Within a few short lines, we're treated to a painting of the real, the genuine, the unpretentious, the base, the intriguing Hymie Stiehl.

That's another thing writers need to remember when painting their creations: memorable characters don't need much to become memorable. A few carefully chosen words, a couple of descriptive passages, and the exhibition of a genuine contempt for--or lifelong love affair with--humanity are enough to create a truly quirky character from any novelist or short-story teller.

So, if you spend some time fine-tuning *your* characters' personalities, you'll reap the rewards of success as sure as you're sitting there, thinking to yourself, "Guess who's coming for dinner!"

How important is it to write descriptive scenes in a mystery rather than concentrating on the crime itself?

You can go a long way in writing a mystery without fleshing out the main characters or revealing "Whodunit." But try doing the same without setting the locale--the story's physical scene--and you'll soon wind up in a boatload of trouble.

Readers don't mind having to wait to get all the information they can get about the people in a mystery. They're used to having characters developed slowly, a little at a time, as events take place and the story unwinds. Characters, after all, show the reader what they're made of by reacting to action and relating to specific events--and those things take place in due time. It's hard to know just how selfless a hard-boiled P.I. is until the reader witnesses his leap off a towering bridge to save a hapless suicide victim or swim the English Channel to nail a counterfeiting ring in France.

But readers can and *do* object to being kept in the dark for too long when it comes to setting a mystery scene. And they do so for good reason. The scene sets the stage for the element of mystery and triggers a readiness in the reader to be, well, *mystified*. Does the story take place at midday in a bright, sunny park filled with tittering children and chattering old maids? Or does it unfold at midnight in a rainy alleyway where the only sign of life is a stoop-shouldered ghost of a man shuffling slowly along ... and the only way out is up? It makes a difference. Whereas the one creates within the reader little speculation about mysterious activities soon to take place, the other fills the reader with trepidation and tension--two of the staunchest allies of the eternal mystery.

Take one of the earliest scenes in Arthur Conan Doyle's tales of the exploits of Sherlock Holmes, *The Hound of the Baskervilles*. The lord of the manor, in hosting a dinner party for some friends, took time out to run food and drink down to a young maiden, whom he held captive, when he discovered her cage empty.

Racing back through the house, he asked his guests to help find her.

".... Whereat Hugo ran from the house, crying to his grooms that they should saddle his mare and unkennel the pack, and giving the hounds a kerchief of the maid's, he swung them to the line, and so off full cry in the moonlight over the moor.

"Now, for some space the revellers stood agape, unable to understand all that had been done in such haste. But anon their bemused wits awoke to the nature of the deed which was like to be done upon the moorlands. Everything was now in an uproar; some calling for their pistols, some for their horses, and some for another flask of wine. But at length some sense came back to their crazed minds, and the whole of them, thirteen in number, took horse and started in pursuit. The moon shone clear above them, and they rode swiftly abreast, taking that course which the maid must needs have taken if she were to reach her own home.

"They had gone a mile or two when they passed one of the night shepherds upon the moorlands, and they cried to him to know if he had seen the hunt. And the man, as the story goes, was so crazed

ABOUT WRITING RIGHT

with fear that he could scarce speak, but at last he said that he had indeed seen the unhappy maiden, with the hounds upon her track. 'But I have seen more than that,' said he, 'for Hugo Baskerville passed me upon his black mare, and there ran mute behind him such a hound of hell as God forbid should ever be at my heels.' So the drunken squires cursed the shepherd and rode onward. But soon their skins turned cold, for there came a galloping across the moor, and the black mare, dabbled with white froth, went past with trailing bridle and empty saddle. Then the revellers rode close together, for a great fear was on them, but they still followed over the moor, though each, had he been alone, would have been right glad to have turned his horse's head. Riding slowly in this fashion they came at last upon the hounds. These, through known for their valour and their breed, were whimpering in a cluster at the head of a deep dip or goyal, as we call it, upon the moor, some slinking away and some, with starting hackles and staring eyes, gazing down the narrow valley before them.

"The company had come to a halt, more sober men, as you may guess, than when they started. The most of them would by no means advance, but three of them, the boldest, or it may be the most drunken, rode forward down the goyal. Now, it opened into a broad space in which stood two of those great stones, still to be seen there, which were set by certain forgotten peoples in the days of old. The moon was shining bright upon the clearing, and there in the centre lay the unhappy maid where she had fallen, dead of fear and of fatigue. But it was not the sight of her body, nor yet was it that of the body of Hugo Baskerville lying near her, which raised the hair upon the heads of these three dare-devil roysterers, but it was that, standing over Hugo, and plucking at his throat, there stood a foul thing, a great, black beast, shaped like a hound, yet larger than any hound that ever mortal eye has rested upon. And even as they looked the thing tore the throat out of Hugo Baskerville, on which, as it turned its blazing eyes and dripping jaws upon them, the three shrieked with fear and rode for dear life, still screaming, across the moor. One, it is said, died that very night of what he had seen, and the other twain were but broken men for the rest of their days ...."

D. J. Herda

Just a light-hearted ditty? Hardly. When you read that at any time of day or night, the scene inspires chills and even fear in the reader--this, in part, for the remarkable clearness with which the author detailed the scene. Using words that still today--a hundred years later—inspire images of such clarity and reality, Doyle has dared anyone to get up and walk away undisturbed.

In that "simple" passage, he described the moon *shining bright upon the clearing.* The unhappy maid *where she had fallen, dead of fear and of fatigue.* The thing *plucking at [Hugo's] throat ...* a *foul thing, a great, black beast, shaped like a hound.* When suddenly the thing *turned its blazing eyes and dripping jaws upon them.*

As in the best descriptive passages in literature, Doyle used imagery as a painter uses oils on canvas. A stroke of his literary brush evokes not only a mere understanding of the artist's words but also a feeling, a string of emotional responses, that a more careless or lazy writer might never have revealed.

Unlike descriptions of people or things, however, Doyle's descriptive passage was designed to set the *scene* and--in so doing--set the stage for the rest of the novel. Something evil lurked among the moors of Baskerville manor. Something frightening and unearthly, some devil of a creature unlike any other known to man. Something hideous. Something immortal. Something ... well, you get the point. By the time the passage ends, the stage is set for mystery.

So the next time you prepare to pen a mystery--whether a novel or a short story--remember to pay special attention to the setting. That is, after all, where everything within the story lives, from characters to action, from storyline to story's end. Set the scene properly, evocatively, and early, and you'll find the rest of the story practically writes itself. Oh, yes, and your readers will thank you for it, too.

I know how important strong dialogue is to writing a novel, but how do you know whether it's strong enough and when you should leave well enough alone?

There are several ways to judge the strength of dialogue. Here's one of them that you can take to the bank. If you have to describe your character's dialogue to your reader, you're not writing strong, believable dialogue.

ABOUT WRITING RIGHT

Sad but true, and it's all too common a shortcoming in writers of *all* calibers and experience.

Now, admittedly, different writers handle dialogue differently. That's one of the things that helps to establish a writer's literary voice. Dialogue is one of the elements that defines literary style. But there are effective ways of handling dialogue, and there are ineffective ways. Take a look at this example:

"I hate you," she screamed shrilly.

What's wrong with that, you ask? The writer tells us that she screamed and that her voice was shrill. Isn't that a good example of strong, descriptive dialogue, of being specific?

Well, it may be specific, but it's not good dialogue--not by a long shot. Why use the adverb, "shrilly," to get the point across when there's a better, sharper, more effective way of delivering the same message. Take a look at this:

"I hate you!" she screamed.

Surprise, surprise. By leaving off the adverb "shrilly" and emphasizing the word "hate" through the use of italics, we've killed two birds with a single deletion. We've economized the writing, and we've strengthened the dialogue. Now, when a reader reads "I *hate* you!" he gets the message at a glance. In fact, provided there are only two people in the conversation and it's clear who is saying what, you may not need the words, "she screamed," at all, thus strengthening the dialogue even further:

"I hate you!"

Of course, there are ways to strengthen dialogue *without* putting words in italics. Take a look at this example:

"I don't want to see you anymore," he said with a defiant, final tone in his voice.

Short, sweet, and ineffective, pure and simple. Now this:

"You're out of here. For good!"

Wow, totally different words delivering the same message, although the second example does so through the clarity and finality of the words. And there's no awkward explanation needed. *Hmmm.* You know what? There really *is* something to this effective dialogue thing.

Another way of creating strong, realistic dialogue is by replacing the word, "said," with a stronger, more defined, more graphic word. Here's the weak way:

"Bring him to me," he said. There was a certain authority, a terseness to his voice that Charlie couldn't mistake.

Now, we have not only weak dialogue, but also weak supporting structure in the explanatory sentence following the quote. A sure way to get around those shortcomings?

"Bring him to me," he growled.

Do you see how changing a single word--deciding how the speaker's voice is supposed to sound and then using a more powerful verb to communicate that thought to the reader more effectively--improves the dialogue? A word of caution, though, when using this technique. Use dialogue-defining verbs such as "growled" sparingly. Use the general word, "said," as the rule-of-thumb and all other verbs as the exception. See how overusing other verbs can end up sounding stilted:

"What are you doing?" John demanded.
"Washing my feet," Bill explained.
"That's a queer thing to do at this time of night," John offered.
"It's a queer thing to do at any time," Bill proffered.
"I guess so," John admitted.

Ouch! Does that sound a bit awkward, as if the writer is just *aching* to be precise? As if he's hung up on telling the reader more than he needs to know? *Uh-huh*, I think so, too. Here's a much simpler way of handling the same exchange:

"What are you doing?" John asked.
"Washing my feet."
"That's a queer thing to do at this time of night."
"It's a queer thing to do at any time—*day* or *night*."
"I guess so," John said.

Notice how leaving out most of the attributes helps to move the dialogue along. Assuming the reader knows there are only two people in the conversation--John and Bill--it's pretty easy for the reader to determine who said what after the introductory question is attributed to John.

By now, you're beginning to see how using descriptive words and rambling explanations to illuminate a character's dialogue only weakens the exchange and slows down the reader's progress. Descriptive passages belong in all writing, of course, but not where dialogue is concerned.

What's that, you ask? What if you have a whole lot of information to get across and don't want to sound as if you're rambling? Check out this example:

"Go get me my hat and coat so that I can put them on and leave here, because I no longer feel wanted," Mary said.

Well, there's an easy way around *that* rambling, disjointed dialogue, too. It's as easy as cutting Mary short, as in this example:

"Get my hat and coat," Mary snapped. She knew when she wasn't wanted.

By shortening Mary's dialogue and moving part of what she was feeling out of quotes and into a straight narrative, we've made the dialogue crisper and more believable without sacrificing any of the thoughts we wanted to get across--namely, that Mary knew when she wasn't wanted.

Are you getting the point here? Dialogue has to be crisp, sharp, and pointed to be effective. Once you begin stringing it out in a prolonged effort to drive home all of your thoughts, once you fall into the trap of using adverbs as descriptive modifiers to enhance your dialogue, you've lost game, set, *and* match.

So, keep your dialogue believable; keep it simple; keep it crisp. You'd be amazed at how far you can go in creating a powerful piece of writing. Make your dialogue ring with the sound of reality, and you'll keep your readers coming back for more.

Can you give me any tips about how to develop a stronger literary voice? I know what that is, but I'm not sure I know how to get it.

Funny you should ask because I was thinking the other day about how lucky some writers are to have a strong literary voice. I say "lucky," because some writers are literally born that way. Others who weren't have had to work their proverbial butts off to develop one.

As for your question, I understand that you said you know what a literary voice is, but do you really? Let's see.

A literary voice is the previously all-too-often or underemphasized strength of the written word. Take, for instance, the following two relatively equivalent sentences. The first:

"Frank knew what he had to do but couldn't do it for some reason as of yet unknown to him, although he was convinced he could do it in the end."

And then the second:

"Frank knew what he had to do; he just didn't know where to start."

The first sentence is weak and wandering with very little focus and too many lame words. The second sentence comes across as more exciting and believable because it has a strong literary voice behind it.

Think of a literary voice as the written equivalent of the spoken voice. Some people (you know the ones—those radio and TV mood music jocks on the Public Broadcast System?) have naturally strong speaking voices. Others haven't.

But even those who haven't can work at developing stronger voices. They can lower the pitch of their voices and talk more clearly, more distinctly. They can insert timely pauses into their speech for dramatic emphasis. They can enunciate more clearly.

The same holds in developing a stronger *literary* voice. Everyone can do it, although it does take a little know-how and practice, practice, practice. Here are some tips to help you develop a stronger literary voice.

    1. Write conversationally.

    By that, I mean write the way you speak. You'd be amazed at how many people write in a completely stilted, unnatural fashion. Yet, when you talk to them face-to-face, they come across just fine. The problem is something I call "Writerese." Writers—especially new writers, although others can also fall victim to the disease—often feel that they need to write differently than they speak. Are you one of them? Here's how to find out.

    Write what you think to be a few strong sentences. Edit them until you feel confident that they say what you want to say in a strong literary voice. Then walk away from them for 30 minutes.

ABOUT WRITING RIGHT

When you come back, read the sentences *out loud*. Listen to yourself as you read. Ask yourself if the sentences are as strong as you had initially thought. Chances are, they're not.

So, why didn't you catch the problem reading the sentences to yourself? The answer is that the human ear has far more training in "hearing" than does the human mind, or our "inner ear." By reading something out loud, you can usually pick up on weaknesses, faulty logic, and even improper grammar and punctuation more readily than by reading something to yourself.

2. Scrap all of those "writing" words you've come to know and love over the years.

   Instead, replace them with something more real. Don't say, "He prognosticated the outcome long before it happened." Instead, say, "He predicted it." The meaning will be more apparent to the reader right from the start, and he or she will thank you for it.

3. Vary the length of your sentences.

   Using paragraphs or even entire pages of similar-length sentences, you create an unnatural rhythm to your voice that can put nearly any reader to sleep.

   "Bob wanted to go shopping. His wife didn't want to go. Bob decided to go alone. He didn't need his wife to come. She would be just as happy at home. That's where she enjoyed being anyway. So Bob decided to leave her behind."

   Do you see how similar in length the sentences are? Same-length sentences create a sing-song effect that can make for damned hard reading, even though the sentences are short. Now see how this one plays out:

   "Bob wanted to go shopping. His wife, he was sure, would have preferred to stay home. Hell, he knew she'd be perfectly satisfied to stay anywhere, *as long as she was indoors. She could go through the rest of her life without ever setting foot outdoors and never miss a beat. That was her."*

   By varying the length of your sentences, you'll lessen the risk of putting your readers off while strengthening your literary voice.

4. Keep the use of long, rambling sentences to a minimum.

   Once again, this literary dictum aims at keeping your reader happy. Readers tend to get lost when reading unwieldy sentences—especially those with lots of punctuation in them. See what I mean with this jawbreaker:

"On the plains, the morning mist rises softly, gently, always at the same time and with the same lack of intensity each day, bringing, as it does, the stillness of the savannah that is inherent in Africa to the dawn—or, in fact, bringing the stillness that is inherent wherever civilization has yet to encroach upon the horizon that is Mother Nature, however lofty its ultimate goals may be."

Hey, that's kind of poetic! But it's also kind of boring and just plain tough to read. Now see how breaking that pup into a few smaller bites works.

"On the plains, the morning mist rises softly. With it comes the stillness. This stillness is Africa, both on the savannah and everywhere else civilization has failed to touch."

Much better. And, for that matter, much stronger, which brings up yet another point.

5. Don't be afraid to use incomplete sentences.

As a rule, good writing dictates that your sentence structure contains a subject, a verb, and sometimes an object (or objective compliment, depending upon the verb used). Your writing can be more effective when you break that rule with an occasional sentence fragment, as in this example:

"Margaret was a kind and loving woman. You could see that in her eyes. Yet, her kindness was betrayed by a hardness that had somehow managed to creep into her makeup over the years. It was not mere hardness. It was ferocity. Threatening. Foreboding. Even deadly."

I know, I know. Mrs. Lemke would turn over in her grave if you'd turned in a composition written like that. But until Mrs. Lemke starts buying your books at Barnes and Noble, she's just going to have to live with it.

Remember that people often talk in non-sentences. Single words or incomplete phrases not only lend emphasis and reality to an idea, but also help to strengthen your literary voice. Just don't overdo things here. When the rules call for breaking, do so. When they don't, don't!

ABOUT WRITING RIGHT

6. Make your direct quotations sound like real dialogue.

    You'd be amazed at how many times I come across writing that reads pretty well...until I get to a quote. You're in trouble if your quoted passages sound like this...

    "I don't know, Michael. I'm as puzzled as I can be. Michael, I think that the best thing for you to do is to just trust me this one time. I know I've said that before, but I think this time you should really just put your faith in me and believe that I won't let you down. Can you do that, Michael? Can you just trust me so that we can get through this thing together?"

    Ouch! Those lines are so stilted, they make my teeth ache! If you know people who talk like this—or, worse still, if *you* talk like this—I have only one question for you. *Where on earth did you grow up?*

    Listen to how much more simple, how much more realistic this version of the same dialogue sounds.

    "I don't know. I really don't. But I if we're going to make it through this thing, you're going to have to trust me."

    See my point? Why would anyone address the person to whom he's talking by name? And three times, no less! Yet, writers—including some proven pros—fall into the trap far too often for their own good. The solution? Always read your dialogue out loud. *Always*. It's the only way to be sure that the dreaded "Writerese" hasn't slipped in between the quotes.

7. Vary your sentence structure...but not too much!

    Sentence structure is the order in which you assemble your words. The natural flow of things is, as I said earlier, subject, verb, and sometimes object. If you tinker with that order too much, your writing will sound stilted and weak. But you are certainly entitled to use an occasional introductory adverbial phrase, parenthetical remarks, and other pieces of grammar to break up the otherwise sing-song *See Spot run* effect.

    "Bob chased after her. He chased after her as fast as he could. As he did, he realized that, no matter how fast he ran, he would never catch up to her. Something had to be done. But what? And then he recalled her one major weakness—her vanity. 'Hey!' he called. 'Your dress is torn!'

D. J. Herda

8. Avoid adverbial phrases.

    In fact, avoid most everything but the bare minimum required to attribute a quote to someone. In such situations, adverbs often sound weak and stilted. Other verbs sound contrived. Check out this nightmare.

    "I didn't know it was you," he admitted hurriedly. "I thought it was the cops. They've been looking for me," he deftly continued, "and I thought they found me." He breathed out loudly.

    Inexperienced writers tend to use adverbs (you know, the dreaded "ly" words?) where they shouldn't. And they tend to use *any* verbs other than the ones they should have used in their attributes. See how much stronger this sentence reads:

    "I didn't know it was you," he said. "I thought it was the cops. They've been looking for me." His breath came in short, quick spurts. "I thought they found me."

    Note, too, that by breaking up a long quote with a descriptive passage ("His breath came in short, quick spurts"), you vary the timing of the sentence and side-step the need for an adverb or any additional attribution.

9. Dump the clichés and colloquialisms.

    They impart very little information and waste the reader's time, as in this abomination:

    "He went over and over it in his mind. His mind was racing. There was a time when he could have thought more clearly. Those days were gone. He knew that, come tomorrow, a new day would dawn, and everything would be just fine and dandy."

10. Read a few pages of a work written by an author you admire most.

    Read them out loud. Listen to the words and try to figure out what makes that author's writing admirable. Does he have a strong or weak literary voice? How does that voice compare to yours?

    Write something similar in theme to one of the passages from your favorite author. Then read both the original and your version out loud. Can you see the similarities? Is your literary voice getting stronger? Can you tell a strong voice from a weak one?

ABOUT WRITING RIGHT

Remember that none of this happens overnight. Developing a strong literary voice can take months or even years. But once you begin working on strengthening yours, you'll be off on a life-long journey that will make you a better writer tomorrow than you are today. And your writing will continue to improve every day of your life.

What is some advice you can give about writing successful mystery stories?

Easy-peasy. Here you go: Give them a few solid clues, point them in the right direction, and yank the rug out from under them. *Ahh*, now *that's* good mystery writing!

Okay, so writing top mysteries is a bit more complicated than that. And it's far more complicated than reading them. Mystery readers want to be 1.) entertained; 2.) surprised; and 3.) challenged, not necessarily in that order. It stands to reason, then, that a well-written mystery will entertain, surprise, and challenge.

In reality, a top Whodunit does that and a whole lot more. And the top mystery scribes writing today know it. So, just about the time a reader gets complacent, the writer stirs up the pot with a big black stick. For example:

Cheevers looked over the body. "It's not that difficult to figure. Mauston hated his boss and had the most to gain from seeing him killed. He had the gun, he had three years' experience in the Green Berets, and he had the motive--the presidency of the company."

Greer shrugged. "True. But he didn't have the opportunity."

"What do you mean? Why not?"

The cop bent over the body, placed his fingers against the man's neck, and looked up. "This guy's been dead two, maybe three hours at the most."

"Yeah," said Cheevers. "So?"

"So, Mauston died yesterday."

This little setup does a couple of things for the reader. First, it prepares him for the resolution of the crime--in this case, Mauston's murdering his boss. Then, just as quickly, it yanks the rug out from under the reader, jarring him back to reality. And, suddenly, instead of being solved, the mystery has deepened.

More than that, the scenario expands the writer's options, opening up an entirely new set of possibilities to pursue. The most obvious is that, with Mauston out of the running, the writer gets to name the *real* murderer. Less obviously, he has the option of maintaining Mauston as the murderer, despite the revelation of his earlier death. How? Elementary, my dear Watson.

Mauston could have set the wheels of the murder in motion before dying unexpectedly of natural causes, himself. Or, he could have faked his own death, using someone else's look-alike body, then killed his boss, although that would have negated his motive for the murder-- taking over the presidency of the company (something he could hardly do without exposing the fact that he was still alive, although he could have had another motive).

Mauston could also have planned the murder and shared the fact with a wife or a girlfriend, only to have her turn on him, making it look as though he had committed a murder-suicide, leaving her in the clear--to collect insurance, marry someone else, or just plain be rid of the oaf. Or, Mauston could have planned the murder and then fallen victim to a double homicide committed by a third party, perhaps another employee farther down the corporate ladder--someone who discovered the plan and stood to benefit from the murder of both the company's president and vice-president.

The possibilities are endless, and that's one of the things that makes mystery writing so alluring. For the logical mind that enjoys twisting and toying with reality, the mystery is the ideal literary medium. As long as the writer can stay at least one full step ahead of the reader, the reader is hooked--and both the reader and the writer emerge winners.

Of course, not all mysteries involve murder, and even of those that do, not all withhold the identity of the murderer until the end (often called Suspense mysteries). In *Double Indemnity*, for example, we know from the opening confession of the murderer into a Dictograph machine that he did it. In cases such as that, the mystery is not the murderer's identity but rather the motive and the means to the deed. We discover those only at the very end of the story. In either case, the effect is the same: the reader is hooked, and the writer intends to keep him that way.

ABOUT WRITING RIGHT

That's where the writer has an insurmountable advantage. But he must maintain his edge over the reader at all times, anticipating even the most jaded mystery junkie's penchant for solving the most convoluted of cases. Often, while plotting a mystery from an outline, a writer will have some unanticipated stroke of genius, something he hadn't foreseen or planned. A good writer will take advantage of every nuance available, making an already solid piece of high concept fiction even stronger and more unpredictable.

It's the wildly unpredictable nature of the mystery that makes it so popular among readers. When you think about it, there are elements of mystery in nearly every genre--some nagging questions for the reader to have answered before the story's end. The only difference between a Romance in which a mystery man sets out to destroy someone and a Mystery in which a woman sets out to ruin a man's life is that the Mystery zeroes-in on the unknown, dropping small clues and endless side streets for the reader to pick up on along the way. Everything else is mere window dressing.

So keep your mind (and your options) open as you write that next great mystery. Make your stories plausible, keep your readers guessing, and set a lively pace. The bottom line: you'll be selling Whodunits like crazy.

I'm toying with the idea of writing a solid nonfiction book that hopefully sells well. Any ideas?

Sure, plenty. I cut my teeth on fiction, but I made my living from nonfiction for more than thirty years. When I decided to write a nonfiction book about building ponds, streams, and other water features, for instance, I figured I was onto a pretty good thing. I'd had experience building water features, and God knows I've written my share of nonfiction, both books and articles. So I drafted an outline, whipped up a sample chapter or two, and sent the proposal off to my agent for pitching. It was called *Building Ponds, Waterfalls, and Streams*.

Imagine my chagrin when, two years later, we hadn't gotten a single nibble. Worse still, a couple of editorial responses along the lines of "Sorry, but the market is glutted with garden and pond books, so I'll pass" seemed to doom my idea to the dead letters file. It wasn't until I decided to change the title to something more catchy, *From Desert to*

Oasis--Zen and the Art of Pond Building, that we began getting requests for a closer look.

Well, to make a long story short, we finally inked a contract with a major publisher, and the book is now published and available online and at bookstores everywhere.

What makes this story interesting is something I call the *Wow! Factor*. You see, in the nonfiction marketplace, books brimming with information cross editors' desks all the time. But something new and different is genuinely rare. To quote the great bard, "There's nothing new under the sun ..."

That being the case, if you want to sell an editor on your nonfiction proposal, come up with a *Wow! Factor* of your own to help lighten your load. To wit:

You want to write a book on baking. It's going to be competing with several thousand other baking book proposals currently making the rounds; but, adding a little *Wow! Factor* gives you something like this: *Baking in the Nude--Turning Up the Heat in* Your *Kitchen.*

See what I mean? The *Wow! Factor.*

Let's take another example, this one a travel guide on Alaska. You could call it *Alaska--The Last Frontier* and virtually guarantee yourself a roomful of rejection slips. Or you could add a little *Wow! Factor* and end up with something like this: *There's Nome Place Like Home: Surviving the Wife, the Kids, and a New Life in the Alaskan Wilderness.*

Of course, to go along with a catchy title, you're going to have to do something equally catchy inside the book. Your cookbook, for example, could offer a checklist of how to increase the "sexiness" of your baked items. Or you might break it down into Low-, Medium-, and High-Intensity Goodies, depending upon the chef's mood.

The Alaska book could open up with a central look at Nome, from its history and people to its museums, restaurants, and cultural events, and then branch off from there in concentric circles. Alaska sites within 50 miles of Nome, within 100 miles, within 200 miles, etc. It could further offer checklists of places and events that might appeal to men, to women, and to children.

Besides attracting more attention along Publisher's Row, a good nonfiction book with a lot of *Wow! Factor* is going to sell better than just another *ho-hum* property once it's published. That's because people, including those all-important book reviewers, will notice it and instinctively want to read it. It's a win-win situation!

So, the next time you sit down to write a proposal for a nonfiction book, spend some time asking yourself what kind of *Wow! Factor* you can come up with to work into the title and the content, and then go for broke. You just might be amazed at the results.

Is it important to have a strong opening to your writing, or should you gradually build up to it?

Funny you should ask. I was thinking just the other day (something that comes dangerously close to an oxymoron) about how editors function. I mean, what pulls an editor toward one piece and pushes him away from another? And how many editors actually *read*--from start to finish--every word of every manuscript placed before them?

I know the answer, of course. But before I break the bad news to you, let me share a little bit about the way one particular editor works.

Sam (not his real name) edits a monthly magazine called *Family Journal* (not its real name). The publication has been around long enough so that, even though it has space to run only five or six freelance articles a month (the rest of the publication is staff-written), it receives 30-40 submissions *a day*.

Still, Sam is a lucky editor. He has an assistant, Chester. One of the first duties Sam gave to Chester when he hired him was to peruse the "slush pile"--the stash of unsolicited manuscripts that comes in "over the transom."

The reason Sam gave this assignment to his assistant isn't that he doesn't want to be the one to pick and choose what articles the magazine runs. On the contrary. Sam has Chester weed out the articles that are obviously not suited for publication in the *Journal*. Those include all fiction, poems, and personal reminiscences ("When I was a bombardier in WW-II ..."). They also include all off-color stuff or pieces of an overtly sexual nature (the publication is family-oriented, remember). They include pieces that are too long for the magazine (which lists a maximum word length of 3,000 in its market report but actually prefers shorter articles and stories).

Finally, the magazine excludes departmental pieces, fillers, jokes, and other things that the staff can assemble themselves or pull from the wire services free of charge.

By the time Chester finishes culling the obvious misfits from the slush pile, he has reduced the day's workload to ten articles.

The second thing Sam trained Chester to do was to recognize bad writing when he sees it. Conversely, it might be reasonably argued, Chester can then be relied upon to recognize *good* writing when he sees it. Another five articles drop out of the running.

Finally, once Chester has culled the five good articles from the day's submissions, he asks Sam if he has time to review the survivors. Naturally, Sam--being busy laying out the book or coordinating the editorial content with the advertising department or working with the art director on the upcoming issue's cover and interior article illustrations or finding appropriate illustrative photographs to go along with next month's articles--hasn't. But, not wanting to discourage Chester from doing his job, Sam humors him by asking for a brief oral run-down of the five articles. It goes something like this:

Chester: "This one is about growing squash in containers on the patio or deck. It's pretty cute and could be useful to our readers."

Sam: "Does the writer have any gardening qualifications?"

Chester (scanning the writer's cover letter): "*Umm*, he doesn't say."

Sam shakes his head.

Chester: "Well, here's one that's a comparison of the quality of automobiles today versus fifty years ago. It's really well written. The author used to work for General Motors."

Sam: "What's his conclusion?"

Chester: "He says today's cars can't hold a candle to the ones made even two decades ago, let alone in the Fifties or Sixties."

Sam (shaking his head): "Nope. Can't do that. Advertising is running a special automotive spread this month. Ford would shit green apples."

Chester (sighing): "Here's one I really like. It's about how parents need to spend more time with their kids, do more positive things with them. The writer is a child psychologist and a former fifth-grade teacher. It makes a lot of sense."

ABOUT WRITING RIGHT

Sam: "Does he say how parents are supposed to find the time when both of them are out working so they can afford to buy a car that's inferior to the last car they bought?"

Chester (setting the article off to one side): "*This* one you're going to love."

Sam: "I love 'em all."

Chester: "It's a piece about how the White House has failed to protect our borders from illegal aliens. It makes some good points in light of 9-11. I think it's terrific. A good investigative journalism piece. Scarier than hell, but it really cuts to the chase."

Sam: "I agree. I read a similar piece in *Reader's Digest* last month. Anything else?"

Chester (shaking his head): "This is the last one."

Sam: "What is it?"

Chester: "It's a little weak, but you might like it. It's the story of the PT-109 and how Jack Kennedy saved his crew's lives during World War Two."

Sam: "Any photos?"

Chester: "A couple of old Navy black-and-whites, one of the ship and the crew, including Kennedy, and another of Kennedy in the hospital after they were rescued."

Sam: "Bingo!"

By the way, Sam is not that unusual an editor. And if you think book editors are any different than magazine editors, you're right-- they're worse. More selective. More demanding. Pickier. Imagine some poor working stiff with forty book-length novels to plow through before the editorial meeting on Thursday morning. Do you honestly believe he'll read every word of every book? And, if not, how much *will* he read?

Here's the answer. Nearly all editors read the first sentence of a manuscript. If it's a book, they read the first sentence of the synopsis. If that catches their attention, they'll likely go on to read the first paragraph of the manuscript. If that "sings," they'll probably read the first page. If the work is still in the running after that (and by now, most aren't), the editor will likely set the manuscript aside for more careful review later.

If, after a week or two, he goes back to the piece and still likes it, he may read the first few chapters of the book. With that done, the editor now has a solid enough understanding of the project to take it in to his publisher or editorial board for review. If they come back with a thumb's up, he'll likely read the entire thing and then contact the writer with the good news: they're going to publish his work.

What this means for you (and if you're reading between the lines the way a good writer should, you already know) is simple. You need to re-think your approach to writing. Your work has to fly from the very first line. *Especially* from the first line. It has to have a dynamite opening paragraph. If it's a book, the first chapter has to sing like a soprano on steroids.

Check out these two leads, or openers, to the same piece of fiction to see which one would prompt *you* to want to read more. Lead One:

It was a cold and dreary night. The rain pelted the windshield. Inside the car, Jack Trembleau, a fisherman on his way back from a day on the lake, struggled to see the road that stretched out ahead of him. It wasn't easy. It was harder, in fact, than it had been the last time he'd gotten caught in a Nor'easter--a torrential storm that blew havoc in toward shore from somewhere out in the Atlantic. And that storm had been so bad, he seriously doubted that he'd ever see Annabelle Lee again. Now, it seemed even less likely.

Not bad. Not really. But take a look now at the same piece with a revamped lead. Lead Two:

Jack would not survive the night. Everything that he knew, all that he loved. Gone. Eliminated. In a split second. He wondered what it would feel like ... the end. He wondered if it would be horrible, filled with terror and wrenching pain like in the movies. Or if perhaps it would quietly slip over him--death--like a comfortable old sweater. He could pull off onto the shoulder. Hold up until the storm settled down. But if he did that, he'd never see her again. And that would be even worse than death. No, it was better this way. Far better.

In Lead One, the writer began with a cliché before promptly following with another. Then he wasted more valuable time and space by specifying that Jack Trembleau (who needs to know his last name, anyway—or even his first at this point, for that matter?) was inside a car--something even less astute readers might have figured out themselves from the previous reference to a windshield. He wasted more time and energy by defining what a Nor'easter is, even though it doesn't matter. Finally, he bogged the lead down even further with the awkward introduction of the name of some woman who means absolutely nothing to the reader.

Do you see my point? When you lay out your leads, keep them short and punchy. Make them gripping. Ask yourself, *Will this catch the reader's attention and hold it through the next sentence.* If the answer is "no," (or even if you're not sure), re-think your lead. Revise and rewrite and keep doing so until you divine something grippy, grabby, and tense, as in Lead Two. Then--and only then--will you be sure that the editor's eye you're trying to grab isn't going to wander from your manuscript to someone else's after the first few words.

Don't worry about not providing all the details in the first paragraph. You have an entire article or book in which to do that. Writers who waste precious real estate by loading it with unnecessary facts are a dime a dozen--and their writing is worth even less than that.

Remember, if you think your lead sounds trite, weak, and uninspired, you'd better believe that some jaded editor on the business end of an editorial desk will think the very same thing—and more so. Your job as a successful, *marketable* writer isn't to show the editor that you have all the facts right from the start. Your job is to convince the editor that he *hasn't* ... and then make him want to read on to learn more.

What's that old phrase about men and women and their eternal quest for love? *He chased her until she caught him.* Well, it may be something of a stretch, but when the words you put into your lead chase an editor until he catches them, you've done your job and done it well. And you can start planning on getting published ... soon. And *often.*

What phrases should I avoid using in my autobiography?

Hmm. Good question. Here's another: What are the names of the stars in the sky?

Actually, there are two main categories of phrases you should avoid in autobiographies and virtually any other writing. One is clichés, which you should *avoid like the plague,* and the other is mixed metaphors (*let's make like a tree and scram*). Between those two groups, I estimate more than a couple thousand frequently encountered examples exist. You should avoid using each one *unless you can't find anything better* with which to replace it. Sometimes (rarely), a cliché nails down an image better than anything else you can think of; so, in that case, you might want to leave it in. *Or* work a little harder to try to find a more original and creative substitute.

Warning, warning, Will Robinson! With that said, don't get overly "cute" in trying to *force* a cliché replacement with something that sticks out like that proverbial sore thumb. Don't, for example, say something *sticks out like a sore foot*. Clichés are clichés because they're used to death. Avoid using them whenever possible, but alter them only at your own risk.

Why worry about clichés at all? Well, the problem with using clichés and mixed metaphors isn't in their very existence within your writing, it's in the frequency of their use. Readers (and editors, should you be interested in selling your work for publication *down the line*) can accept an occasional overused or misused phrase; they'll balk at your reliance upon or overuse of them.

Clear? As *clear as a snowy night in August*!

How does a high-school student whose writing sounds as if he's in high school make his writing sound like that of a real author?

Justin, Justin, Justin—I hope you'll take some of the answers you've received to your question here with a grain of salt. Those who missed the thrust of your question and those who don't understand what you're asking are nearly as bad as those whose answers are outright wrong.

Let's see if I can nail it by starting with another high-school student who wanted to be a writer.

When I began my writing career at fourteen, I felt incredibly lost. I had no idea of what a writer was supposed to sound like (his literary voice) or write like. Zero. None. Furthermore, I felt as if my own writing style was boring and pedantic and that it needed some definite "punching up."

So, I turned to those writers whose works I'd read and liked—Hawthorne, Melville, Poe, Doyle—and taught myself to write the way I thought they wrote. The only problem was that, while they and other

ABOUT WRITING RIGHT

writers of the era were famous, their literary style was peculiar to one particular era in time. Victorian. Today, we would call their writing old-fashioned and stilted. At the time, it was considered cutting edge and modern.

Cutting to the chase: I wasted nearly ten years of my life writing in someone else's stilted, outdated voice simply because I had no idea I had a voice of my own that I could have—and should have—cultivated. My early writing sucked. It probably would have gone over well in the early 1800s, but it was a "No-Sale" in the 1960s (yes, I'm that old).

Finally, once I realized that adopting someone else's literary voice wasn't going to work, I ever so *S-L-O-W-L-Y* began recognizing my own. I started writing the way I talked. Even at that, I often found myself slipping into what I term Writerese (the way writers think writers are supposed to write) before recognizing what had happened and scrapping my stilted writing to start over again, concentrating on sounding like *me*!

Now, here's where my advice to you gets a bit dicey. It took me ten years to undo the bad writing habits I picked up from emulating someone else's literary voice. That means I was twenty-four by the time that finally happened. Are you willing to devote the same amount of time to finding your voice? If you haven't picked up too many bad habits, you can probably find it in a lot less time than I needed. (Call me a "slow study.")

How? I'm glad you asked.

Record yourself talking sometime. Not when you set out to record yourself and are speaking self-consciously, but rather when you're talking to someone on the phone or in person. Then play back that recording. If you weren't hamming it up for the sake of the recording, you'll hear what you actually sound like to others. That's what you should "sound" like in writing.

Do you?

Here's a good way to find out. Take a few pages of something you're written, print them out, and read them out loud. You'll hear a *lot* of words and phrases you don't like. Things you'd never say to a friend but that you nonetheless said in your writing. Cross them out and replace them with your own voice.

Keep doing that with everything you write. Read everything out loud, hear where you've gone astray, and make the corrections (along with a mental note to yourself to avoid writing that way in the future).

The reason it's critical to read your material out loud is that the ears hear far more accurately than the "mind" does. When you read something to yourself, the mind fills in gaps, changes words to more understandable ones, and forgives a whole lot of "junk" writing. Your ears aren't that forgiving. They hear what you tell them, and they send what they hear to your brain for processing.

So, I get where you're coming from. You're not happy with your "high-school" voice because it's not your voice; it's the voice in which you've begun to write. The only way you'll ever be satisfied with your own literary voice is to discover what it is and work hard at maintaining it in everything you write.

And take solace in the fact that you now know more than 99 percent of all other high-school writers in the universe. Hopefully, it won't take you nearly as long to find your voice as it did me. Congratulations on a well-considered and thoughtful reflection on your own writing. Let me know if you have any other questions. But I think if you take this advice, you'll be writing like who you really are in no time. And people will *love* it!

Should book titles always be italicized?

Italicizing book titles (as well as titles to any standalone creative work, such as the film *Bell, Book and Candle* and the song *Ticket to Ride*), is the norm, although today, that norm can vary from one style guide to another. The definitive rule used to be that placing titles inside quotation marks pertained only to sub-works within a larger whole work. So, while *Ticket to Ride* is italicized when referring to the song as a standalone creative work, it's placed in quotation marks in regular face when referring to it as one of the songs on the album, *Help!*

- The Beatles' album Help! includes "Ticket to Ride" and other popular songs of the day.

In referring to an article in *Time* magazine, one might further refer to the articles within that publication, "Just Left of Center" and "Washing Out in Washington." The main creative work is placed in italics (*Time*) while the sub-works (which we call articles) included

ABOUT WRITING RIGHT

within that main magazine are placed in regular face in quotation marks:

- Check out *Time* magazine's articles, "Just Left of Center" and "Washing Out in Washington."

Over the years, some sources have attempted to simplify the rule (which, I admit, does take a modicum of thought) and resorted to what I call the "cancel culture" of literary style. Placing all titles, regardless of hierarchy, inside quotation marks creates more problems than it solves from a reader's point-of-view, but it simplifies things for the *writer* who, apparently, is some poor, brainless twit incapable of understanding and applying conventional rules to his writing. And God forbid the writer should have things made any tougher for him or her than absolutely necessary!

Bottom line: If you're writing for a specific publication or publishing house, follow the organization's in-house style rules. If you're writing for yourself, weigh the advantages and drawbacks of doing it either way, choose one, and be consistent in your use of italics and/or quotation marks.

TWO: The Structure of Writing

In writing, the word, "structure," means the same thing it does elsewhere outside of literature. It's the physical appearance, the form, the representation of the object to other elements surrounding it. Just as a building may have the structure of a two-flat or a high-rise, a literary work has its own structure upon and around which the work is built. It may be a novel or a short story, a novella or an article, a poem or a play.

It's similar to creating a drawing. When you start out, you begin with an outline of the image you want to create. From there, you add darker lines, shading, colors, texture, and finally end up with a finished masterpiece. One can hope.

An author follows a similar set of steps, each one of which leads to the creation of the complete work. While all authors' works vary depending upon style, choice of words, story line, and skill, all rely upon structure of some sort to get to the final product.

In its simplest term, structure is how a story is organized. It is the framework of the story, much like a foundation, rough framing, and roof trusses form the framework of a building.

In creating the framework, an author includes several disparate elements—the plot, setting, characters, and theme. All four of these elements create the structure.

The *plot* of the story is the story line, or what happens within the story. An author generally tells the story in some sort of order, most often chronological or time-related. He or she may also choose to begin in the middle of the story or even at the end, such as in a traditional suspense novel in which the reader knows what happens but reads on anyway to find out *how*. An author may also rely upon flashbacks or flash forwards in time to add color or to reveal certain elements of the story.

The story's *setting* includes the place and time where the story takes place. Its *characters* are the people inhabiting the story. And the *theme* is the overriding message the author hopes to resonate throughout the story and at its conclusion.

Structure in writing is greatly determined by traditional use, stemming back to ancient Greece and the three-act tragedy that includes a beginning, a middle, and an end. A modern short story follows that basic narrative structure. The author introduces a plot, creates some complications or a crisis, presents a turning point, and provides a resolution.

A novel, which due to its longer length, is often more complex and traditionally includes more descriptive and explanatory passages to paint with a broader stroke. It rarely employs obvious, sustained rhyme or syncopation the way poetry does, and it's not written in scenes and acts the way a play is. But it still contains a beginning, a middle, and an end.

Lots of different elements go into determining the structure, or the makeup or physical appearance, of a piece of literature. Length is a traditional definer of structure. Under 10,000 words, and a story is a short story. Under 50,000 words, and it's a novella. Over 50,000 words (or 60,000, depending upon who's doing the labeling), it's a novel. Each story structure employs the use of characters and their development through the work; the sustainability of plot; the placement of individual scenes; the author's choice of words (which also comes under the auspices of "style," and other elements. I also like to include audience in structure: Is the book written for general adult reading enjoyment (an adult trade book) or for a juvenile? For a scientific or technical audience or a student? A book's intended audience plays a major role in determining its structure, what elements to include, where to put them, and how to develop the story.

Sound confusing? It can be to a writer who just wants to sit back and relay a story the best he can. But even for a writer who hates outlining (a "pantser" who writes by the seat of his pants), some level of structuring the story takes place, either subliminally or otherwise. And that makes structure in writing a perennially hot topic for college-exam questions and trivia buffs.

For you, the reader and writer, if you understand the basic elements of the Greek tragedy as they apply to all forms of writing (beginning, middle, and end) and how you can move from one to the other without bogging the story down, you'll be well on your way to understanding your own writing better ... and to creating better writing on your own.

What is "structure" in writing, and why should writers pay any attention to it?

Structure, in its simplest form, is a basic framework around which you build your writing. It's present in all types of writing—fiction, nonfiction, business, academic, trade, children's. If it's part of the written word, it has structure. And that's a good thing, because knowing the structure of what you're about to write will save you time, energy, and paper while keeping your work from wandering all over the place.

But knowing that everything has structure and creating *effective* structure are different things. If you think about how you want to structure your writing—what happens, what happens next, what is the result of what happens next, and what is the result of *that* (ad infinitum), you'll be ahead of the game from Page One.

How do you develop structure in writing? That's easier to do than to answer because everyone's writing structure is different, based upon how each writer perceives his or her work, what his emphasis is, and what his goal will be.

Think about the structure of a textbook. You have a title, of course. And inside, you generally have some type of Table of Contents. That TOC contains chapter headings and often sub-chapter headings, both of which serve as an outline for creating the work's structure.

The TOC exists primarily for the benefit of the reader. It helps to define the book's structure and enables the reader to anticipate what happens when, what takes place where, and how the book will end. In short, it's a navigational tool, both for the reader and the creator or writer. Even in books that don't have a TOC, *you*, as the writer, will need to know where the chapters are, where they break, what they include, how they segue into the following chapters, and so on. That's all part of a book's structure.

If you begin writing a long work such as a book without giving any thought to its structure, you're going to end up with a mess. You'll misplace information (something you should have placed nearer to the front of the book than to the back and vice-versa), omit information that should have been included, and include information that should have been left out.

Remember back in Mrs. McReedy's third-grade English class when she had you outline a paper before actually writing it? Or perhaps she gave you an outline to follow, and you had to flesh it out into a report? Well, that's what structure is all about—providing the framework for the written piece.

While each writer's structure varies from one person to another, some structure exists because the reader needs that framework within which to place what he's reading. And, while there's no single structure for all forms of writing, there are a few elements common to all. Each piece of writing has a beginning, and each has an end. Presumably, each also has a certain amount of information in between (if not, you'd better re-think your goal here), and that information is divided into sets and sub-sets.

Structure, then, makes the most sense to a reader and *should* make the most to a writer when it is logical, clear, and precise. If, as either a reader or a writer, you find yourself asking, "Why is this here?" or "Isn't something missing from this section?" you know the work is something of a disaster.

So, yes, structure is essential to all writing. And, no, it's not the same from one writer to another. Nor is it the same from one genre to another. A Romance is structured differently than a Mystery or a Science Fiction/Fantasy, and all are structured differently than a textbook or an academic paper.

But keep in mind that framework is never carved in granite. It's always subject to some flux and variation—for good reason. As you write, you think. As you think, you question. As you question, you respond. As you respond, you reevaluate. As you reevaluate, you make changes.

What may start out as a simple Boy-Meets-Girl story that ends happily ever after could just as easily end up a Boy-Meets-Girl-Meets-Ex story that ends anything *but* happily.

So, regardless of how your structure unfolds, make thinking about your work from a structural point-of-view a regular part of your writing routine whenever you sit down to "crank something out." Think first; write second. That's always good advice. It's particularly commendable when deciding upon a structure for your next writing project—whether or not it morphs into something different along the way.

I can see how structure is important in novels and in nonfiction books, but is it something to worry about in business correspondence, which seems pretty cut and dry to worry about much of anything besides the point you're trying to make.

That's true—except that making your point is much easier and more effective if you structure your writing logically. Just as in other types of writing, business correspondence relies upon specific frameworks that result in more effective communication. More effective communication in business can mark the difference between success and failure, funding and being rejected, or even expanding or going out of business.

Although the framework for various types of business correspondence varies and is subject to the whims and calculated guesses of each author, here are a couple of typical examples based upon the purpose and goal of commonly encountered business formats.

As with all types of writing structure, begin with the basics—the main points or section headings--and expand from there into what to include in each type.

1. The Written Report

Reports traditionally contain a large amount of information that you must organize to have it make sense to the reader. To do so, you'll want to structure your piece something like this:

Report Title
Table of Contents
List of Illustrations (if any)
Abstract or Summation
Introduction
Background or Review

ABOUT WRITING RIGHT

Research Methodology Used
Findings or Analysis
Conclusion
Recommendations (if appropriate)
References and Bibliography
Appendix

That may seem like a lot of work to do simply to structure your report, but it's necessary because the proper report format is expected, anticipated, and desired. Leave something out, and you could wind up in big trouble.

2. The Press Release

For this type of business correspondence, you'll structure your piece quite differently. A press release is an announcement presented in a palatable format to be read and used as a basis for research, usually by the media.

Keep in mind when writing a press release that journalists and editors review dozens if not hundreds of releases every day. The key to structuring a successful release, then, is to keep it short, concise, and understandable. It must also contain contact details so that the recipients can follow up in requesting additional information or interviews.

Although the structure of a successful press release contains specific elements, these are hidden from the reader and only serve to benefit the release's creator (you!). The finished product should look something like this:

<u>Press Release Heading Includes:</u>
Date: "For Immediate Release" or "For Release after [insert date]
Headline: (make it short and grabby)
<u>Press Release Body Includes:</u>
Paragraph 1 - Lead: This is where you summarize the story, telling everything the reader might want to know. Use the Five W's of journalism: who, what, when, where, and why. Include only the most critical information and a bridge to the next paragraph.

Paragraph 2 - Follow-Up: Add more details to flesh out the information in the opening paragraph.

Paragraph 3 - Documentation: Supply pertinent facts and quotes from major players in the story, or site industry studies. Brevity and precision are still key, so write precisely and economically. *Do not editorialize or otherwise give your opinion on the subject.*

Paragraph 4 - Conclusion: This is where you finally summarize the relevant information with a satisfying and believable conclusion.

Paragraph 5 - Contact Information: Say something such as "For additional information, background material, or in-depth interviews, please contact [insert name]."

Developing a structure first and then expanding it into a finished press release will help assure that you've included everything you want or need and in the proper order. And that's the most crucial role a structured outline can play.

Of course, just as with creating and following a structure for other types of writing (novels, academic books, feature articles, etc.), once you design a structure for your business correspondence, you'll want to stick with it until you discover that something doesn't work. If that happens, go back, find out what seems out of place or what needs additional fleshing out or trimming, and make the appropriate adjustments.

Be sure to read your finished press release out loud (as you should all of your writing) so that you can pick up on any awkward wording, sudden jumps of thought, or unsubstantiated logic or facts. Pay special attention to the ending of one paragraph and the beginning of another so that the transition reads smoothly and effortlessly.

Remember, structures in business writing, just as in all writing, are meant to be followed only as long as they prove useful. If the time comes when they don't, make whatever adjustments are necessary, and pick up from where you left off.

Can you give an example of how to structure an academic assignment so that even I can understand it?

Piece of cake. But first, let's start by defining structure as an ordering of ideas. Structuring (or outlining, framing, or however you like to think of it) ideas is important because you want the end product—your finished work--to read smoothly and logically. You don't want your concepts jumping around from one sentence to the next.

In other words, you want your main points to be linked together so that, by the end of the piece, they work together to create a single, logical conclusion. Structuring your work then becomes critical in producing effective academic writing. That means starting with a premise (a question or a goal), proceeding through your examples (arguments), and ending with a conclusion.

If you don't structure your writing correctly, you're likely to end up with illogical, confused, or scattered thoughts at odds with one another. That will not make for a happy reader. Or a good grade or successful business venture!

One of the best tests for evaluating a document for effective structure is summing up the information included in a single sentence. In Hollywood, film people call such a summation a logline, and films are often made or passed over based upon how successful the logline is. Here are a couple of examples:

Gone with the Wind - A high-spirited southern girl falls in love with her cousin's man during the Civil War, but he eventually tires of her petty shallowness and, in the end, leaves her to her beloved plantation.

It's a little long-winded, I know, but, hey! It's a complete film condensed into a shoebox. Here's another example:

Overboard - A snobbish heiress suffering from amnesia is tricked into thinking she's married to a crude tradesman with whom, upon regaining her memory, she falls in love.

Okay, and one more just for good measure:

Stagecoach - A wanted man falls into the hands of a sheriff who sets out to bring him back to jail before the outlaw redeems himself in the end.

If you can't summarize your written piece into a single sentence, you're probably guilty of trying to squeeze too many different points into something that should be more tightly focused. You may need to reconsider your premise and how you reach your conclusion.

Of course, before you can evaluate your writing's structure, you need to develop a plan. So, think about the premise of your work and focus on the ideas you want to use to advance that premise before you begin writing. Jot down your notes so that you don't forget them. Eliminate extraneous ideas that don't contribute to the conclusion. If your topic is the role women play in society, for example, your notes might look something like this:

Rough List of Ideas To Include
- Biology and sex
- Traditional women's roles
- Feminism and chauvinism
- The "Right To Vote" movement
- Other women's movements
- WWII
- The industrial revolution
- The technological revolution

Next, ask yourself which of these ideas can be linked together: Which belong in the same sub-sections of your work? You're likely to refine them in this way:

Traditionally Limiting Factors
- Biology and sex
- Traditional women's roles
- Feminism and chauvinism
- *Organized Calls for Change*
- The "Right To Vote" movement
- Other women's movements
- *Societal Factors Affecting Change*
- WWII
- The industrial revolution
- The technological revolution

These three groups of factors work together to form a consistent view of the overall role of women in society. If you remove any one of the groups, you'd be left with a gaping hole or an incomplete argument and would have to revisit your thinking to fill in the gaps.

If you follow a guide such as this, you'll find greater clarification in your work and increased reader satisfaction. If you don't, opting instead for the "easier" route of merely "winging it," you're going to end up with a piece filled with holes and riddled with repetitious, unconstructive, and even contradictory points.

And that's not what you want. Nor is the grade of "D-" you'll likely receive.

Can you tell me how to settle on a word count for my novel?

Sure. Choose exactly the right number of words. Not too many, and not too few. And stick to them.

ABOUT WRITING RIGHT

How? The easiest way to adjust the length of a novel that's too long for its own good is, of course, to get out the old pencil and begin red-lining the manuscript. Take out everything that doesn't add to the story or the characters, setting, etc. Watch especially for long, rambling paragraphs or even entire chapters that don't contribute much to the book and could be replaced by a single sentence or two—or not at all!

Adding material to a novel that's too short, on the other hand, is usually trickier. Most fledgling authors start on page one, add a word or a sentence here or there, and find out that, in the end, they've expanded the book by a paltry 500 words or so. Not a good use of your time.

Instead, think through the story from start to finish and ask what *major* additions would work to advance the narrative. Perhaps a new character enters, creates some havoc, and departs in some logical fashion, leaving his or her mark and perhaps raising a few new questions for the reader to ponder. Or maybe a new event involving the existing characters occurs. In short, whenever expanding a shorter novel into a longer one, it's always easier to think big and add significant chunks of the story than to think small by adding a few words here and there.

One of my favorite techniques for expanding a book is to add a "prequel" chapter before the original first chapter. In other words, add a chapter explaining some event that occurred that leads into the main story. Something that serves as an introduction and whets the reader's appetite to continue. Just be sure in adding any new material anywhere that it's relevant to the story's advancement and not merely empty filler.

How does anyone write a novel of 100,000 words or more?

Good question. First, you need to ignore most of the answers so many "experts" give to this question and realize this: You write one word at a time. *Period.* When you've finished telling your story, then you check the word count. If it's 3,000 words, congratulations, you've just written a short story. If it's 30,000, you've written a novella. If it's 60,000 or more, you've written a novel. What matters here is writing one word after another and to continue until the story is told. If it turns out to be 100,000 words or more, so what? It's still a novel.

But shouldn't length come into play in deciding how to write your book? Actually, yes. And no. Length becomes a factor only when deciding analytically how much "real estate" you're going to need to eat up to *get your story told*. The number of words you require to do so is immaterial.

But, what if, when you're partly through the writing process, you think the finished product is running too short? Can you elaborate? Include multiple side-stories? Different settings? Different timeframes? Introduce new characters?

Well, *yes* to all of the above, but *only* if doing so doesn't harm and, in fact, *helps* advance the main story.

The starting point, then, is not a preconceived notion of how many words you need to crank out. It's the way in which you can best tell the story. And that begins with an outline. It can be written down on paper (which I highly recommend) or running freely through your brain (which works for some writers). From there, you set about filling in the blanks, expanding the details, providing background material, describing the characters and their motivations, detailing their history, etc. Writing as faithfully and interestingly as your skills as a storyteller and as a creative writer allow will dictate whether or not the work will be a critical, financial, or creative success. And that's *regardless* of its length.

So, once again, the best and *only* legitimate answer to your question is this: Write one word at a time. When you're finished, and only when you're finished, go back and re-read from beginning to end, noting where the *story* dictates additional info may be required, some information may need to be cut, and when the story as you envisioned it is "perfect."

Remember: No one remembers novels for their length. Everyone remembers novels (and even short fiction, for that matter) for their content and how that content is presented to the reader.

Should a writer vary the word count of his chapters or doesn't that matter?

I don't think the answer to chapter lengths is written in stone. With that said, I sometimes work overtime to avoid all chapters being 10 or 15 or 20 pages in length. It seems to me that various writers have a set amount of words (an internal counting machine, perhaps, that works subliminally in the background?) with which they're comfortable working. Many books published over the years have chapters that are roughly the same length.

As a reader, you know what I'm saying. You start reading a short chapter, and then you read another like it, and, after a while, you begin to feel as though each new chapter will be about the same length. Perhaps you even scan ahead in the book to see if you're right—and you usually are!

I think writing chapters of the same length is probably a trap into which too many writers fall. While it's true that a chapter is as long as a chapter needs to be, as the creator of the book, you have the ability to make adjustments to your chapter lengths and still have each one be as long as it needs to be.

For example, you find yourself writing in chapter "clumps" of, say, 20 pages or so. What's to stop you from going in after the first page or two of a new chapter, inserting a "hook" to keep the reader guessing at what comes next, and making that the end of that chapter? You'll probably have to adjust the next few lines of the following chapter to align with what you wrote for the hook, but that shouldn't be too difficult.

The result? Just about the time you lull your reader into expecting chapters to run for X number of pages (or number of minutes or pebbles on the beach or whatever), *wham*! You throw a one-pager at him or her. The result, if done right, not only wakes him up but also intrigues him enough to want to keep reading, wondering if there are more of those hidden gems in the book.

That brings up another point, although it's slightly off-topic. Don't go out of your way to make chapters too long. Often, writers feel they have to keep a specific train of thought going without interruption. Or they don't feel comfortable deciding where one chapter should end and another, begin.

But overly long chapters can be death to a reader. If you doubt me, check out a copy of your local newspaper. See how long an average paragraph is, and then check out the number of paragraphs in a "section" (usually denoted by a sub-head introducing a new section in the story, similar to a book's new "chapter"). Newspaper editors learned long ago that the average reader wants quick, easily navigated sentences, paragraphs, and "chapters" to avoid growing eye-weary or bored. That's why experience journalists often make some of literature's best (or at least most successful) novelists. They write with easily digestible sentences, paragraphs, and chapters.

That's not a universal dictum, of course. Every "rule" has its exceptions. But it's something you might want to check out in your own work and at least consider making some alterations. After all, you don't wear the same suit and tie to work every day, do you? Why would you present the same chapter lengths to your readers?

What are the maximum number of main and important other characters should I include in my novella?

The answer is simple: As many as you need.

No, really. Of course, if a character is necessary to a scene or a chapter or an entire book or short story, you should include him or her. If not, write him out.

Simple, no?

The point is that everything in writing reflects a condensation of reality, whether it's a novel or a novella or a short story or even merely an image. That means that, if you're going to capture the essence of the true meaning of that reality, you can't waste time or words frivolously. That means, too, that you can't waste space on meaningless characters.

If you're looking for a specific number in response to your question (three characters are enough, four are too many), sorry, Charlie. That dog won't hunt. There is no magic number for how many characters inhabit your prose, nor should there be. Let the story dictate who's in it. You, as the author, get to bring those characters to life.

Or death.

How many characters should I write into my novel?

Just as many as it requires. *Seriously.* Forget about "guidelines" for determining the number of characters you should have and other such nonsense. Each novel is different; each writer is unique; each story is one in a million. As a rule, you'll begin your novel with the storyline already firmly entrenched in your mind. You'll also have identified several characters, including the main character and some primary supporting persons. You may well end the story in just that way. It has happened before. Remember *The Big Chill*?

ABOUT WRITING RIGHT

What I'm wondering, though, is if you asked that question because you face the terrifying fact that you may need a new character to keep the story going, and you don't have a clue as to who he is or how to introduce him.

Am I right?

I bring this up because I faced the same terror when I was a young novelist. That's before I had any formal training in fiction writing, before I had any experience in fiction writing, before I had any knowledge of just what the hell fiction writing is! I remember getting to a certain point in my story, feeling the need to introduce a new character, and running through the four or five characters I'd already introduced.

If none of those earlier characters fit the task at hand, I knew I had to create a new one from scratch. But who? How? What would the character be like? How would he or she think, act, talk, *look*?

That was always a frightening moment in my early writing development. The terror ended when I finally learned to E-N-V-I-S-I-O-N my characters. Even the new ones. Once I took time to analyze the situation, I reviewed the different types of people who might fit into the scene and decided on whether or not to make him a throwaway character or someone to develop into a three-dimensional human being.

You see, when you think things through, imagine them, create imagery around them, describe them to yourself, and do that until you can actually *see* them in your mind—as if you were watching them on a movie screen or stage or your television set—you make your life easier. And your creations seem more real because you're not relying upon some spur-of-the-moment caricature that might fit every other character ever created. Seeing is believing. Or, rather, seeing is to coax your *readers* into believing. Remember: See it and show it, don't *say* it.

So, give that a shot the next time you get to a place in your book's development where you know you need to introduce a new character but can't for the life of you figure out who. Think things through until you can hear the character, see him, smell him, pick him out of a police lineup—whatever! Then, you'll know intuitively whether or not you need to add him to your story.

Of course, if you'd begun your book with a detailed, chapter-by-chapter outline, you might not have found yourself in just such a predicament. But, that's another matter over which I can chastise you some other day.

How do you write nonfiction chapters?

You know, this is a bit of a guessing game because there are numerous ways to interpret your question. What I assume you're asking is how you know where to begin and end a chapter in a nonfiction book. Right? If not, please feel free to rephrase the question in a response.

If so, here's the down-and-dirty answer.

Chapter one? No problem. You begin at the beginning of what you want to say. How and where you end it, though, depends upon your subject matter and how long the chapter is running.

For instance, in a how-to book on planting trees and shrubs outdoors, you may want to begin with Chapter One: Finding a Spot for Your Plant. In that, you discuss the pros and cons of finding a suitable location for your plant; what to be aware of; getting the city to come out to mark any underground lines if it's a large plant; and taking such things as exposure, light, and shade into consideration. Once you do that, you might be ready to begin Chapter Two: Preparations for Planting. End that chapter after you've beaten the topic to death. Follow up with Chapter Three: Watering and Pruning Your New Plant, and end it at a suitable spot, as well. Your chapters should have *logical* concluding points before you move on, just as when you're talking. You don't plan on stopping for a breath every five or six seconds, and you certainly don't plan ahead to do so; it merely happens. The same is true with concluding points in chapters.

In short, you want to begin a new chapter with a new activity, even if all the action is related to a previous chapter (as in planting a tree or shrub). Take things step-by-step or, in this case, chapter-by-chapter, elaborating on all aspects the reader may need to consider within the scope of that chapter, utilizing the journalist's Five W's: *Who*, *What*, *When*, *Where*, and *Why*. And then, of course, throw in that sixth element: *How*. You should also discuss in each chapter the potential problems the reader may encounter and how to resolve them.

ABOUT WRITING RIGHT

In other types of nonfiction books, such as biographies, memoirs, histories, and the like, you'll similarly group similar aspects of the subject matter into their respective chapters. Those aspects may be governed by the passage of time (Young Abe Lincoln, Abe's Teenage Years, Senator Abe Lincoln, etc.) or by any other logical measure.

The key to knowing where to end a chapter is in *grouping*. You need to make sense. Keep chapters relatively short to prevent the reader from going crazy or falling asleep, and keep your chapter progressions logical. First this, then that, then the other. Chapter One, Chapter Two, Chapter Three. That's how the mind works, after all. So, why mess with Mother Nature?

What's the best way to ruin a book in one sentence?

I'm not sure if it's the best way, but starting out a book with your main character's first and last name is so amateurish that it's a sure-fire way to ruin your chances for publication.

Joe Smith wasn't sure why he'd gotten the call, but he had.

Who on earth cares what the guy's name is when you haven't even established a plot or a reason for his existence yet? What's that you say? But, don't you have to establish about whom you're writing to give the reader a heads-up from the very start?

No! In fact, if you keep the reader guessing, you'll get him to read farther along than if you'd spelled everything out for him from the beginning:

He wasn't sure why he'd gotten the call, but he had.

Now, the reader is wondering not only why "he'd" gotten the call and why "he" wasn't sure himself but also just who the heck this mystery "he" is! Someone important? Someone inconsequential? Someone likable? Someone to hate? Remember, your primary goal in writing for a reader is to snag that person and goad him into reading on … and on … and on. Of course, you can overdo it, too, failing to assign a name to your character until Page 396. But that's just silly. It's best to give your character a name when the time presents itself. That means when it benefits the reader to know who the character is without stumbling over his identity from the very first words.

Even then, think twice about listing both of your character's names at once. Often, a first name will suffice for a while (and, occasionally, for the entire book). Again, you can hold off on revealing the person's last name until the time is appropriate (as in when it's essential to do so), thus continuing to build suspense.

Now, with that said—and taking my word that beginning a novel with the character's full name will turn off an editor *instantly*—guess how many novelists fall into making just that mistake? Well, I don't know, either. But from the books crossing my desk, searching for an editor (or a book doctor or even a publisher for that matter), I'm going to say eight out of ten. That's a lot of commonly committed writing mistakes that can cost an author dearly.

So, be smart. Be cagey. Be wily. Be *mysterious*. As with all other elements of a novel (and, often, with a nonfiction book as well), reveal the character's first and last names only when it suits the advancement of the story. And quit slamming the door on your success from the very first line!

What's the name of the page in the book where it cites the sources? And where within the book can it usually be found?

I think you're referring to a book's Bibliography, which appears in a book's back matter. What's *back matter*? It's the polar opposite of *front matter*. Here's a breakdown of the commonly encountered parts of a book (most relevant to nonfiction, since novels don't require many of these sections):

FRONT MATTER

This includes the information that appears at the beginning of a book, before the book's content. It's a bit like the nuts-and-bolts information in a legal contract before you get into all the technical stuff (the body). In a book, front matter consists of title and author (of course), publisher and address (or at least city/state), ISBN, and Library of Congress data. The front matter pages are either unnumbered or numbered with Roman numerals (x, iii, xix, etc.).

A description of the front matter includes these pages:
- Half Title (Sometimes Called the Bastard Title): Actually, this is just the book's title appearing on an inside page, sometimes shortened for long titles.
- Front piece: The artwork on the left (or "verso") side of the page opposite the title page on the right (or "recto") side of the page.
- Title Page: The full page with the book's title, authors, and publisher.

ABOUT WRITING RIGHT

- Copyright Page: The page with the declaration of copyright, meaning the copyright owner (almost always the authors) and the credits, such as illustrator, editorial staff, and indexer. Sometimes, this page has notes from the publisher and copyright acknowledgments for reprinted material that requires permissions, such as excerpts, photographs, illustrations, song lyrics, etc. This page also includes the edition number or printing of the book (First, Second, Third, etc.).
- Dedication: This is a page of acknowledgement in which the author elaborates upon the contribution of others by stating that the book is dedicated "To So-and-So, without whose help its writing wouldn't have been possible" (or something similar).
- Acknowledgments: A page thanking those who have donated their time, resources, and talent toward writing the book without being specific.
- Table of Contents: The page or pages outlining (or at least listing) each chapter of the book.
- Foreword: The "set up" or rationale for the book's existence, usually written by someone *other than the author*.
- Preface or Introduction: Another "set up" page, usually written by the *author*, explaining his/her motivation or reason for writing the book.

BODY MATTER

The main "story" or core content of the book, often divided into chapters. The body matter is numbered with Arabic numerals beginning with the number "1" on the first page of Chapter One and concluding with the last printed page of the book.

BACK MATTER

This includes information that appears at the back of the book, although some or all back matter is optional, depending upon the publisher and/or author.

- Glossary: A listing of the book's terms and definitions unique to the book's subject matter.
- Bibliography: A page or pages in a nonfiction book listing the references and sources used in researching or preparing to write the book.

- Index: A section of nonfiction pages acting as a roadmap to different places, persons, and references mentioned within the body matter of the book.

That's it—a brief description of what's included in the Front Matter, Body Matter, and Back Matter of a book.

For writing, is a new paragraph line needed in dialogue when a character responds with actions?

I think whether or not you should start a new paragraph following a line of dialogue depends upon how closely the dialogue and the following narration are to one another. Here's an example of how to handle each:

Example One:

John said, "I think I'm going to rest here for a while." He pulled out a chair and sat down.

Example Two:

John said, "I think I'm going to rest here for a while."

He didn't know why, but he suddenly felt tired, weak, confused—too much so to carry on their conversation. What had begun as a simple exchange of words had somehow escalated into a war.

While there's no "right and wrong," simple common sense dictates that closely tied thoughts should remain together in the same paragraph (as shown in Example One above), even if part of that paragraph contains a quote. Disparate thoughts, on the other hand (as shown in Example Two above), should get their own distinct paragraphs to distinguish between the two trains of thought for the reader.

With that said, all rules are meant to be broken—*if* you understand them before cracking a few grammatical eggs. If you're not sure which way to go, try reading your copy out loud, listening to the words as they fall on your ears, and deciding only then whether or not to hit the return key between sentences.

How do I write a dynamite, captivating first page to my novel?

How do you write a compelling first page to your novel? Think about it. Ask yourself the question, What's compelling to me? Or What's outrageous? Or What's remarkable? Or What's the most amazing thing I could imagine ever happening to me?

ABOUT WRITING RIGHT

Once you've come up with a list of four or five things, choose the strongest, most outrageous, most compelling, complex, alluring, frightening, incendiary, and just about every other shocking adjective you can think of. Here are some examples:

I came home, and all my furniture was gone.

I went out to my uncle's restaurant, but I found a sign saying 'Out of Business' on the front door.

I walked in to find her body in the center of the room, with both wrists slit but no blood to be seen. Anywhere!

See what I mean? Next, ask yourself how that could be. Have your character wonder about it aloud (use italics and first person to show an internal thought), as in this example:

Maybe she was killed somewhere else and the body moved here. That explains the lack of blood.

I placed my hand against her neck. No pulse. But her skin was soft and warm.

She hasn't been dead for more than a couple minutes. I'd better call the cops. They'll want to know ... oh, crap. They'll want to know about the fight we had the other night. I'll tell them ... I'll tell them what? That it wasn't serious. Just a lover's spat. And then they'll say it was serious enough for someone to call the cops on us. Someone who has something against us. Or someone who had something against her!

There's your compelling first page. Simple when you take the time to think about it in advance. The key is to create the element of surprise, and then to keep the mystery behind it alive to entice the reader to read on. A lot of people like to take a peek at a book's first page—either on Amazon's "Peek inside the Book" feature or at the corner book store—before deciding whether or not to buy it. Don't give them a choice in the matter. *Make* them *have* to buy it, if for no other reason than to answer an apparently unanswerable question: Who did it, and why.

After that, the rest of your book will damned near write itself. *If* you're lucky!

What's a basic structure for a simple novel?
A simple first-novel story structure? How about this suggestion:
Boy meets girl; boy loses girl; girl winds up dead.

Now, all you, as the author, have to do is to convince the reader that her boyfriend murdered her while he struggles to convince the cops (and the reader) that he didn't. There's your universal murder theme, as simple as it comes. Except that nothing, in the hands of a good, creative writer, is simple.

New characters come and go. New motives appear and vanish in the night. New clues surface and get squashed like so many bugs against a car's windshield. Then there are the nearly unmistakable signs that the cops know more than they're letting on—*much* more. So much more, in fact, that the reader begins to think that maybe it was John Law who had a reason to put the bag on the old gal. Perhaps they found some secret she was harboring that could be damaging to their reputation or even land the District Attorney in prison!

All you have to do as a novice first-book author is to keep all the loose ends straight, build a strong story arc with several sub-arcs unfolding around it, and write believable dialogue.

Oh, yes, and you will need two more things as the author of this convoluted yet simple tale: The girl's real murderer and a logical rationale for how he, she, or they got caught.

Along the way, introduce another girl—perhaps a formerly spurned girlfriend or even a lover or even a simple bystander who hates to see injustice carried out—to help the main character through some of his perils, and you're home free.

And do let me know when you've finished writing the book. I'd like to read it.

Is there a standard format for self-publishing a book?

There really is no "standard format" for a self-published book. There are commonly produced sizes, ranging from pocketbook to coffee table and everything in between, plus custom sizes (which cost more to produce, of course). And, you can publish in paperback, hard cover, eBook, and sometimes audio book. Beyond that, there are some self-publishing guidelines for setting up the formatting of the interior (the copy) as well as the cover that you should follow for the best results.

With that said, all POD (Print On Demand) publishers have different requirements depending upon the software they use to prepare your manuscript for an acceptably good job of production and

ABOUT WRITING RIGHT

printing. Amazon's Kindle Direct Publishing has an entire free course that you can access simply by signing up and clicking on the link for their KDP Tools and Resources. Other publishers, such as Ingram, Lulu, Draft2Digital, etc., have their own guidelines. Depending upon where you decide to publish (including multiple places), you would be wise to follow their suggestions to the letter.

Can I switch points-of-view with different characters from third-person omniscient to third-person limited? Are editors fine with that?

Is it "fine" with editors? Probably not. The reason is that it's not "fine" with readers. But let's slow down and take a closer look at what you're talking about here.

Third-person point-of-view is a means of storytelling in which the narrator relies upon someone besides himself to relay the events. To do so, the writer uses third-person pronouns such as *he*, *she*, and *they*. It's the most natural way of relaying a story and, thus, the easiest. That means that, not surprisingly, it's also the most popular and frequently used perspective in writing fiction, particularly among new writers.

But, as you intimate, there are two different third-person points-of-view. One, called *omniscient*, gives the narrator complete (or omniscient) knowledge of what all the characters are thinking and feeling. One example:

> *John felt as if he had been betrayed, but Mary couldn't have felt more comfortable.*

While John is perfectly capable of assessing his own feelings, the only way he could know about Mary's feelings is through the use of the third-person omniscient point-of-view—the point-of-view of an all-knowing narrator.

Another third-person point-of-view is called *limited*. That's when the narrator's knowledge of what the characters are thinking and feeling is *limited* to those held by the specific character, namely, the protagonist. For example:

> *John felt as if he had been betrayed, but he could only guess at how Mary felt.*

Since we're writing from the third-person limited point-of-view, John can't possibly speak for how Marry feels, although he may certainly speculate. That inability for your character to know all is a very real (although not insurmountable) limitation to writing in third-person limited point-of-view.

Often, new writers feel most comfortable writing in the first-person point-of-view since that often seems most familiar to them. For example:

I felt as if I had been betrayed, but I could only guess as to how Mary felt.

Notice that, although the first-person point-of-view seems to be a comfortable approach for the writer to take, it's also extremely limiting because, just as in third-person limited, the narrator can only *know* what he knows from his particular perspective. That means he can't make pronouncements about how other characters may think or feel, where the story is going, what happened previously (when he wasn't present), or what happens elsewhere in the tale farther on in time.

For that reason, alone, writing in the third-person omniscient point-of-view presents the writer with far more latitude in developing the story.

From the reader's perspective, the third-person omniscient is likewise the most satisfying because it's the most trustworthy. After all, the narrator knows all, and he's revealing to the reader what he knows about the story a little at a time. That includes intimate and often critical details that no one else but the narrator and God, Himself, could possibly know. Who else but the narrator would the reader put his faith in?

From the writer's perspective, both third-person limited and first person points-of-view are the most difficult to pull off because the writer must rely upon other characters and his own observations to tell the story. In other words, there are no shortcuts for the writer, who must constantly ask himself, *Would the narrator know that about another person, and, if not, who would?*

Now, for the crux of your question: Can you switch between third-person omniscient and third-person limited points-of-view, depending upon the character? The short answer is *no*. The long answer is *maybe, providing you do it obviously, effectively, and with the complete understanding and acceptance of the reader.*

ABOUT WRITING RIGHT

Therein lies the problem. A writer can't know how a reader will react to a shift in point-of-view. The reader might reject it outright and give up on the book. At the very least, he's going to feel cheated.

As a rule, then, the point-of-view should be consistent. If the writer even *attempts* to switch tracks in the middle of the journey, the reader will question the writer's authority to tell the story. And he'll reject the story outright as being contrived or bogus. No one wants to play in a card game where the deck is stacked.

If you begin telling a story in limited third-person and suddenly reveal a secret that another character harbors, even though that character never said a word about it, you can kiss the reader goodbye. You've lost his or her trust in the narrator (you!), and you've lost a potential five-star review. The only way you can pull off a switch in perspective is to have the main character (limited perspective) overhear the other person's secret, be told the secret by the other person or a third party, or read about it on the Internet (unlikely) or in that character's diary (even more unlikely).

That brings up my question to you: Why would you even contemplate changing perspectives in mid-stream? To me, it says you're looking for a gimmick, an earth-shattering, logic-bending, contrived mechanism to *wow* your reader to keep coming back for more. If that's the case, take it from me and several hundred thousand other successful fiction writers over the years, there is no *wowing* your reader except, perhaps, through great, strong writing. Just buckle down, decide upon your point-of-view, forget about the gimmicks, and tell the story the best way possible so that everyone will want to read it.

That's what writing is all about, after all. Isn't it?

What's the best font to use to write a book?

If what you mean by "to write a book" is to *create* a book for your personal use, use whatever font you desire. The key in such a situation is to use something that's non-obtrusive so that the font doesn't slow down your output or otherwise distract from your productivity.

On the other hand, if what you mean by "to write a book" is to p*ublish* a book, numerous studies conducted over the eons show that serif fonts (such as Times New Roman, Courier, and Garamond among others) are easier, faster, and more enjoyable to read than are sans-serif fonts (such as Arial, etc.). And, since your goal in publishing a book is to entice readers to buy, read, and enjoy what you've written, why buck the odds? I picked up five books at random off the corner of my desk, and all five were produced with a serif typeface, most in 11 or 12 point Times New Roman, which size makes for easier reading than smaller or larger fonts.

Which brings up an interesting supposition that has been bouncing around the world of graphic arts for decades. Courier, the long-time king of serif fonts, was for years the *only* font used universally by newspaper publishers for distribution to the masses. Thus, readers were raised on Courier, grew comfortable with reading Courier, and have made it and other serif fonts similar to it their favorites ever since. In this case, it seems that familiarity, rather than breeding contempt, breeds *comfort*.

Of course, as in most things in life, there's a contrary supposition that, since serif fonts are intrinsically easier to read than sans-serif fonts, early newspaper publishers adopted Courier as their number one go-to font to satisfy their readers' expectations. What came first, the chicken or the egg?

Whichever may be the case, think of serif fonts as the GOP of font-face styles while sans-serif fonts are more like the upstart Democrat Party. For years, one was far more common and universally grounded than the other. Today, they both have their place in the publishing industry.

And you thought this question was beyond the reach of politics!

Just what in the world is Narrative Nonfiction anyway, and how do you go about writing it?

Narrative Nonfiction? *Ahh,* the words roll off the tongue like *buttah*. They roll off the tongue ... and plop to the floor with a thud. Narrative Nonfiction? Just what in the name of Aunt Nellie's mare is *that*?

At first, the phrase seems like an oxymoron. A narrative is a story. Nonfiction is journalism. So, this pup is a true story? Or a made-up story that just happens to be true? What's going on here? Double talk? Jabberwock? *Exactly*! Whether you call it Narrative Nonfiction, Creative Nonfiction, or Literary Journalism, it's one-in-the-same. What we're looking at here is nonfiction that reads like a novel.

ABOUT WRITING RIGHT

The keyword in Narrative Nonfiction is *nonfiction*. Narratives must be fact. Unlike the Historical Novel that uses a real-life element as a focal point and then loads up on fictional elements and characters, the Narrative Nonfiction tale starts with fact and ends with fact (and, in fact, has fact sandwiched in between). It's a story told as a story, complete with a beginning, a middle, and an end.

Sound like a piece of cake? Seem like the most natural thing on earth? Yeah, sure. After all, every article you read in the newspaper, every story you see on *60 Minute*s is factual. Each one is a story. Each one has a beginning, a middle, and an end. So, what's the big deal that sets Narrative Nonfiction apart?

Well, writing an 800-word article versus a 90,000-word book is one big deal. While it's relatively easy to write Narrative Nonfiction in short form, it becomes dramatically more difficult to sustain the exercise over hundreds of pages.

Writing compellingly is another big deal. No one expects to fall in love/hate with the subject in a newspaper article. But for a Narrative Nonfiction book (or long magazine article, etc.) to be a success, the author must make the reader feel something, must make the reader care, must make him want to learn more.

How does a writer do that? The answer lies in presentation.

The Narrative Nonfiction book is a hybrid, a melding of the art of storytelling and reporting. It's a way of taking the very real world of people, places, and events and relating them in a story-like fashion. Instead of "just the facts, ma'am" (remember the "lean-and-mean" admonitions you learned in J School?), NN demands that the author set the scene, unleash the drama, flesh-out the characters, and relay the story in a compelling voice that the reader wants to hear.

Nabokov once remarked about narrative: "If I tell you that the king died, and then the queen died, that's not narrative; that's plot. But, if I tell you that the king died, and then the queen died of a broken heart, *that's* narrative."

In other words, Narrative Nonfiction bridges the gap between happenings (plot) and emotions. It tells not only what happened but also why it happened, how people were affected by its happening, and what happened as a result. It's a Whodunit with real characters. It's a historical novel without any fiction. Narrative Nonfiction must make the reader want to read on, whereas basic nonfiction reporting doesn't—the reader can stop anywhere without feeling he's missed much. The Narrative Nonfiction writer not only needs to tell a story but also to tell it compellingly. Here are a couple of examples:

Nonfiction:

George Jensen, 26, of 5353 Los Alamos Blvd., died in his home last night, February 23, of suspicious causes. Jensen, who was last seen alive at 7:30 p.m. by his girlfriend, Marsha Franks of 2735 Glenwood Ave., was a victim of suffocation. Police suspect foul play.

Narrative Nonfiction:

George Jensen had entered the prime of his life. At 26, the world had finally opened its portals to him, and he had decided to explore them. Affable, outgoing, boyish in his charms yet street-wise and shrewd beyond his years, he was the ideal candidate to make his way through life successfully. He was the doctor people feel comfortable visiting, the clergyman in whom people feel safe confiding. He was everything to everyone. But when Jensen's girlfriend said good night to him that snowy evening in February, all that would change. Jensen's dreams--and his girlfriend's--would come crashing down around them and disappear forever.

You get the point. This isn't merely meat-and-potatoes reporting; this is something more. And, the good news is, editors are looking for Narrative Nonfiction *to publish.*

Where can *you* find a publisher for *your* Narrative Nonfiction? The Web is a good proving ground. Many writing sites are all too happy to showcase a new writer's work.

Also, newspapers and magazines are publishing increasingly more NN, which is good news for *all* narrative writers. After decades of *USA Today*-style underwriting, where news bites, charts, graphs, and sidebars told only the meat of a story, it's heartening to see the trend swinging back the other way. Newspapers and magazines are at last returning the word "story" to the phrase "true story."

Book publishers, too, are turning increasingly toward Narrative Nonfiction as a reliable source of income. One glance at the pages of the *New York Times Review of Books* confirms that NN is here to stay and only growing stronger.

ABOUT WRITING RIGHT

"I'm getting an increasing number of requests from editors for Narrative Nonfiction," says literary agent Faye Swetky of The Swetky Agency. "Several editors who used to handle fiction are now acquiring Narrative Nonfiction exclusively. That's a pretty good indication that there's money for Narratives in the marketplace. Otherwise, publishers wouldn't touch them."

And that, for freelance writers everywhere, is the best news of all.

I'd like to get into home and garden book writing, but I'm not sure what to write about other than some aspect of growing plants. Help!

I can identify with you. It's not easy taking a subject as broad as garden writing and narrowing it down to a few specific topics. It's not easy, but it's imperative. And that's where the problem comes in. Here's what I mean:

There is *nothing* new under the sun. And that is particularly true with garden writing.

What's that? Do you question my veracity?

Then tell me this.

What's new about tomatoes? What's different about growing vegetables from seeds? What's unique about soil, water, and light? What's *different* about *any* gardening topic you can conceive?

Answer: Absolutely nothing. That is both the challenge--*and* the resolution to--selling a new gardening book to a publisher. It's tough to come up with some angle on gardening that hasn't been done before, granted. But it's even tougher *not* to. Try bouncing the usual "Why My Garden Grows" concept off an editor at Crown or Random House and see just how far you get. Try convincing an editor at Simon and Schuster that yours is a revolutionary method for producing more fruits, vegetables, and flowers per square foot of garden space than ever before known to man, and see just how much progress you make.

Do you get where I'm coming from?

Now, I'm not saying that there's no hope for you to bring out a new gardening book—just the contrary. What I *am* saying is that there's no hope for you to bring out a new gardening book that has been done to death. Even if yours *is* better. Editors know all about Amazon.com, too, you know. And they *always* check out the competition before asking to see some proposal (or finished manuscript) from you. If, God forbid, they find that the very same topic you're proposing has been written about some twenty times before, the results are etched in stone: Can you say "rejection slip" boys and girls?

So what do you do? How do you get a wink and a nod from a publisher for your next gardening book proposal? Think *outside* the box. For example:

How about a book on water gardening? And not just *any* old water gardening, but water gardening from scratch? Water gardening from scratch with *edible* plants? You know, building your own pond, planting your own plants, harvesting the crops, and reaping the rewards?

Or how about a book on growing tomatoes--without soil? Sure, hydroponic gardening books are a dime a dozen, but perhaps yours tells how to do it organically.

Or how about a book on growing trees from seeds. Everybody can buy a tree from a nursery, plant it, and nurture it to fruition. But damned few gardeners know how to plant trees from seeds and get the same results!

I think you get my point. If you're going to sell a gardening book, you're going to have to come up with a unique angle. So, put your thinking cap on, do your research, and find an angle that hasn't already been done to death. When you come up with it, I virtually *guarantee* that it will sell.

Growing corn in a shoebox? Who knew?

If I set out to write a historical novel, how much accuracy must it contain versus creative writing?

Well, let's just say that you can be historically *inaccurate* and proud of it. If you take your cue from some of the most successful authors in the world, when it comes to historical fiction, don't forget that you're a novelist first and a historian second

But, won't book reviewers crucify you? Won't your readers abandon you? Won't you have to live out the remainder of your life in shame and ignominy? Is that what's bothering you, bunky?

Well, step right up and pay attention because the answer is *no*.

If you like history (you got good grades in Mr. Ferguson's history class in high school; you joined the history club in college; you belong to the *History Book of the Month Club* today), the historical novel is a natural for you. Even better, many publishers are *anxious* to see well-written historical fiction. Think about it. It's like publishing two books for the price of one: a novel *and* a history. The novel is admittedly a hit-or-miss proposition, particularly with untested authors. But history has a built-in market attached to it. And that translates into dollars, which every publisher *loves*.

Will your historical novel be about the Civil War? Huge following. Will it involve Marie Antoinette? Massive audience. President Hoover? J. Edgar Hoover? The Hoover Vacuum Cleaner Company? Tremendous name recognition and built-in appeal. See what I mean? No wonder editors are so receptive.

That doesn't mean you can pluck virtually any subject out of thin air and hope to strike it rich. For starters, your subject (or, in a broader scope, the people within a historical framework, such as World War II, The War of the Roses, or the Great Depression) should be easily identifiable. If you have to explain to people who a historical figure is and why he/she is important, you've lost your audience before you've even started. So, select someone or some time that is easily identifiable. That can either be some readily identifiable big name (George Patton) or a relatively unknown person at a famous location (Dunkirk).

Be careful, though, when choosing historical figures. Avoid living subjects. Sure, a historical novel about Hillary Clinton would make for popular reading; but it would also make for lucrative lawsuits. Unless you're prepared to go to battle to defend your first amendment right to write (or your publisher is, and that's highly unlikely unless your name is Tom Clancy or Stephen King), choose someone who can't sue the daylights out of you. Corpses usually make better subjects, anyway. They're farther removed from everyday news and susceptible to reader speculation, which is what a historical fiction writer offers his audience, in any event.

Also, choose a compelling historical event around which to build your story. I'm currently working on a historical novel about Ernest Hemingway in Cuba during the Marxist revolution. Hemingway met Fidel Castro only once at a marlin fishing tournament long after Castro had seized power. But I speculate in the book about Hemingway not only meeting Castro *before* the overthrow but also working with him to help unseat Batista. Suddenly, we have not one, not two, and not three enigmatic characters to follow throughout the book (Hemingway, Castro, and Castro's second-in-command, Che Guevara). We also we have a host of easily recognizable historical bit players in the form of Hemingway's friends (Ava Gardner, Gary Cooper, Spencer Tracy, Howard Hawks) and Washington politicos (J. Edgar Hoover, Dwight D. Eisenhower, John F. Kennedy). The book overflows with name recognition.

Finally, get inside your historical characters' minds and make them real. Read up on them so that you know how they might have thought, talked, and acted when faced with a particular situation. Write as if you're quoting them from a news source.

In one place in my book, I have Hemingway searching the San Maestro mountains for Castro's rebel camp several weeks before the overthrow. He locates them, and while he wants to meet Castro to tell him what he knows about Batista and Washington's probable reaction to an attempted coup, he has to settle for Guevara. Here's a slice of the action

* * *

"I was hoping *Senor* Castro would join us, yes?"

Guevara pulls a cigar from his fatigues, bites off the end, and proceeds to light it. He extends one to Fuentes and another to the writer, who takes him up on the offer.

"Is he here?" Hemingway asks.

Guevara blows a long plume of gray smoke across the compound, where it hangs in the thick afternoon air, casting shadows from the crackling fire beyond. "I'm afraid not. He took some men with him to Camagüey, to the monastery to pick up some supplies. He will not be back before morning."

Hemingway looks disappointed.

"But, Ernesto," Fuentes says, "you can tell Che anything you would say to Fidel. He is *el comandante* of the Revolutionary Army of Barbutos. He is second in command only to Fidel."

Hemingway raises his brows. "Well. I didn't realize."

Guevara shrugs. "It's a job."

The men laugh. Guevara leans forward.

"This information ... it concerns your country's government?"

ABOUT WRITING RIGHT

Hemingway stares squarely into his eyes. "Yes."

"We have been waiting for word from our operatives about Washington's reaction to our little revolution here on the island."

Hemingway smiles. "*Senor*, in my vast experience, I have learned that there is no such thing as a *little* revolution." The men laugh again.

"This is true," Guevara says. "And when this revolution is completed, the island of Cuba will no longer be slave to the dictator Batista. The glorious and vaulted People's Revolution will see to that just as surely as the people of Argentina put an end to *that* corrupt regime." He pauses, draws on his cigar, and exhales slowly. "But tell me, Ernesto. Why is it that you are so willing to share information of value with the leaders of a socialist revolution? Could it be that deep down inside, *you* are a socialist?"

Hemingway laughs. "Deep down inside, *everyone* is a socialist. It's just that you have the courage to *act* on your feelings. No, no. But I *am* a writer. A writer who happens to hate political injustice and corruption. What I have to tell you involves some high-ranking people within the U.S. government and their view toward the revolution ... toward Castro."

"Yes? It is not good news, I imagine."

Hemingway shakes his head.

* * *

Within this exchange, we find realistic dialogue. That's because of the research that went into what Guevara would think and say and how Hemingway would talk and act to make this fictitious meeting sound historically accurate and *believable*. That, of course, is critical to pulling off *any* historical novel.

So, if you have a penchant for history, think about writing a historical novel. And then do a little research before diving in. The worst that can happen is that you'll end up getting some invaluable experience. The best is that you'll end up getting published.

And isn't that, after all, every writer's goal?

I read your advice about coming up with a new angle for a garden book, but I still don't get it. How do you know if it's "new" enough to appeal to a publisher?

D. J. Herda

Okay, let's try again, but only because garden writing is a natural for so many writers who have a penchant for gardening and a need to earn a buck. Unfortunately, far too many garden writers today are too damned boring?

Case in point: I used to write a gardening column. It was syndicated to nearly 2 million readers a month. I was an expert, and I wrote with expertise. That, after all, is the most significant part of being a garden writer. Isn't it?

Well, yes and no. Anyone writing about any topic as specific as gardening has to know his beans ... no pun intended. But he has to remember that being an expert and being an expert gardening writer aren't exactly one-in-the-same.

We've all read "experts" who were dull as stripped screws. (You draw further conclusions.) At least, we've all *started* reading those experts. Whether or not we finished is open to debate. I have a feeling it's the rare reader, indeed, who will plow through those heavy-as-molasses tomes simply because they're written by an "expert."

On the other hand, what a joy to find an expert in *any* field of expertise who writes in a flip, lively, imaginative way! What a pleasure... and what a rarity! Why is that? Why can't experts also be expert writers?

Well, the simple answer is, they can. The tough solution, though, is that it takes a whole lot of energy to write with vim and verve and vigor and ... oh, hell, I'm running out of "V" words. But you get the point. It's one thing to know your subject well. It's quite another to know your subject well and to know how to write it up so that *everyone* finds it interesting and not ho-hum, as in this pathetic example:

> *The tomato is a fruit. Its habitat ranges from the near-Arctic to the Equator. Its habit, too, is similarly wide-reaching. It can be anything from short and squatty to vining. It's one of the most versatile fruits in the world.*

Excuse me while I *excuse* me, but, hey, what's going on here? That sounds as if it were written by a writer who thinks that, as an expert, he need only put words on paper to capture everyone's imagination. Apparently. And *wrong*. Just how many pages of writing like that would *you* be willing to endure? *Oops*, and here's a thought. If you can't tolerate such mindless dribble, how do you suppose the average *editor* (jaded, stilted, saturated with clichés, longing for creativity) feels? So, what's the lesson to be learned?

Take a dull subject (sorry, I love to garden, but it's a dull subject to most people who couldn't care less whether a tomato is a fruit or a vegetable, only that it's 99 cents a pound at Safeco and not $2.99 at Wal-Mart), figure out where the dullness lies, and avoid that chasm like the plague.

I give you the resurrected example of a rewritten paragraph:

The Tomato. Humble, unassuming, and common? Actually, anything but. If your supermarket has a produce department--and I know it does--it's deluged by the ruby reds 12 months a year (okay, yeah, sometimes they're yellow or orange, I know, but 99 percent of the time, they're red). And why? The question is, rather, why not. Tomatoes are the most popular fruit (technically speaking) on the face of the earth, mostly because they're so versatile, partly because they're so prevalent, definitely because they range from the near-Arctic to the Equator and down as far south as just this side of Antarctica. And absolutely because they're so damned tasty*!*

Okay, okay. I set you up. It's easy to write a bad paragraph; it's not much more challenging to write a better one. What's difficult is to write a good one *all* the time, even with potentially dull subjects. Are we beginning to see eye-to-eye here?

My philosophy about writing nonfiction is simple. Make it interesting.

Fiction is a breeze. You have something to say; it's extraordinary, remarkable, unbelievable, mind-boggling, made-up. But nonfiction? *Ahh*, there's the rub. That's where we, as writers, tend to want to let the "facts" (*Just the facts, ma'am*) speak for themselves. But facts, as any good fiction writer knows, are deadly dull. Do you think you could write an intriguing novel using "facts" alone? Well, neither can you write an interesting nonfiction piece.

Facts, to experts, are the end-all and be-all. That is their downfall. Facts, to a good writer, are a jumping-off point. What do they tell us? How can we relay that information to others in a lively and entertaining way? In short, how can we use factuality as a *tool* to animate our writing styles, rather than as a writing style itself to deaden our effectiveness as writers?

The answer lies within every one of us. Read the "facts" that you wrote, and then ask yourself--be brutally honest with your answer here--just how interesting what you've written would be to someone *outside* your field of expertise. If the answer, on a scale of one-to-ten, is anything but an *eleven*, you'd better drop back and punt.

And tomatoes, by the way--as far-flung as their empire flies--are far less impressive in that respect than the ordinary pepper. Or even the pole bean.

Take *that* to the table and consume it!

People tell me I have a good sense of humor, and I'm a decent writer, so how hard would it be for me to write humor books or articles?

Possibly not difficult at all, as long as you can keep 'em laughing and coming back for more. But I know you. You not only want to be a humor writer but also you want to be a *rich* humor writer. Am I right?

Well, here's the deal. Let's say you have this once-in-a-lifetime chance to crack a really big market. Or, better still, you know a book publisher just dying for a big humor book--*now!*--and you think you can fill the bill. Except that you don't know a damned thing about writing humor.

Is that what's bothering you? Your lack of humor? Or, *umm*, your lack of confidence in being able to write comedy? If so, step right up, 'cuz Uncle Deej is gonna show you how to be funny in two dimensions.

The first thing to do when writing humor is to relax. Humor isn't humorous if it's forced or contrived. Take a deep breath. And then move on to Step Two.

The second thing to do is a no-brainer: Pick a subject. Let's say it's dogs. Now, if that's not a subject ripe with humorous possibilities, what is? But when are dogs funniest? When they're eating (or waiting to be fed)? When they're sleeping (or looking for a place to curl up)? When they're running around outside (or begging to go out)? When they're hunting?

ABOUT WRITING RIGHT

Hunting! That's it. That triggered something in me. I remembered suddenly an experience I had with my own two dogs in Steamboat, Colorado.

Chaucer was an extraordinarily accommodating golden retriever. Shortly after we had moved to the country, he had attempted to befriend every porcupine in the neighborhood. And succeeded. In his first run-in, his barking at a cornered porkie led our young Corgi down the steps and out into the field to follow, and both dogs jumped the animal before returning, howling, to the house. A good pair of pliers resolved the dilemma.

On Chaucer's next encounter, the Corgi once again went barreling down into the field to see what was happening. This time, she pulled up short and started barking some three feet away from the porcupine as Chaucer, once again, charged in. Back at the house, he growled when I approached with the pliers, so I ended up paying my local veterinarian fifty big ones to play the heavy.

On Chaucer's third run-in with a porcupine that summer, the Corgi lay shivering under the bed. When I went down to grab the retriever and pull him back to safety, he caught sight of me and—mistaking my presence for the universal sign to attack--leaped upon the cornered beast, only to go running, whimpering and yelping, back to the house a third time. That trip to the vet cost me a cool hundred-and-a-half, what with the lateness of the hour and the anesthesia required to knock the dog out so the vet could extract the quills farthest down his throat.

Growing tired of spending all my discretionary income on my veterinarian's ballooning retirement fund, I finally asked him why one dog continue attacking porcupines while the other had apparently learned her lesson.

"Well," John said thoughtfully. John was a big, burly Irishman whom you couldn't help but like no matter *how* much money he sucked from your veins. "It's been my experience that some dogs get stuck by a porcupine once and say, 'Oh, no, I remember what happened the last time. I'm not going through *that* again!'

"Other dogs see a porcupine and think, 'Oh, you're the son-of-a-bitch that got away from me last time. But you won't get away today!'"

See what just happened here? That brings up another point pertinent to humor writing: Take your time in development. Don't race to the punch line. Sometimes, a humorous anecdote is short; other times, not. The point is, let the story develop naturally. If you force it to get to the punch line more quickly, no one will find it amusing.

Once you've committed the image to paper, go back over it. Read it out loud. Listen to its cadence, its literary "voice." When it sounds natural, start analyzing it for injections. Can you stick some humorous word or phrase in here? Can you shoot a short quip in there?

Don't feel that every sentence has to be a thigh-slapper, though. If you try to work too much funny stuff into a short anecdote, you'll simply wind up confusing your reader to the point where *nothing* will seem funny.

Remember: the recipe for humor is a straight line followed by a punch line. Take the time to set your reader up before bowling him over, and you might end up laughing all the way to the bank.

What makes a literary novel different from a genre novel, or is it?

More than any genre fiction, the literary novel demands careful, creative construction. That's because the "growth factor" must be cultivated from early on.

When I was younger, I thought every novel was a literary novel. I believed that every work of fiction was as fully developed as it could be and that every writer's goal was to see that it got that way.

Today, I know better. Not necessarily because I'm so much wiser, more so that I'm more experienced.

In essence, after more than half a century of writing, *I* am a literary novel. Or, rather, I *would* be if I were any type of novel at all--much more so than I could have been when I was, say, 20, 30, or 40. Do you see what I'm getting at here?

A literary novel is a well-developed read. It features full, rich characters that have lived full, rich lives, albeit not necessarily long ones. The characters must virtually crackle with emotions--and not merely one or two, but the whole riveting gamut of them. By creating fully developed, rich characters, we give the readers of our literary works something into which they can dig their teeth.

The same is true with the setting of a literary novel--both the time and the place. Literary fiction paints a broad canvas of setting, and then it moves in to fill in the details even more completely--adding the rocks and stones and pebbles and sometimes even the most minute grains of sand that all go into making up the literary novel's tableau.

Whereas a genre novel can (and usually does) get away with a paragraph or two about the setting of the story, literary fiction requires passage after passage of intimate details. What does the landscape look like today compared to fifty or a hundred or even a thousand years ago? How are the characters who inhabit the literary novel alike; how are they different, and how, in the end, did they get that way to begin with?

What makes the people in a literary novel tick? What makes the setting work for or against the characters effectively? Why did Melville set *Moby Dick* almost entirely aboard a ship, while Hawthorne set *The House of Seven Gables* on land? The answers to those questions are the very things that the literary novel portends.

The reason for all this attention to detail in a literary novel is simple. The reader wants to know everything about the characters and the place they inhabit. They crave to know how they relate to one another and to their history (and their family's history). They're curious as to how the characters of today vary from their ancestors.

Think of the typical literary novel reader (my God, is there such a thing?) as meticulous. This reader is the same anal-retentive human being who sorts table salt by the size of its grains. Throw out some information in a literary novel, and the reader immediately reacts by raising a dozen questions, all of which he expects to have answered in full by the novel's end.

Contrast that with the reader of the typical modern genre novel (Detective, Romance, Sci-Fi, etc.) in which the main character develops just enough to advance the storyline and keep the reader wondering what's going to happen next. (That's always a big part of the genre novel--a continuing string of unfolding events, usually unexpectedly and almost always right in the path of the main character's goal.) A typical genre novel reader is about as far from anal-retentive as one human being can get. Table salt? You'll find it in the genre-novel reader's home in the same five-gallon bucket as he stores the rock salt, pellet salt, and block salt for feeding to the broodmares. Throw out some information in a genre novel, and the reader immediately wants to see some action.

D. J. Herda

There is some room for crossover, of course. A literary novel often has its share of action, but it's considerably less action than in the typical genre novel. The reader doesn't need to learn about the characters in a literary novel by observing how they react to dramatic, exciting, or even life-threatening situations; the reader learns through the writer's fleshing-out of the characters' thoughts and emotions and through the painting of each elaborately detailed scene.

If all this jabber sounds as if I'm saying the literary-novel characters are developed more thoroughly than the typical genre-novel characters, you're right. In a literary novel, we expect our main character to grow, to change, to morph into something deeper, more understanding, and more illuminated. That's the "growth factor."

Which brings up the question: Is the literary novel more challenging to write than the genre novel? It is if you buy into the premise that it's much more difficult and time-consuming to learn all about a person--both inside and out--than it is to receive a cursory introduction to someone and then move on.

And that's precisely the challenge facing the writer of a literary novel: how to relay a voluminous amount of information about the novel's characters in the relatively short space of a few hundred pages. More demanding, yet, is to do so without boring the reader to death.

And that, in a nutshell, is why so few writers are up to tackling the beast. It's much easier to create a work of fiction that moves and excites and inspires in the reader familiar and exalted feelings than to create a work of fiction that leads the reader to a greater sense of personal understanding of the human condition that surrounds him. Just as it led the novel's main character. That is where the true genius of a Herman Melville or a Nathanial Hawthorne or even a Phillip Roth shines brightest.

So, the next time you toy with tackling that literary novel that's been bouncing around the back of your brain for eons, better give it some serious thought. Are you up to the task? Ready for the demands? Prepared for the rigors? If so, the literary world awaits. Just remember: do it right ... or don't do it at all.

Are western novels dead? Or are they only dying? I'd love to be the next Louis L'Amour, but I'm not sure there's a suitable market for westerns anymore.

ABOUT WRITING RIGHT

So, you have a hankerin' to ride off into the sunset, tame the Chisholm Trail, and throw all the bad guys in jail. Is that what you're saying? If so, I can't blame you. But think about this first: Before you decide to knock out a quick Western or two, you'd better understand what it takes to make 'em *last*. Here's what I mean.

Thanks to the wonders of cable and streaming television--and now of re-issued DVDs *ad nauseam*--is there any doubt that every human being walking the face of the earth is intimately familiar with the genre we call Western? Even before Hollywood began gobbling up such fare and spitting out true-to-celluloid reality, most Americans knew the genre as well as they knew their own names.

Either they grew up cutting their literary teeth on the likes of Zane Grey and Brett Hart, or they thumbed through the slough of western fare in the form of pulp magazines and, later, comic books, novels, and Cliff's Notes. In a way, nearly *everyone* is an expert on westerns. Or everyone *was*, at least, until Larry McMurtry came along.

McMurtry rejuvenated and revitalized the steadily declining art of western writing by de-glamorizing the American West. Unlike most of his predecessors, he didn't paint his characters or their surroundings with a broad brush swathed in black and white. He created a canvas of what the Old West was really like, the *real* West, drawing on a palette of a thousand different hues.

The good guys no longer wore white hats and rode stealthy Paints. The bad guys no longer dressed in black and lumbered along on Chestnut geldings. Suddenly, everyone was more complicated. You won't find a single John Wayne or Lee Marvin character among the hundreds McMurtry has created over the past half-century. With McMurtry's new brand of western writing, suddenly the Old West became more alive, more vibrant, more real, and less predictable. People of the West are a combination of good *and* bad. Indians are trustworthy and dependable as often as they are savage and bloodthirsty. Entire towns sprout from sticks and old, rotting boards and sod roofs that look as if they are about to blow away at any moment.

That's the kind of western most editors look for today. And the next Larry McMurtry is the kind of western writer they hope to discover.

So, what's a writer to do? For starters, research!

D. J. Herda

If your entire perspective of the American West has come from old films and rotting clichés, you're not going to make it as a writer of western Americana. Not in today's competitive marketplace. If your knowledge of the West comes from painstaking trips to the library, thumbing through old *National Geographics*, watching *History TV* about the *real* characters of western lore, what they did, how they lived, and how they died, well, pardner, you might have a chance!

Ditto if you've studied McMurtry's realistic western classics, such as his lauded *Lonesome Dove* mini-series, or read his books. You recognize immediately the amount of research he's done on the Old West, beginning with his earliest writings and extending to the very twilight of his career. You know in a heartbeat that this western writer was eons apart from those who came before him.

You can also research the Old West on some of the many educational Websites on the Internet. One of them is a PBS-associated site listed under the "Storyline Resources" page at the American Society of Authors and Writers Website (http://www.amsaw.org). It's called New Perspectives on the American West, and it's worth a look even if you *never* plan on writing a western novel.

Once you've done enough research to give you the confidence you need to start that very first Western, the rest should come easy. Just remember to tell the story from your characters' own perspectives--the way you imagine they felt, acted, talked, and lived, warts and all. Make your "good guy" characters likable (or at least tolerable); make your "bad guy" characters multi-faceted (even bad guys do good things every now and then), and place them in relationships that would be similar to those in which living people find themselves today--tempered, of course, by the restraints of the era. After all, people are people, no matter where or when they lived.

Once you've completed your book, go back and read it out loud. Edit it two or three times, read it aloud again, and sit back and smile. Then go ahead and round up the usual suspects--a list of editors currently hot after realistic western novels. Then, start cranking out those pitches!

And remember, if your book doesn't sell at first, try, try again. There is an editor for every marketable property ever conceived. It's

ABOUT WRITING RIGHT

only a matter of time until you find the one who's right for you. *And your new western.*

What elements go into the creation of a horror story like Stephen King writes?

That's a pretty good question, considering how everybody likes a good ghost story. Everyone likes to be frightened nearly to death by a good vampire tale. Everybody likes to watch a good horror flick.

And that's what makes your question so timely.

But what, exactly, does a "good" horror story mean? And how can you set about writing a horror story--regardless of its subgenre--that is actually good enough to get published?

I've thought about this for a while now, and this is what I've come up with.

1.) Make it unique. If you want to write about the reanimation of dead tissue, forget about the obvious. You can write until you're blue in the face, but if your story is a recalculated telling of the road-weary tale of Frankenstein, I'll tell you right now, it won't work. Mary Shelley did it *par excellence* long ago. How can you expect to challenge perfection?

2.) Make it universal. A story that affects twenty percent of the population might get you a contract with a publisher that pays an advance of 20 percent of what the Big Boys pay (if that), but even that isn't likely. Appeal to 80 percent of the population, and you're talking a great chance of finding a publisher and for making big bucks. Remember John Russo's *Night of the Living Dead?*

3.) Make it believable. Tell the tale of a one-armed, one-eyed cyclops come down from the heavens to make life miserable for planet earth, and you're going to have a hard sell. Tell the tale of an average Joe (the Plumber or otherwise) who has something very small go very, very wrong, and you're likely to win over converts from the start. Remember Edgar Allen Poe's *Telltale Heart?*

4.) Include a familiar. In witchcraft, a "familiar" is a being that, in everyday life, is safe, sane, and unthreatening. Most common familiars during the Salem Witch Trials were cats, thought to be the cavorting consorts of witches and warlocks. A familiar makes everything seem more real (who actually knows what a cat does after you turn in for the night?), making everything seem more believable. A familiar can even do most of the dirty work in your tale, leaving the more readily identifiable "human" element of your story to bond with the reader. Remember Arthur Conan Doyle's *Hound of the Baskervilles?*

5.) Be frightening. And I mean unbelievably, *believably* frightening. The terror need not be physical to make a horror story work: psychological horror sells well, too, and is often easier to create. In fact, because of the obscure workings of the human mind, psychological terror is often the most frightening kind. Remember Stephen king's *Christine?*

Writing horror stories can be immensely satisfying and extremely lucrative, as any horror genre junkie will tell you. But if you, as a new, untested writer, hope to have a chance at success in a weak economic climate and glutted literary environment, you'll have to take that extra step toward making your property stand out from the thousands of others currently making the rounds.

Keep these few points in mind, and you'll be well on your way to success.

I recently came across a reference about a "literary memoir." I know what a memoir is, and I know what a literary novel is, but what's a combination of the two?

Of all the subjects available to you as a writer, the one you know best is yourself: your past and your present, your thoughts and emotions, your strengths and your weaknesses. Yet, "you" is very likely the subject you try hardest to avoid writing about. Why?

Well, nobody knows for sure, of course. But the pros would make book that you simply don't have the courage. Writing about yourself takes tremendous *chutzpah* on two counts. First, you need to have the confidence to permit yourself--the "right"--to do something so "egotistical" as writing about yourself. Second, you need to be able to take the heat resulting from your decision.

The first obstacle to overcoming the "you" factor is simple enough. You're a writer, and your job is to write about what you know. You know yourself better than anyone else on earth (assuming you're not schizophrenic). Therefore, you have the right--bordering on an obligation--to write about you. (Sort of a warped take-off on Kierkegaard ... "I think; therefore I am ... a *writer*"?)

ABOUT WRITING RIGHT

The second obstacle is less subject to rationale. Either you have enough intestinal fortitude to expose yourself, your thoughts, your desires, and your innermost *you* to the world, regardless of what the world may think, or you haven't. If you fall into the latter group, nothing I can say will make you write a memoir. But if you fall into the former, here are some tips to help you get that memoir off and running on the right foot.

1.) Recognize that having the "right" to write about yourself comes with the responsibility of doing so properly. You absolutely may *not* write poorly or incorrectly. Few readers have the patience for sloppy artistry or lazy crafting, particularly as they pertain to a writer's own memoirs. If you're not a good enough writer to make a good enough showing, take lessons, and practice, practice, practice, or forget it.

2.) Forget, too, about writing for an audience. The non-fiction memoir is literary, not genre-driven. By that, I mean its goal is to flesh out the meanings, the makeup of the people about whom you write (*numero uno* being you, of course). If you try to satisfy your audience by gearing your writing toward them, as you might a detective or romance or sci-fi novel, you're going to get screwed. Memoir readers read memoirs to learn something about someone that they never knew before. To see that person evolve and grow. The only way you can give your readers what they want is to write from your psyche, from your perspective, from the inside-out. If you end up writing to appease your reader or an editor, you'll end up not writing anything of merit for *anybody*. If you write for yourself, you'll reach the people you want to reach--the memoir readers.

3.) Writing a successful memoir is directly proportionate to one's age. I don't care how exciting a life even the most extraordinary 14-year-old has lived, it isn't varied or deep enough to hold an audience of one past page 17. What reader wants to read about the school sock hop or that weekend's basketball game?

Of course, that doesn't mean that young writers shouldn't write memoirs--or at least attempt to do so. At any age, the creative act of writing is a powerful psychoanalytical tool that often sheds light on the depth and nature of one's desire to write and the ability--or lack thereof--one possesses toward reaching that goal. Thinking in terms of memoir--reaching back to recall something that happened last year or last decade and remembering the feelings created by the event, the triggers that unleashed them--is a tool one develops more fully in time. Once learned, its mechanisms will pop up at the most remarkable of moments. A free-reigning memory is almost always good for material when all other avenues fail.

Working once on a literary mystery entitled *The Death and Life of Hymie Stiehl*, I had just entered a passage where the protagonist (ostensibly *Moi*) had made arrangements to have his friend, Hymie Stiehl, interred. While going over the last-minute details with the funeral director, Mr. Elgars, something struck me. And out it came pouring--the memories of Aunt Mary. And into the book they went:

* * *

I looked at the man [Mr. Elgars] standing next to me more carefully now. His eyebrows were thin and weak, his lips practically nonexistent, if present at all. He wore a white shirt with a tattered collar held in place by a silver-studded pin and a tie the color of the sea on a moonless night. In his lapel, a carnation carried the smell of death. I know. I had smelled it once before, on my Aunt Mary—fat Mary, they called her—at her wake.

One of the reasons she was so fat, of course, was that she ate like a pig. And not just ordinary food. Oh, no. Being of Italian-Polish descent, she ate gnocchi and sauerkraut, pigs' feet and cacciatore as if it were going out of style. She had the same smell about her as Elgars, even as she lay in the casket, peering up at me through sealed lids.

Fat Mary had always liked me, I guessed because I had been scared to death to go near her when I was a child and had to be dragged to her home to visit, kicking and screaming, by my parents. Inside, she would lure me with pleasant talk of beautiful young children with wholly beguiling manners and wait until I was within striking distance. Then, from her straight-backed chair set to one side of the kitchen table, she would lunge at me with those two stumpy tentacles and snag me, unsuspecting and amazed that anyone so large could move with such grace and alacrity. Once she had snared me, she would reel me in, her prized catch of the day, and breathe that awful breath on me, all the while squeezing me until I was sure the eyeballs would pop right out of my head.

ABOUT WRITING RIGHT

Part of the reason I dreaded her so was her size, of course. She stood five-foot-three and weighed five hundred pounds easily. Four-eighty on a good day. She wore three or four chins as comfortably as most people carry one. Her eyes were set so deeply inside the folds of her cheeks that it sometimes looked as though they were closed permanently. But when she moved, or, worse still, when anyone else around her moved, she would draw her head in their direction as surely as a handful of metal filings are lured to a magnet, and you would know after all that she could see perfectly fine from behind all those layers of fat, thank you very much.

So that was a good part of my repulsion. But there was more. There was the story. The tale of a young man—Adolph, I believe his name was—who had been a doughboy in Europe during World War I and, while on a leave of absence from the war, had taken to frequenting a particular dance hall known by the name of That's Fats, or something to that effect. Inside That's Fats, he discovered a most remarkable thing. All of the twenty or so women who periodically climbed the steps to the stage—the broiling spotlights casting eerie shadows across their faces, their limbs, their torsos—were fat. Enormously fat. They were called The Beef Trust. I could only imagine why. The lead dancer, naturally, was Fat Mary.

Well, as my grandfather, who—it just so happened to be—was the brother to Fat Mary, liked to tell it, when Adolph the soldier first laid eyes on Mary the Fat, sparks flew. Or maybe fat grams. But whatever they were, Adolph knew in an instant that he had finally met his fate.

So he dated her once or twice, poked her a few times in between—how, I can't imagine, since Adolph was four-feet-eight and weighed in at a scant eighty-five pounds—and then brought her home with him to Chicago and married her. He set the two of them up in a comfortable brick bungalow on Chicago's great if economically undistinguished South Side, and preceded, like all good Italian men of little-to-no upbringing, to pork every available woman in the neighborhood. And a few who were unavailable, if you know what I mean.

Well, it didn't take long for Fat Mary to catch wind of Adolph's indiscretions, and when she confronted him with the evidence, he calmly proceeded to pluck a belt from a hook inside their bedroom door and beat the living hell out of her. After that, Fat Mary would periodically show up at various family functions with bandages stretched across her cheeks and ice packs tucked beneath her chins.

All of which made her that much more alluring in my eyes, I can assure you.

So, while I stood beside the casket, looking down at Fat Mary and thinking about how badly she looked but how lucky she was to be free at last, I could not help but inhale the thick, pungent, sickening smell of all the herbs and spices, the strange conglomeration of meats and vegetables mixed in with her Italian-Polish heritage, the odd combination of sweet and stinking cheeses that she was wont to devour on a regular basis and which, I was convinced, continued to rot long after they had passed down her esophagus, through her gigantic stomach, and out into history. And that, I was convinced, along with the sweat that poured out of her constantly—even at death—was what made up that smell.

Now I realized that I may have been wrong all along, because for the first time in nearly twenty years, I smelled that smell again. This time, it was coming from Elgars.

* * *

I would not--*could* not--have written that at fourteen. I doubt that I would even have *recalled* it until I was 45. Time has a way of making us more conscious, more cognizant of those things that happened to us when we were young, melding one set of reactions, feelings, and dreams with another to produce a perfectly wonderful anecdotal tale.

4.) There's a thin line separating memoir from egotism. A small dose of ego is healthy; no writer can go far without it. Egotistic writing, however, is a bane, and a memoir is not a license to commit mindless prattle.

To avoid excesses, make sure that every component in your memoir serves a useful purpose. Write about yourself with confidence and satisfaction. But see to it that *all* of your details—people, places, events, anecdotes, ideas, emotions—are there to move your story along. If they fail to do their job, the reader will stumble over them and fall, and you will look like an arrogant ass.

ABOUT WRITING RIGHT

Why write a memoir at all if doing so is such risky business? Mainly because no other nonfiction form goes so deeply into the roots of personal experience—to all the drama and pain and humor and surprises of life. Great memoirs are some of the finest reads you'll ever enjoy--books such as Andre Aciman's *Out of Egypt*, Michael J. Arlen's *Exiles*, Russell Baker's *Growing Up*, Vivian Gornick's *Fierce Attachments*, Pete Hamill's *A Drinking Life*, Moss Hart's *Act One*, John Houseman's *Run-Through*, Mary Karr's *The Liars' Club*, Frank McCourt's *Angela's Ashes*, Vladimir Nabokov's *Speak, Memory*, V. S. Pritchett's *A Cab at the Door*, Eudora Welty's *One Writer's Beginnings*, and Leonard Woolf's *Growing*. Now *that's* writing.

5.) Focus is most effective when honed to its narrowest point. What creates power in a memoir is the book's concentrated, illuminating beam. Unlike an autobiography, which busies itself in laying out the entire life of a person, a memoir assumes the reader is less interested in the whole than in a tiny slice of it--a period within the writer's lifetime, an experience to be savored, examined, sniffed, tasted, remembered, and possibly even related to.

An effective memoir writer takes us back to some corner of his or her past that was unusually intense—childhood, for instance—or that was framed by war or some other extraordinary social upheaval. Baker's *Growing Up* is a box within a box, two stories for the price of one. It's the story of a boy growing up, set inside the story of a family battered by the Depression. Nabokov's *Speak, Memory*, regarded by some as the most elegant memoir ever written, elicits memories of boyhood in Czarist Russia, a world strewn with private tutors and summer houses that the Russian Revolution would soon relegate to the pages of history. It is history frozen in time.

Think narrowly, then, when you try your hand at writing this genre form. Memoir isn't the summary of a life; it's a tiny window into a realization, a glance at a photograph whose image remains indelibly etched in the mind to haunt and illuminate long after the photograph is gone. The memoir may look like a casual and willy-nilly recounting of some of life's most trivial events. But it's much more than that: It's an examination of how such events came to affect a human being. It's a look at a piece of that person's life.

D. J. Herda

Thoreau allegedly wrote seven different drafts of *Walden* in eight years. If so, then few American memoirs have been more painstakingly pieced together. To pen a good memoir, you must become both critic and editor of your own life's events, shaping an ungodly potpourri of half-remembered occasions into a well-organized narrative. Memoir is the art of reinventing personal truth.

6.) Sweat the details--they are the primary secrets in making the artwork called memoir succeed. Any details will do, as long as they are keen and quickly perceivable by the reader. They can be smells or sounds, visual images and more--as long as they trigger in the reader an instantaneous, "Oh, yeah, I get it!" Here's a small slice of something that triggers memories in nearly everyone, a slice from Eudora Welty's *One Writer's Beginnings*:

* * *

In our house on North Congress Street, in Jackson, Mississippi, where I was born the oldest of three children in 1909, we grew up to the striking of clocks. There was a mission-style oak grandfather clock standing in the hall, which sent its gong-like strokes through the living room, dining room, kitchen, and pantry, and up the sounding board of the stairwell. Through the night, it could find its way into our ears; sometimes, even on the sleeping porch, midnight could wake us up. My parents' bedroom had a smaller striking clock that answered it. Though the kitchen clock did nothing but show the time, the dining room clock was a cuckoo clock with weights on long chains ...

My father loved all instruments that would instruct and fascinate. His place to keep things was the drawer in the "library table" where lying on top of his folded maps was a telescope with brass extensions, to find the moon and the Big Dipper after supper in our front yard, and to keep appointments with eclipses. There was a folding Kodak that was brought out for Christmas, birthdays, and trips. In the back of the drawer you could find a magnifying glass, a kaleidoscope, and a gyroscope kept in a black buckram box, which he would set dancing for us on a string pulled tight. He had also supplied himself with an assortment of puzzles composed of metal rings and intersecting links and keys chained together,

ABOUT WRITING RIGHT

impossible for the rest of us, however patiently shown, to take apart; he had an almost childlike love of the ingenious ...

* * *

How much we learn in those words about Welty's familial beginnings, the kind of home in which she lived, the lovely peculiarities of her father who influenced her so! In the continuum of a few short sentences, she opens the door to her Mississippi childhood, admitting us into her own home to hear all the clocks chiming, up and down the stairs and even out onto the sleeping porch, where sleeping-- especially at the stroke of midnight--was often anything but easy.

I, too, once lived in a house with chiming clocks. So long ago, so many memories past. And I was aligned with the author the moment I realized where she was going ... which was where she had been. A successful memoir writer can't ask for more than that. For, once you have the reader on your side, conquering the rest of the world is easy.

What errors are commonly made when writers write nonfiction?

Hmm. That's a good question. But it's unanswerable the way you phrase it. "Common" errors? What errors are common to one writer may not be common to another. So, to cut to the chase, let's rephrase that question into, "What are the most *frequent* errors authors make when writing nonfiction books?"

Well, that's a *little* easier to answer, and it all starts with research.

All too often, nonfiction authors have a point-of-view with their prejudices intact, and the authors tend to skew them into "facts." If they were facts, they wouldn't be points-of-view. So, with that in mind, here's one frequently encountered error:

1. Not providing enough documentation. If I had a nickel for every unsupported premise I've read in nonfiction books, I'd be wealthy today. No kidding. It's one thing for an author to believe passionately about something; it's another thing entirely to present that author's belief as fact. Unless your nonfiction book is a treatise or an extended personal essay or autobiography, personal premises have no right masquerading as facts. Yet, far too many authors want to structure their books that way. Instead, do your research, evaluate your findings (some will be pro-conclusion and others anti-conclusion), and present them *to the*

reader to assess. You can, in the end, extend your point-of-view, but *only* after identifying it as such. *Never* masquerade your point-of-view as fact. Doing so will destroy you and your reputation as a nonfiction author.

2. Writing in a personalized tone. "Tone," as I'm defining it, is the slant you give your writing. Positive, negative, upbeat, downbeat, authoritative, personal, formal, informal—all are examples of different tones you may choose to use, usually to affect or influence your reading public. If you're writing nonfiction (unless it's a memoir or an autobiography), you need to use an objective tone. You neither stand for or against something but merely present an argument. Following that, you may choose to draw your conclusion, but only after clearly identifying it as such.
3. Writing something that has already been covered to death. Some examples: Amelia Earhart's last flight. Lee surrendering to Grant at Appomattox. Wyatt Earp's shootout at the OK Corral. If you want to write nonfiction that sells (and I assume that's the goal of every nonfiction writer), pick a subject that hasn't been covered to death and is still of interest to the majority of readers. Otherwise, make sure you have something *new* or potentially revealing about your subject.
4. Letting personal feelings intrude in your work. Doing so might make you feel good at the time, but it will turn the entire reading universe off. How do you prevent that? By questioning every statement you make as a "fact" or as a "conclusion." But can you do that? Unless you're writing a treatise or an autobiography, you can and you *must*. A point in fact: A publisher once commissioned me to write a book on abortion. As a Catholic, I felt strongly opposed to the concept at the time. Instead of letting my personal feelings interfere with my narrative, I bent over backward to question every statement I made that even hinted at a biased conclusion. I took all alternative views into consideration. The resulting book was a critical success. Every reviewer loved it—except for one who said that the book's only flaw was the author's obvious bias in *favor of abortion.* When I read that review, I knew I had done my job. I had presented the

ABOUT WRITING RIGHT

topic subjectively by sublimating my personal views. And that's what every nonfiction writer should do.
5. Structuring your nonfiction book as fiction. Fiction reads uniquely unto itself. (How do you like *that* phrase?) Nonfiction does likewise. The two are not interchangeable. While fiction relies upon storyline, characterization, and description for its allure, nonfiction depends upon facts. Verified facts. If your reader can't tell whether or not he's reading nonfiction when he begins a book, you have failed in your goals as an author, and your reader might as well quit reading.

Is there a good way to end a story with a dream sequence, as if something had never really happened?

Yes, there is a "good way" to write a story with an "it was all a dream" ending. In fact, there are many *great* ways of doing so. Unfortunately, that's speaking from an esoteric point-of-view. From a practical point-of-view, the answer is an unmitigated *no*!

The reason for the *no* is that readers reject such endings as contrived and simplistic. They see them for what they are: endings that writers use when the author runs out of steam, ideas, creativity, or time. *When in doubt, fantasize it as if it never happened.* But that's precisely why the reader feels cheated. After investing thousands of words into reading a story, and plenty of time and energy in following along, guessing at conclusions, and putting themselves into the characters' mindsets, the author comes along and says, "Wait a minute. King's X. Only kidding. Sorry you wasted your time."

Such a cop-out is the mark of an amateur writer. Can any writer find a simpler, less creative way to end a book-length story than by claiming it was all a dream and, therefore, anything goes? I mean, really. How convenient.

That's not to say that dream sequences have no place in fiction. *Wrong*! Dreams play a *significant* role in creative development, foreshadowing, problem-solving, and more. Or they *can*. They simply don't work as endings, because the readers *always* feel cheated, and everyone resents that feeling.

It's a little like going to the store, tallying up your grocery items one-by-one so that you don't go over your $100 limit, and then checking out for a total of $97.85 just before the checkout gal says, "Sorry, but those prices on the items are there for a rough estimate only. They're not the actual prices. The actual prices total $212.53."

What? Would you stand for that? Not much more than a reader would stand for investing his time and feelings in a novel that ends by having the writer pull the rug out from under him.

So, in answer to your question, yes, you *can* write a story with a good dream ending, but *no*, you can't expect the reader to accept it. Two different slants on your question; two entirely different responses.

Follow me?

Can a first-person narrator change into a pseudo-omniscient character?

Can he? *Yes.* Should he? *No.* Here's why.

A reader approaches a new novel with a certain degree of confidence and a large dose of trepidation. The confidence is that he or she saw the book somewhere, was attracted to the cover, blurb, or descriptive copy, and decided it was worth buying. Or perhaps the reader read a review or received a personal recommendation from someone: Same results.

The trepidation arrives when, shortly after starting the book, the reader isn't yet convinced it's worth continuing. That results in some degree of hesitancy in the reader's mind. It does, at least, until the reader becomes comfortable with the elements of the book—particularly the characters.

When you begin a novel using first-person, which is by definition a person of limited omniscience or understanding (people know nothing more than what they have learned personally and can only speculate as to everything else), you create a specific vulnerability to that character. He or she becomes a potential target to whom bad things happen because of that very vulnerability. The reader, of course, picks up on that character flaw and either roots for or against the person, depending upon how you present that character. That's structuring a novel conventionally, and it works.

Now, assume the reader's position when he discovers that the character he'd been following was a sham all along and that suddenly and mysteriously (not to mention miraculously), he "pseudo" knows all (whatever that means). Suddenly, the reader realizes he has spent X number of pages and untold hours worrying about someone who turns out not to have required all that worry in the first place.

The reader feels cheated: He wasted his time. The writer is ostracized for attempting such a cheap, sleazy, literary "trick." And the book goes down the tubes with reviewers.

If that's what you want, go for it. Such a one-trick pony isn't likely to generate enough interest or readership to harm your reputation as a writer, anyway. On the other hand, are you willing to take that chance merely to attempt to be different?

Remember, different doesn't always mean better. It simply means different.

Right?

What's so special about Tolstoy? He only does what all average fiction writers do.

It's all rather subjective, isn't it? Some people hate Herman Melville; others idolize him. Some think Hawthorne was the greatest American writer of all; others believe he was overrated. Personally, I'm not a fan of Tolstoy's literary skills, which I find to be rather plebeian because of the time in which he wrote and his literary voice, choice of words, and use of punctuation.

But, while I may not appreciate Tolstoy's swordsmanship, I'm a huge fan of the longevity of the longevity of his stories. *War and Peace*, *Anna Karenina*, and *The Death of Ivan Ilyich* are considered classics for a reason, less for the author's writing expertise than for the stories' impeccably classic novel structure and universal human appeal. The storylines, characterizations, and descriptive passages of a time long ago and far removed from western civilization resonate with readers from all walks of life to this very day. And with writers, too, who have emulated his universal, humanistic examples for nearly two centuries. That's one of the reasons those three books alone average 4.5 stars with reviewers on Amazon.

D. J. Herda

Not that Amazon's book reviews are the sole or even a primary arbiter of literary greatness. Still, what was it that Abraham Lincoln said about fooling all of the people all of the time?

But, forgetting all that for a moment and getting back to your comment that Tolstoy does what "all average fiction writers do," do you mean he writes works that last an eternity? Do you mean he writes books with voluminous sales? Do you mean he writes stories that resonate with most people walking the face of the earth? Is that what you mean by saying he does what all average fiction writers do? If that's the case, I think you need to take a closer look at "all average fiction writers." You know, those whose books are published (self-published, the majority of them), languor in obscurity, and suffer an ignominious if not premature and welcomed death.

All average fiction writers should be so lucky. That's merely my take on the matter, of course.

Do short-story skill sets vary much from those of novelists or are they pretty much the same?

Absolutely they vary. Vastly different writing skills are required when structuring a short story as opposed to a novel. It's the rough equivalent of a monkey scribbling some colored lines on a sketchbook at a zoo and Vincent van Gogh finalizing his world-renowned self-portrait. Or maybe it's more like the guy next door grabbing a cell-phone selfie with his new car versus Ansel Adams trudging out to the wilds of Yosemite, setting up his 8 x 10″ sheet-film camera on a tripod, and waiting for just the right moment to capture the grandeur of Half Dome.

While a short story and a novel are both fiction, having a storyline, plot, characterization, conflict, pacing, and resolution, the similarities end there. What a novel has that a short story doesn't have are long, lazy passages of narrative (often too many, in fact), in-depth character development, over-the-top descriptive passages, and plenty of "revolving-door" or inconsequential "flat" characters.

Think of a short story as a novel on steroids. Instead of taking 100,000 words to develop, it utilizes 5,000 to 10,000 or a few more in which to accomplish roughly the same thing. That places a tremendous burden on the writer to be concise in his writing, precise with his storyline and plot, and economical with his character development. Instead of taking five or ten pages to develop a character, a short-story writer can afford no more than five or ten lines—and even *that's* stretching things.

And, by the way, if you're thinking right about now that a short story due to its very brevity can't match a novel for overall impact and memorability, think again. And read some of Edgar Allen Poe's works. Or Hawthorne's. Or Melville's. Or even those of Donald Barthelme. Some of the most memorable pieces of literature ever written just happen to be short stories *because* of their very conciseness and focus. So, while novelists are served well by an ability to take into account numerous facts, figures, descriptions, and events and juggle them successfully for thousands of words on end, a short-story writer is required to be concise and effective in using the English language. No side-trips allowed!

But which of the two is more difficult for a writer to write? That depends upon whether or not that writer is skilled at writing one and not the other—or at both, which seems to be a dying art these days. In much the same way as successful screenwriters usually make poor novel writers and vice-versa due to the very different skill sets required of each specialty, successful short-story and novel writers need training, practice, and more practice to become masters at the craft of cranking out both novels and short stories.

Are there any fiction novels in which the main character is a writer or a storyteller?

Are there any novels in which the main character is *not*?

Every first-person account ever written, to my knowledge, involves the telling of a story and, thus, contains a storyteller. Does the phrase, "Call me Ishmael," sound vaguely familiar? If not, Google it, and then obtain and read the book.

Numerous novels also include as a first-person narrator a character who just happens either to be a writer or someone who is destined to become a scribe by the end of the story. Far too many to mention.

D. J. Herda

But, why, I'm wondering, do you ask such a question? Are you planning on writing a novel (all novels are fiction, by the way; so, the phrase "fiction novels" is redundant) in which your main character is a writer/storyteller? If so, you won't be the first. Still, it's a good structural mechanism for justifying the telling of a story and a great way for a writer to immerse him- or herself into the work and blend into the storyline.

Some things are just damned hard to improve upon, so why try?

"In those days cheap apartments were almost impossible to find in Manhattan, so I had to move to Brooklyn."

Sound familiar? Probably not. But it's the opening of *Sophie's Choice* by William Styron, the narrator of which just happens to be a writer, retelling the story of his experiences with a rather, *umm*, extraordinary couple following the war. It, too—while written nowhere nearly as elegantly as Melville's *Moby Dick*--is just as moving in its way and also worth reading.

Just my two cents worth on a couple of outstanding examples.

What is the best fictional structure for a literary novel, if any?

Hmm. It sounds as if you look upon the structure of a novel as a high-rise blueprint or a Mayan message etched in stone when, in reality, it's more like a movable feast. Structure, as it relates to literature, doesn't exist outside of a piece of writing, either fiction or nonfiction. It develops only as the author begins creating the written work. It follows him into existence, not the other way around.

That's one of the reasons structure is sometimes difficult to define: It doesn't exist the way a phone booth or an automobile or a cloud does. It's not a noun or a verb or an adjective. It does not have a life of its own. It takes on whatever life the author creates for it only after stringing words together into sentences and sentences into paragraphs and paragraphs into chapters. An author decides when and how to hone the structure of a work as he determines what goes where and who does what. The structure for one piece of literary fiction may very well have several features in common with that of another, but it also will vary, often significantly.

ABOUT WRITING RIGHT

So, to answer your question, the fictional structure that's best for a literary novel, assuming it's a well-done work of art, is exactly what came from how the writer put the story together. Nothing more, but nothing less.

Is it acceptable to write an introduction, prologue, and short introductory chapter to a book, introducing something that took place five years ago?

Yes. You can structure your book however you desire; there are no prohibitions on doing anything. But if by "acceptable" you mean is doing so the normal practice in literature today, the answer is "no." It's definitely *not* the norm simply because most books don't have short first chapters. That's unfortunate because a short (super-short?) chapter can snag the reader's interest, set up the storyline, and start the book off with a bang. As an example of the role a short opening chapter can play in a novel, regardless of when the action took place), check out Paula Favage's *The Mynah's Call* currently available for free as a review copy (along with several other of the publisher's books) at Elektra Press. Click on the book's title (Favage: The Mynah's Call) to learn more about that particular book and receive your complimentary copy.

Although I'm talking here about fiction, you can also write a nonfiction book with an introduction, prologue, and short opening chapter. Again, since you're the author, you have the option of choosing the structure that works best for your book.

One more word of advice: Never be afraid to innovate and break with the "norm," whatever that may be. Sometimes, publishers, editors, and readers are aching for something "new" to come along. As examples, just look at Jack Kerouac's *On the Road* or Hunter S. Thompson's *Fear and Loathing in Las Vegas*. Oh, and, no—you don't have to be stoned to create something different right out of the box. It might not hurt, but it's not a prerequisite.

By how much can I increase the word count when a publisher asks me to add depth to my characters and expand upon their world-building?

I'd advise you to be reasonable. A few thousand words more or less won't sink a manuscript if the editor falls in love with it. Doubling the length, though, is a bad idea for several reasons. If the story is fairly strong as it stands, adding tens of thousands of words will only dilute and weaken it, and that's something you *don't* want to do.

Naturally, when an editor asks for expanded characterization and enhanced details, he's going to expect a different word count than the original. That's not what should concern you. This is:

The editor just gave you the opportunity of a lifetime. You have a completed story and someone who likes it enough that he might actually buy it (with a few changes). Take advantage of the opportunity to go back, re-read the work, cut out extraneous material (and there's plenty of that, I guarantee you), expand upon critical references, and sharpen the entire work. This is your chance to turn back the clock and hone the book to perfection. *Don't blow it!*

Most writers never make it as far as you did. Few get requests from editors to revise and resubmit their manuscripts. So, follow the editor's directives and rework, rework, rework. While you're at it, get rid of those typos. Dump the passive voice for active. Strip all the adverbs you can and replace them with descriptive verbs. Tighten the dialogue so that it's crisper and more realistic. Expand areas of conflict and resolution. Strengthen the opening chapter and the ending.

Once you've done all that, you'll have a better property for your efforts and a greater chance that the editor will not only like it but also be able to talk his editorial board into publishing it.

Should I mention how my orphaned character's parents died or devote more time to it in keeping with "Show not Tell"?

You're mistaking the concept behind the admonition of "Show it, don't say it." The commandment to "show it" doesn't come with a word count. There are no minimum words required to show something. The key is differentiating between empty words and imagery-charged words and phrases. Here are some examples.

- BAD: *He let out a sudden noise from his mouth.*
- GOOD: *He belched.*
- BAD: *A sudden storm came up, and the winds and rain began falling down on us.*

ABOUT WRITING RIGHT

- GOOD: *The skies exploded, and the wind hammered (or peppered or pelted) us with rain.*

See what I mean? Most definitely, show it whenever possible. There are times when showing it, though, seems awkward and out of place, right? That's because you're failing to convey to your reader the *imagery* you want to drive home. Or, worse, you're *forcing* imagery that doesn't work. It's called the difference between effective and ineffective writing.

As for how your character's parents died, spend some time in a flashback (still "showing" instead of "saying" via your choice of imagery-charged words) *if* their death is a critical part of the story and needs to be expanded upon. If it's not, have your character reference it in passing—possibly in dialogue with someone else or in a short inner dialogue (or thought).

Simple? That's the way good writing always seems to the reader. Although it often seems anything *but* to the writer.

My first-person characters aren't working for me. Every time I try straightening things out, I end up dissatisfied. They're either under-developed or over the top. How can I fix that?

Most likely, you're trying to squeeze too much into too short a time frame. Think of the film, *The Big Chill.* It's one hundred percent about college friends, how they have matured over the years, and how they fit back together after one of the group commits suicide.

You know everything there is to know about the group, their camaraderie, and their motivations within the first ten pages of the script, right?

Wrong! It's not until nearly 1 hour, 45 minutes later that we have a solid understanding of who's who and what's what. And, most importantly, what motivates them to remain friends despite having grown apart over the years.

So, how do you expand upon *your* characters' relationships? I thought you'd never ask. Here are a few suggestions.

1. List the characters and their motivating characteristics.
2. Find two group members who vary dramatically in at least one characteristic. Say, one loves classical music while the other eats, drinks, and lives Zydeco.

3. Have those two interrelate, quarrel, bicker, and then grudgingly come to some understanding about there being nothing wrong with how the other person thinks. This is a great opportunity to work in some snappy, humorous, revealing dialogue.
4. Do similar things with all the group members. Some feel strongly about one point, and others feel just the opposite. But everyone comes to respect everyone else in time.
5. Have the group gang up on one member until he can't take any more criticism and storms off. Then, have another member go after him, talk to him, and calm him down. Have that person explain that the group is only a bunch of dumb jerks, anyway, so why is he letting them get the better of him? In the end, they still love him.
6. Have some if not all group members be self-deprecating. One or two can have a hard skin, but even they eventually show understanding, empathy, and concern.
7. Continue with the group members coming together, splitting apart, and then coming back together as they spar with one another. In the end, they become better acquainted with and more accepting of one another.
8. Spread everything out throughout the book instead of squeezing it all into a few pages or a single chapter.

Remember, fine wine wasn't built in a day. Or was that Rome? Anyway, treat your character like a fine Cabernet, giving it plenty of time to develop its nose and bouquet, and you'll wind up smiling yourself to sleep at night instead of grinding your teeth until the first rays of dawn.

Or, maybe it *was* wine.

Also, there's one more thing that might be keeping you up nights. It's called being too close to the story. Or, in this case, the characters.

You mention you're writing in the first person, which at least intimates that you're writing about your own friends and acquaintances. Yet, you can't understand why the writing doesn't flow out of you like sap from a maple tree.

But, when you're too close to your subjects, you view them through your personal lens--your perspective, your feelings, your thoughts and experiences with them. Instead, try objectifying them. If Mary is like

ABOUT WRITING RIGHT

this, name her character *Celeste* and add *something else* to her character (something not in the real Mary but would be an interesting addition if it were). Perhaps she has a soft spot for kittens or a weakness for fine shoes. Do the same with all your characters. Make them alter-egos of your friends—not exactly duplicates--and build upon their characteristic natures until you have a field of fictional people populating your book.

Sometimes, writing about others in first person becomes frustrating. If you learn to compartmentalize your characters (including thinking about yourself as an actual fictional character based upon you but not the real you), things flow more smoothly.

It's called fictionalizing, and it works. Give it a try. I think you'll enjoy the experience.

After seven years of work on my story, how can I stop rewriting it and move on with the next step when I want to make sure the first draft is perfect?

Unlike dozens of other omniscient responders to your question, I don't have the definitive answer because there isn't one. I only know what works for one perfectionist with whom I'm remotely acquainted.

But, before I let you in on a little-known secret, understand that perfection is a curse. Nearly as much as a blessing. So, if you're a perfectionist (and you have virtually admitted that to the world), understand that you'll benefit from your abnormal behavior more than you suffer. And recognize that relatively few people in this universe are true perfectionists. Type-A personalities. Obsessive-compulsive temperaments. Tormented souls. You know what I'm saying: We both belong to the same club.

So, how do I handle my writing, rewriting, and re-rewriting ad infinitum as a perfectionist? Obviously, I've figured something out. You don't write tens of thousands of articles and other short pieces, a hundred conventionally published books, and several full-length plays in production over half a century by letting your perfectionism stand in your way. So, here's what I do.

I compromise. Knowing I'm a perfectionist is a great starting point for each writing session. I write a chapter. I leave it for a day or two. I come back and start "warming up" by reading the chapter I recently completed. *"Oops.* No good. This isn't right. That's not what I meant.

This isn't the best way to say that. I've got to change that line."

After fine-tuning that chapter, I force myself to move on to begin creating the next one. This is not an option. This is the law I set down for myself. Re-read and edit the previous day's session, and move on. If I violate the law, I go to writer's prison ... or hell.

Once I finish with the new chapter (or two, or however much I create that day), I set it aside. When I return a day or two later, I begin my work on the book by reviewing what I wrote the previous session. *only* what I wrote the previous session. Not what I wrote or revised prior to that. Just the newest material. That's law number two: Review the previous session and move on. And, guess what I find when I review that previous session: *"Oops.* No good. This isn't right. That's not what I meant. This isn't the best way to say that. I've got to change that line."

I continue in that manner, starting each writing session with a review of what I created the day before, until I've completed my book. It doesn't matter what draft you call it. First, second, third, *Thermopolis*. Hell, give them Greek letters of the alphabet for all anyone cares. What matters is that you've finished the book.

But, of course, you haven't.

So, after waiting several days for my mind to clear its literary prejudices, I go back and begin re-reading Chapter One. And I rework it. The following session, I begin re-reading what I reworked the previous session and re-read the next chapter or two or ten—however many I'm up to that day. The session after that, I re-read what I reworked the day before and plow on to the next chapters. By the time I've gone through the book a "second" time, I'm *relatively* satisfied with it.

Of course, being a perfectionist means you're never completely satisfied with *anything*. But, being a professional *and* a rational adult means you have to make a decision to stop reworking something and let it go out into the troposphere sometime.

How can you force yourself to "give up the ghost" and stop tinkering with your work? Keep in mind that, should an editor somewhere actually ask to see the piece and--*yeow!*--believe it or not, buy it, you'll have yet one more chance to edit the hell out of it before the publisher's editors tell you: *Enough!*

ABOUT WRITING RIGHT

Once again, this system might be perfect, or it might be perfect for me only. All I know is that it has worked for many years for one perfectionist. Perhaps, it can work for another.

Hope this helps.

How many chapters does a 200-page book contain?

At the risk of sounding condescending, have you ever read a book?

Have you ever *seen* a book?

Because, if you have, you'd know that your question has no definitive answer.

Now, if you're asking how an author determines how many chapters should be in a book of X-number words (pages don't count and don't matter because they vary too greatly from one format to another depending upon numerous variables), that's another story, and someone else already answered that for you. The author is in charge of determining the length of his chapters depending upon story flow. Tiny breaks in thought dictate the need for new sentences. Somewhat larger breaks call for new paragraphs. Larger breaks, still, dictate the use of new chapters. *Normally.* But, again, that's all up to the author.

See?

Of course you do. But, it's all water under the bridge, anyway, since that's not what you asked. Which makes me wonder why you asked that question when you already knew the answer. I mean, *if* you ever read or saw a book.

Anything else I can help you with today?

Can an author put too many things into a novel?

No. Not if they all work together to sweep the reader from Point A to Point Z. Characters, setting, plots and subplots, flashbacks and flash-forwards, description, dialogue—everything you include in your novel should eventually prove valuable to the reader at the end.

That's not the same as saying you can't have a wasted character or two or a false line of pursuit to confuse your protagonist (as well as to throw your reader off the trail). These ploys, too, eventually help the reader to a satisfying conclusion of the book and thus can be useful additions to the work. Just make sure you don't deliberately set out to "cheat" the reader out of something you as the author intimate you'll resolve and then don't. That can be very frustrating.

On the other hand, even two "things" in a book can be one too many if one of them is totally removed from your storyline or plot and serves absolutely no purpose in the book's development other than to completely confuse and frustrate your reader or waste his time and energy.

Also, a uncomfortably large number of "things" (whatever you mean by that) in a shorter work might prove frustrating reading, while in a longer book, they might work out just fine. You can fit more elements into *War and Peace* than you can into a typical O'Henry short story.

Got that? Good. Next question, please.

In a screenplay, should I reveal a major secret up front, or should I save it until the end and use it as a plot twist? What's your preference?

It's nice to see that some respondents to your question really answered with their preference, because that, in the end, is what you asked for … their preference. As for my response? It all depends upon the author, the author's intents and goals, and the storyline. That means that all those answers regarding your ultimate question: *Do you have a preference?* are right on target. But they're nothing you should pay attention to. Here's why.

Only you as the author know what your screenplay is about, where it's going, and how you're going about getting it there. Do you understand what I just said? Your respondents aren't in charge of your play; you are. They can't possibly know your intent for your story; you do. You're the film guru; you're the goddess (or god) of your plot; you're the guider of the action. No one else can give you suggestions as to how *you* should write your play. Especially not in such a potentially earth-shattering area as audience awareness.

My suggestion to you if you're really stuck? Don't ask for advice; try it both ways. Write one scenario one way; write a second another way. After a few days to "forget" about your attachment to the play, go back and read one, and then a short while later read the other.

Out loud! Particularly with scripts, always read what you wrote *out loud*! That's what the audience will hear, remember, and that's what will register with your brain most emphatically. Let me say it again: *out loud!!!*

ABOUT WRITING RIGHT

After reading both, do what I always do when confronted with such a situation: Eenie-meenie-miney-moe. (Okay, just kidding!) Seriously, see which to you "sounds" better. Which works better. Which sets up more conflict and resolution and keeps it going through to the end of the script. I'm betting the answer will be saving the secret until you reveal the plot twist toward the end.

But, then again, I'm only another voice in the wilderness. Don't let me influence you.

How long should an author's novel be?

Subjectively (that is, from the author's point-of-view), a novel should be exactly as long as the author requires to tell the story efficiently and effectively. No more, no less.

Objectively, if you're planning on pitching your book to conventional publishers, pay attention to their published minimum/maximum word requirements, because they matter. Publishers learned long ago that skimpy books won't sell for $28.95—or any price, for that matter. In order to plunk their hard-earned pesos down on a book, a reader has to feel he's getting something in return for his money.

Conversely, a book that's overly long costs more to prepare, print, warehouse, and distribute, which puts a publisher at risk of losing a reasonable return on investment.

While numerous online estimates (*guesstimates?*) of recommended novel lengths exist, depending upon genre and targeted age group, take these with a grain of salt. Each conventional publisher has its own thoughts and marketing reports on what lengths work best for that publisher, and each expects its authors to adhere to them.

More or less.

How can I explain my character's fantasy world without giving away the farm?

Thank you, thank you, thank you, thank you, thank you for asking this question. It's one I relish answering. I was beginning to think no one would ever get around to it, and I'd *never* have a chance to respond. So, here goes:

- *It was a dark and stormy night.*

What? No? Too much information? Okay, then, how about this:

- *They say the world will end with a whimper, not a bang. For me, it was just the other way around. That's how my world began—with a whimper. I had awakened beneath a large boulder shrouded by shrubs to the scintillating, soothing, softening, sensuous, satisfying sounds of life playing out on a distant breeze.*

Now, stepping aside for a moment from that remarkably lucid example, I'm also leaning toward an excellent piece of advice offered from a couple of other respondents who had their fantasy fans turned up to high. They advised you not to start with a description at all but instead with some action—a real fight-or-flight situation. After your character disposes of that menace, he or she can gradually and *g-e-n-t-l-y* reveal the background of that strange new world. That's probably the approach I would take, too.

But, with that said, if you're intent upon doing it the way you suggest, I would use some opening along the lines of the example above (not the *dark and stormy night* thing). Very sensuous, poetic, and appealing. Very short. Very comforting. To lull the reader into a false sense of well-being. And then I would end the chapter with those few lines.

Start out the *second* chapter with the reader captivated and curious—enough to have to read more. That's where you set him up for just the opposite of serenity. Knock his socks off, and have your character's internal dialogue (thoughts) slowly reveal what his world has become and how he's managed to survive in it—despite the omnipresent dangers that lurk round every *yeddith* (corner).

Okay, scratch "yeddith." The world doesn't need yet one more volume of sophomoric future-speak. Let the story tell itself, see the imagery in your mind (envision it clearly) before putting it down on paper, and allow the background to surface slowly as appropriate.

Whichever way you choose (or neither), keep your main goals in mind: to entertain, enlighten, intrigue, frighten, awaken, shock, and ultimately satisfy your reader.

Why does a book need a table of content?

You're kidding, right? I mean, this is a joke, isn't it? Okay, okay, so not everyone is familiar with the purposes served by a TOC. Let's shed a little light—and a touch of history—on the subject.

ABOUT WRITING RIGHT

A Table of Contents (not "table of content") tells the both the current reader and the potential reader who hasn't yet purchased the book what's inside. *Roughly.* If you omit the TOC, you're forcing the reader to pre-judge the book's content based upon its title, which is rarely enticing enough to persuade a viewer to buy a book, and the cover blurbs, if any.

Once a reader sets about tackling a new book, the TOC serves as a roadmap for the reader to navigate. That can be especially useful for readers who take several days or even weeks to finish reading a book, particularly if they tend to forget where they have left off. A quick glance at the contents page can help them recall the story while assisting them to locate what they still need to read.

The contents page originally served still a third purpose. In the late first century, Roman naturalist Pliny the Elder included what we refer to as a Table of Contents in his *Natural History*. He did so to save his readers time, writing that "one may search for what he wishes, and may know where to find it." Pliny refused to take credit for the convention, though, noting that the TOC "has already been done among us" by Valerius Soranus in his treatise entitled *On Mysteries*.

Today, TOCs serve less of a utilitarian purpose and more one of convenience, while the book's Index has been elevated to helping readers pinpoint the specific information they're looking for, most notably in nonfiction tomes.

Still, virtually all nonfiction books and most novels have TOCs of varying complexities, some with chapter and page numbers only and others with chapter headings or even descriptions detailing what each chapter contains. It's information-at-a-glance for the reader's use and appreciation.

Should I write my historical fiction novel using more modern English or the archaic dialect?

Absolutely, write your historical novel ("fiction novel" is a bit redundant, no?) 100 percent in more modern English. Do so for two reasons.

One, the reader is not conversant in older English and will have a difficult time deciphering what you mean. And slow, labored reading makes for easy, pain-free stopping. It's the surest way to condemn your book to the "No, thanks" pile.

Two, *you're* not conversant in older English, which means you'll make some horrendous blunders in trying to piece together natural-sounding English from a vastly different era. And as soon as the reader recognizes that fact, he or she will be gone.

Remember, you don't need to use period language to get the message across that you're writing about a different period. In the end, your reader will thank you for it.

Has anyone ever written a book in second-person point-of-view?

Yes. In fact, several. At least according to some literary analysts who claim to know about such things. And do you know which of those books is universally acclaimed for its literary brilliance?

Exactly.

The reason the two main points-of-view in writing are so popular is because they work. First-person and third-person POVs are conducive to storytelling. Second person isn't. I suspect that those writers who attempt to force something into second person do so just to see if they can. Either that, or they're trying to *prove* that they can. In either case, the results are an ignominious flop.

By the way, would it be heresy to say here that there is no way to write a book in second person? *Period?* That *all* second-person stories are usually written in third person by an external narrator who refers to "*you*" as a means of seeming to write in second person? Yet, the use of the word "you" as the target of the narration doesn't negate the fact that the narrator is not speaking from second person because he *can't* speak from second person; he's speaking usually from third person omniscient or limited omniscient or, on rare occasion, first person.

But *why* can't a novel be written in second person technically? I thought you'd never ask.

In order to narrate a story to someone, the narrator must have *access* to or *knowledge* of the story. That means either "I" have to be the narrator (first person) or "he, she, it, or they" does (third person). Attempting to assign the story-telling to neither first nor third person is to admit defeat. How can a person outside of someone telling the story to someone else tell the story to *anyone* without becoming a first- or third-person narrator? *I* can tell a story to you; *he* can tell a story to you, but *you* can't tell a story to you because you already know the story, and you can't be both the narrator and the person being narrated to. As soon as "you" as the narrator tell the story to "you" as the person narrated to, "you" as the narrator become the third-person. Calling something second-person simply because you address the narration to someone you refer to as "you" doesn't make it so. It's not logical, which means it doesn't make sense, which means it can't be done, which means it doesn't exist.

Of course, that won't stop writers everywhere intent upon inventing a legitimate second-person point-of-view from trying. Still, as Moustache, the French saloon-keeper in *Irma La Douce,* says throughout the film, "But that's another story …"

I'm writing a book about my mother's life story, told by her. I'm wondering whether it's a biography or an autobiography. Someone said it depends upon whose name is on the book. Is that right?

Well, the answer to that isn't quite as simple as whose name is on the book, yours or your mother's. If your mother's story is written in first person and has her name on the book, it's a no-brainer autobiography. And, if your mother's story is written in first person but has *your* name on the book instead of hers, it's *still* an autobiography (an "as-told-to" work). If your mother's story is written in third person, no matter whose name is on the book, it's a biography.

Clear as mud?

Hopefully, it's a little clearer than that!

I'd like to use eight different points-of-view in my novel. Is that too many?

Finally! One respondent to your question actually got it right for a change. And her answer, although somewhat skewed, is correct: Give it up.

But, beyond that advice, why on earth would you ever have considered doing that *ever*? I know the answer, of course, because I was a young, inexperienced (i.e., dumb) writer once, and I probably would have tried the same thing had I thought of it. But, thankfully, I didn't, so I didn't. But I thought about many other dumb things to do, and I did them. *Ouch!*

So, let me jump ahead here and assume I know why you even considered doing such a thing. Because the caliber of your writing leaves you wondering whether or not you desperately need a "gimmick" to succeed. You know, like Jack Kerouac used in *On the Road?*

My answer: no. If you doubt the caliber of your writing, take some courses. Invest more time in writing, read more, study more, think more, and invest more time in writing again. In other words, be patient. It will come to you if you want it badly enough. If not ... Well, there's always grad school.

Short take: In time, you'll wonder why you ever had the nerve to ask such a question here, and, more so, you'll wonder why you even considered doing such a ridiculous thing in the first place. I know I did.

Just my take on things.

How should a writer go about introducing a secondary plot?

Umm, I would suggest you reject one respondent's reference to subplot types: *There are two types of subplots, including the parallel subplot and the independent subplot.* I mean, you didn't ask for an analytical treatise, did you? You asked for practical advice.

So, here it is. Announce it. Just as you did your primary plot. You know, when, in your first chapter, you wrote, "And now, ladies and gentlemen, I'm going to reveal to you my primary plot, which is ..."

Oh, okay. You didn't? Good for you.

And that's my point. You don't "introduce" a secondary plot line. Not any more than you "introduce" a primary plot. You meld it. You weave it. You work it into the existing story. Someone new comes onboard. Something new happens. Some new element arises. Someone takes a cruise and meets someone mysterious. Or someone doesn't take a cruise and instead gets to know the gardener better. (*Much* better.) Or whatever.

You don't ever "introduce" a plot. You *develop* it.

Semantics? Call it that if you want, but I have the distinct feeling that you're asking for a formulaic method for advancing the story into a secondary plot, and that doesn't (or, at least, *shouldn't*) exist.

James Taylor, remember? "Ride with the tide, and go with the flow."

See the story. *Envision* the imagery. *Know* what you want to do. And *write* it as you want it. In other words, "go with the flow."

ABOUT WRITING RIGHT

Simple, no? And you never have to give a second thought to types of subplots, *parallel subplot*s, or *independent subplots*.

Thank God.

Remember: Teachers teach; writers write.

'Nuff said.

Who should I ask to format a screenplay for me?

Wow, it seems that the answer is so obvious, someone else would have thought of it by now. So, here's my response:

A screenwriter. Or any writer with screenwriting experience and software.

How do you find him or her? Ask around. Ask other writers. But don't expect anyone to work for nothing. Work means time, and time means money. I'm guessing, if you're looking for someone simply to provide the proper formatting to an existing screenplay, you're looking at spending $300 - $400. But if you're searching for someone to take your story and convert it into a screenplay, that's a whole different ballgame requiring far more expertise. Now, you're likely facing a tab of a couple thousand dollars or more—if you want it done right. And who wouldn't?

Should I edit and cut my YA book? It's presently over 100,00 words in length.

Wow, you've received a couple decent but also some seriously ridiculous answers to a pretty sensible, straightforward question. Here's the scoop.

First, you're equating basketballs with eggs. Yes, you need to edit your book. You need to edit everything you write from now until the end of time. No writer is good enough to escape this mandatory step. *Ever.* Write, edit. Write, edit. Write, edit. Do it until your vision gets blurry and your eyeballs turn red.

Second, yes, you need to cut your YA book. It's possible that someone would want to publish it regardless of its length—assuming it's well written and has "good seller" scrawled all over it. (Not literally, of course.) But why swim upstream if you're not a salmon? Why not stay within the norm?

In this case, the average word count for YA fiction is 55,000 - 80,000. A little more, a little less. But *not* 20,000 words more! So, you can begin the laborious and always painful task of cutting bits and pieces from every page beginning at the start until you've trimmed the required amount, or you can cut the book into two parts, adding a new ending to where you decide to stop "Book One" and providing a new, smooth-transitioning beginning to "Book Two."

That's probably the easier of the two possible solutions, although cutting a book into two parts isn't quite as simple as it sounds. You'll have to adjust your storyline and plot in Book One to match the new ending you provide for it, and that may entail making some interior changes, as well so that the new ending makes sense.

Either way, it looks as if you've pretty much filled up *your* dance card for the summer!

Should I write my professional biography in first or third person?

That depends upon where the bio will be published and by whom it will be read. The third person point-of-view sounds more objective and, thus, believable. It's as if someone other than you wrote it *about* you instead of you writing it *for* you. The first-person POV sounds more subjective and could be interpreted as boastful or braggadocios, not to mention slanted in your favor. With that in mind, the author needs to decide which satisfies his immediate, as well as his long-term, goals.

For example, I recently received pre-publication copies of my latest book, a biography of Etta Place, the glamorous and mysterious paramour of the Sundance Kid of Wild Bunch fame. On the inside dust jacket is my biography, which I wrote and sent to the publisher at his request. It's written in third person and, thus, sounds as if some independent reviewer news reporter generated it. It reads like a litany of events or a list of facts rather than a bunch of boastful accomplishments that a reader might choose to question or that might turn him or her off.

And, yes, review copies of the book are available for the asking. Just drop me a note at http://www.djherda.org, and let me know what format of eBook you'd prefer.

How can I begin a story where the main characters are leaving for a family vacation?

Do you want me to tell you a sure-fire, can't-miss opening for a vacation story? I mean above and beyond the Chevy Chase vacation-film franchise? One that will guarantee you instant success? One that's so good, you'll wonder why you hadn't thought of it yourself? One that will knock the socks off every publisher ever to hang out a shingle? One that ...

Oh, hell. Never mind. Here it is: "*See* it."

Hmm?

That's right. *See* it. Envision it. Picture it in your mind. Create a mental image of what you think your opening should be. If it rings your bell, it's gold. If it doesn't, go back and dig deeper until you *see* another image—as if watching television or a video or something on a screen as it plays out before you—and another, and another, until it the bell rings loudly.

Doesn't that sound about right? I mean, especially since creative writing is all about imagery—about creating an image in your brain and writing it on paper so powerfully for your reader that he or she can't help but see it, too? You know, as if it's presented *in-camera*. (Look it up; the experience will serve you well.)

With that said, let me ask *you* a question that's even more pointed than the one you asked. "Why on earth would you allow anyone to tinker with, to influence, or to affect your story without putting up a bloody fight? I mean, whose story is it, yours or someone else's? And why on earth would you put your trust in anyone else to be able to tell a story—or even a small part of it—that lives within *you*?"

Now, I suppose there's a chance that this whole vacation episode is not really your story at all and, thus, it doesn't live within you. In which case it sounds awfully much as though you're fishing around for someone else to do all your work while you sit back and collect all the rewards.

Well, here's another invaluable life tip: Ain't gonna happen. You either make it on your own, from your own brain to that of your reader, or you don't. You train yourself to do it, or you don't. You learn how to envision strong, powerful images and then present them to your reader on paper, or you don't. And if you don't, that's not so bad. Remember those immortal words issued by Judge Smails to Danny Noonan in the Chevy Chase film, *Caddyshack:* "The world needs ditch diggers, too.

THREE: The Editing of Writing

If you've been around the world of freelance writing, editing, and even publishing long enough, you've probably heard the phrase, "Good editors aren't made, they're born."

Malarkey.

No one is *born* knowing how to edit any more than anyone is *born* knowing how to be a brain surgeon or a piano tuner. Every occupation comes only after sufficient exposure, a desire to learn, a reliable source of instruction, and practice, practice, and more practice.

None of those prerequisites to becoming an editor has anything to do with birthright or happenstance. They have to do with learning a skill that can be taught to anyone, provided all prerequisites are present.

If what I say about editing is true, that means a couple of things should be obvious.

First, no one can know how to edit simply by having written a lot of words. Writing requires one skillset (or, some would argue, *no* skill set whatsoever, but let's not get into that); editing requires another. Without learning what editing involves—and then learning what *good* editing entails—no one can sufficiently edit anything but the most rudimentary piece of writing with the hopes of improving its readability.

Second, few editors can do all types of editing. And editing does come in a plethora of flavors. Not butter brickle, unfortunately, but things that can be just as enticing, if less indulgent. Depending upon who's doing the defining, an editor can be a proofreader (checking for

ABOUT WRITING RIGHT

typographical errors and basic grammatical and punctuation mistakes), a fact-checker, a copy editor (reviewing the author's copy for readability, proper syntax, and the like), a conceptual or substantive editor (also at times referred to as a content editor, checking a piece for various flaws in logic), a developmental editor (reviewing how the story is put together and marking various recommendations from that point-of-view), a structural editor (specializing in structural issues concerned with a story's readability and involving the use of flashbacks, flash-forwards, linear chronology, and even when and where to break a story into chapters and other divisions), and a line editor (concentrating on the flow of the prose and pointing out any awkward phrasing, etc.).

This doesn't even scratch the surface of those corporate-specific editors whose goals are less concerned with improving the quality and readability of a work than they are on increasing its marketability. These editors wear titles such as managing editor, assistant editor, acquisitions editor, associate editor, fiction or nonfiction editor, photo editor, executive editor, and even publisher. Each of these people plays a roll more specifically geared to producing a quality product once the decision has been made to acquire a specific property.

Obviously, for an editor to gain experience and expertise in all these areas of editorial development, he or she would have to put in a lifetime in the trenches. Think decades rather than years. Just as obviously, while some people can do it all, few even attempt to do so.

Third, even if a writer is skilled in two or three specific areas of editing, he's not necessarily fully qualified to edit his work himself. Often, the writer is too "close" to his work and unable to evaluate it objectively. In such a case, his choices are limited: Hire the right editors for the job, or take the time to learn and work at those areas in which the writer needs to develop his editing expertise.

Guess which one is the more practical of the two!

But why worry about editing at all? Surely writers such as Jack Kerouac and Hunter Thompson wrote by the seat of their pants. Editing must have been the last thing either of them had on his mind, right?

True. You can even stretch that narrative out further to include authors such as Hemingway and Fitzgerald, two huge-name enduring classics. *Ahh*, but Hemingway and Fitzgerald wrote at a time before the Internet and POD printing made writing for publication so accessible. That, in turn, has quadrupled the number of beginning writers searching for their place in the sun. In the Good Ol' Days, simply finishing a book—particularly one with a strong storyline and memorable characters—meant some editor somewhere was going to run the risk of acquiring the manuscript and assigning a publisher's editor to clean up the junk in the trunk prior to its publication. Ditto, Kerouac and Thompson.

Today, however, the problem facing most unpublished and even oft-published writers isn't finding an editor who believes in the work and wants to champion it to his peers as much as it is preparing the work so that it reads professionally enough to catch the attention of that beleaguered editor in the first place. With the explosion of new material that first-time authors are cranking out and shipping off for consideration, the competition to find an editor willing to read past the opening page of a manuscript is far more intense today than ever before.

So, editing is as important today as it ever was—if not more so. Even for those authors who intend on self-publishing their works, a bad editing job will read poorly, and books that read poorly sell poorly. Once a reviewer or two gets turned off by the slough of typos and grammatical errors in an author's book, that author can kiss any hope of literary success good-by forever.

So, with all this in mind, it's obvious that writers can't ignore editing. We must all face up to the demands editing places on us and meet it head-on. Here are some of the most thought-provoking questions writers have asked me about editing, along with a few pointed responses. As someone once said, *Tolle lege*: "Take and read."

Where can I find writers for a new nonprofit magazine startup I'm planning on editing?

Assuming you're talking about paid positions instead of voluntary, which is the difference between finding good editors and coming up empty-handed (no one can afford to work for nothing these days, particularly not good, experienced editors), magazine editors are around. The best of them are still employed but might be persuaded to

ABOUT WRITING RIGHT

jump ship with the right salary and working conditions. Some others are in between employment. I can recommend some people to you in both categories if you're serious. But first, let's take a closer look at what's involved with finding magazine editors.

In many ways, magazine editors are like book editors. Each specializes in a specific area of expertise. While book editors can cross over from acquiring Sci-Fi books to tackling Mystery, for example, so, too, can magazine editors go from editing sports titles to women's monthlies. They can, but often they'd rather not; so, it's wise to match the editor's editorial preference to the type of magazine you'll be publishing.

Also, magazine editors, like book editors, play different roles at a publishing house, depending upon their training and experience. At larger magazines, you may have different editors performing ten different tasks, from acquiring articles to copy editing, proofreading, layout and design, concept editing, fact-checking, etc. Each of these editors may have one or more assistant editors, and those assistant editors may have interns or runners. At smaller houses, fewer editors mean they must of necessity double- or triple-up on the editorial duties at hand.

So, before anyone can answer your question, he'll have to know the type of magazine you're proposing (its audience and its purpose for publication). Also, what kind of editing you need and whether or not these are full or part-time positions. Plus, if the jobs are virtual or physical (remote or on-site) and the staff's hierarchy (who reports or is responsible to whom), and so forth. The answers to all these questions will likely affect how much reimbursement the editors will require.

Are you still with me? Still onboard and serious about launching a new magazine? If so, and you have deep pockets (new magazines are notorious for going out of business after a few issues unless they have some powerful advertising revenue and people behind them), get in touch with me at http://www.djherda.org.

If this project is more of a pipe dream or a fantasy, though, I'm afraid no one of any professional caliber will be able to join you in it.

It's called the harsh reality of life.

Should I hire someone to edit, publish, and market my book or should I pursue those skills on my own?

Hmm. Tough question. Here's another one: If a tree falls in a forest and no one is around to hear it, does it make a sound?

Actually, the last question is a little easier to answer than the first because there are so many variables to what you ask.

For starters, how much time do you have to devote to learning the skills required for editing, marketing, and publishing your book? Remember: Learning is easy if you don't care about how the outcome looks; otherwise, it's not such a slam dunk! Not to mention laying out the manuscript for eBook and Print and then formatting it correctly for acceptance in both formats by Kindle, Ingram, and other distributors. Then, there's also the question of cover design. If you're not a trained graphic artist with book-publishing experience, you definitely shouldn't tackle that job, or you could wind up with a newly published book *no one* looks at twice.

So, unless you have years to devote to learning all the above and years more to gaining practical experience, I'd plan on hiring someone. That, though, is sometimes easier said than done. First, you have to find someone with experience and knowledge in each of those disciplines. Don't plan on finding one person who can do it all, because we're so few and far between! Seriously, good help is hard to find, and it's therefore expensive.

How expensive? That depends upon how rough the shape your manuscript is in. Is it nearly perfect but simply needs someone to dot the T's and cross the I's? Or is it one bloody grammatical mess from start to finish? You'll pay an editor much less for the former and much more for the latter, so a personal evaluation would be necessary before the freelancers you approach can give you a firm price. Even then, you can only hope you'll be satisfied with the finished product. I don't know of many who offer a firm guarantee of satisfaction—they're few and far between and have to be pretty darned good at what they do to make such an offer.

Then we come to layout and formatting. If your book is a straightforward novel, you'll likely get off pretty light. If it's a complex nonfiction volume with lots of footnotes, comments, references, illustrations, drawings, charts, and graphs, figure on paying a professional a lot to whip it into pre-press shape.

ABOUT WRITING RIGHT

Artwork? Again, depending upon how generic or custom you want to go, the cost will vary quite a bit.

With all this said, if you find yourself thinking about hiring the work out, I'll be happy to put on my Publisher's Hat and give you my best estimate of what's involved, what's necessary, and a range of costs you're likely to encounter once you begin shopping the book around.

Of course, there's a down-and-dirty way to go, as well, although I assume someone as articulate as you in the phrasing of your question isn't looking for a wham-bam-thank-you-ma'am job. If that's all you want, you can do that much even without the proper training. To do it right, though, and give your book a chance at success, you'll need to spend a few bucks.

Those are the nuts and bolts. Contact me via my Website if you need additional input: Get Some Help or Just Say Hello!

Meanwhile …

Must a person be a good writer in order to get into the field of publishing?

Not at all. In fact, I know *very few* successful book editors and even fewer publishers who are good writers. They don't need to be. They need to be good at what they do—acquiring books and publishing them to make a profit. Publishers hire out the rest of the work involved in book publishing, from editing and book cover layout and design to formatting, marketing, printing, and distribution.

What you *do* have to be to be a book publisher, then, is dedicated to your job and, as people in the industry know, willing to work long and sometimes crazy hours to acquire and produce the books you want. That means, if you're to be successful, you at least have to be able to *recognize* good writing, good stories, and marketable books and then find and sign up quality talent.

I know that, as a book scout for Elektra Press (www.elektrapress.com), one of few traditional, advance-paying publishers I work with that didn't go "belly up" during the recent pandemic slowdown, I'm always on the prowl for future best sellers. To their benefit, EP has gone right on publishing, marketing, distributing, and most importantly paying their authors over the past turbulent year. That makes me pretty happy as both a writer and a scout, the latter of which means I'm continually looking for quality projects to sign up.

Is that all there is to becoming a publisher? Well, no. But that should do for starters.

Do professional novelists save editors a lot of time by using Grammarly?

Do novelists who use Grammarly save editors a lot of time? Your editors or your publisher's professionals? If you mean yours—maybe. If you're referring to professional editors—*never*. Depending upon how astute you are in English grammar, composition, and punctuation, Grammarly can do more harm than good. Yes, it can find fundamental typos and disagreement in number between subject and verb. And, it can discover misused pronouns with the wrong antecedents. And, sure, it can warn you of overly long or otherwise unwieldy sentences. Sometimes. But not consistently. The program often misses things it should find and mislabels things it should never have pointed out.

It can also make suggestions that are *totally* grammatically or otherwise wrong. Take Grammarly's advice in these cases, and you're consigning your writing to the publisher's slush pile.

The bottom line is this: Spell checkers work only reasonably well, regardless of who makes them. Grammar checkers work even less effectively. So, if you want to use software to check your grammar, you'd better use it to point out minor slip-ups or omissions rather than pinpoint major problems. Only by knowing what's right can you possibly tell what's wrong.

That said, I have used Grammarly to point out areas that needed tightening up or to find a better-suited word than the one I'd chosen. But I also know and have taught analytic grammar at the college level. While that hardly makes me an infallible editor, it equips me with enough knowledge not to accept some of software's most egregious errors. You've heard the old expression, "You have to know the rules before you can break them"? Well, in the case of editing software, you have to know *when* the rules are wrong before you can *ignore* them.

The best way to become a better self-editor? Take a course in editing at a local college or university. An even better way? Take two courses. Or as many as necessary to turn yourself into a top-notch

ABOUT WRITING RIGHT

editing machine with a built-in radar for finding and correcting what's wrong.

Not everyone can be a good editor, of course; sometimes, I think he or she has to be born with that instinct. When I edited a major monthly magazine out of the Windy City, I had an associate editor who I would occasionally call upon for some information. Often, I'd have a sheet of galley proofs in my hand, dangling at my side as we spoke. That means the writing on the proofs was upside down to her as she remained seated at her desk four or five feet away.

On more than one occasion, after we'd completed our talk and I'd turned to go back to my office, she interrupted me. "Oh," she'd say. "You might want to check out paragraph four, line seven. There's a typo there."

Of course, I'd get back to my office, sit down behind my desk, and check out paragraph four, line seven. And I'll be damned if she wasn't right. *Always.*

She was what I call a natural-born editor—and a damned good one. The day someone releases a software program that works as effectively as she, I'll buy it. At any cost.

Where can an author find a good, reliable editor?

You can find editors everywhere. Good ones, however, not so easy. By "good," I mean people who are empathetic and yet knowledgeable, helpful without being pandering, and skilled in all aspects of editing and not only line or conceptual editing or fact-checking or any number of other editing specialties. A good editor can do it all and make the difference between success and failure for a book, particularly one by a relatively new author who hasn't yet developed a large following and a group of publishing-house editors willing and able to work with her on a book.

That said, you can forward several pages of your work, along with a brief summary, and I'll look it over and give you my unvarnished opinion as to my feelings about its chances for publication. I'll also give you some names of professional editors with whom you might enjoy working. Fair enough? You can get in touch with me through the Author's Guild at this URL: http://www.djherda.org/contact.

Get some help, or just say *Hello*!

Will a professionally edited book become a best-seller?

Nothing known to man in heaven or on earth translates into a best-seller. If it did, everyone would know about it, and every book would become a best-seller ... until, of course, that translated into no books selling any better than any other books and, thus, *no books* becoming best-sellers.

With that said, a poorly edited book will not only never become a best-seller but also never get conventionally published, positively reviewed, and widely read. There are *rare* exceptions, of course, when a topic is so timely that a book succeeds despite its shortcomings or when a writer has such a strong following that the book becomes a best-seller based upon name recognition alone.

Extrapolating then, if you want a *chance* at creating a best-selling book, at the very least write it well, have it professionally edited, and hope for the best. Only then does it stand a shot—a long shot, admittedly, but stranger things have happened—at getting published and rising to the top of the *NY Times* list.

Will a self-published book fail to sell because it wasn't professionally edited?

Absolutely. At least, that's *one* of the reasons. Once word of a poorly written, poorly edited book gets out via the grapevine (Amazon grows the grapes), sales can plummet or even drop to nothing. No one wants to read garbage.

But poor editing is only one reason a book might flop. It might fail at the consumer level because of poor timing. A book illustrating the dangers of the spread of COVID-19 released the week after the Feds announce COVID-19 is dead will likely tank. Similarly, if the author is a poor conceptual writer, word will get out, and sales will dry up.

Also, if the book's cover is amateurish or otherwise unappealing, the book won't sell. If the book's title is ridiculously off-message or juvenile, plan on the book's taking a bath.

Finally, if layout, design, and production values are second-rate, don't expect the book to rocket to the top of the NYT bestseller's list anytime soon. It ain't gonna happen.

So, does poor editing translate into poor sales? Yes, although that's only one of a dozen potential reasons.

What's the average age of most professional ghostwriters?

ABOUT WRITING RIGHT

Great question! Not unlike asking how many oranges it would take to fill the Panama Canal.

I don't have the hard, cold statistics in hand about either one, so I'm going to have to make a few assumptions here. First, the age of most ghostwriters is likely greater than twenty-five, since few people know enough about writing, let alone life, before then. And the age group would most likely top out somewhere around ninety, since few people older than that can still hold a red pencil, let alone a ZOOM conference.

Hope this nails it for you, Once again, really great question, something of interest to one and all, I'm sure. Let me know if you have a follow-up. I want to be certain not to miss it.

How can I advance my story from ho-hum to out-of-the-box extraordinary?

Well, for starters, the answer to this question is more complicated than the no-brainer it initially appears to be. And, obviously, some respondents with limited experience in creative writing (and talent to match) feel they know the answer: A story needs two elements!

Why, of course it does. Not three, not four, not more, but two!

Hardly correct. In fact, the "two-element" theory is based as far from reality as the person who espoused it. Here's why.

A story needs as many "elements" (whatever that's supposed to mean) as necessary to make it work. That is, to make it resonate with the reader, stand out in the reader's mind as an extraordinary piece, and leave a lasting impression that will remain with the reader for the rest of his or her life. In all likelihood, that means *you*, the author, have to get to work. Sorry about that.

Here's what I suggest—something I've been teaching in Creative Writing Workshop for more than four decades and what I do with my own fiction, both long and short.

Start reading your piece (let's call it a book, although it could also be a short story, a nonfiction article or book, or even a poem) from the beginning. When you get to some action that you later resolve (or not, depending upon the circumstances and how experienced a writer you are), ask yourself some questions. "Okay, but *what if* this happened or *what if* that happened? *What if* this new person showed up and had a history of this or that? *What if* some unseen force intervened to change the outcome I've already written?"

Do you see any possibilities now for some unanticipated twists and turns to develop within your book? *"What if?"* It's a powerful motivator.

When someone creates a story, he or she needs to explore all avenues for the action and development to occur. Simply pulling an experience from your memory and changing a few names and places as you transcribe the event to paper doesn't qualify as creative writing. Letting your imagination loose and seeing where your inner mind can take you does. That's why we call it *"creative* writing." Understand?

In a way, fiction writing is similar to reporting because both writers constantly have to dig deeper. The reporter has the prescribed mantra that he learned in journalism school or on the job: Who, What, When, Where, and Why--the notorious five W's. Plus, there's a sixth question to ask: How.

The nonfiction writer asks those questions to arrive at the truth, to uncover a logical progression of events leading to an intelligent, plausible conclusion. The fiction writer asks the same questions to arrive at a manufactured but still *believable* conclusion for the characters occupying the world he created. Same questions; different reasons for asking them.

If you don't like the reporter analogy, think of a creative writer as a detective. He has a murder or theft or some other crime to solve. He doesn't do so by observing the existing evidence and drawing a conclusion. He does so by asking himself questions and getting potential answers. Perhaps dozens or even hundreds of them. At that point, he employs logic to weed out the least likely conclusions until he reaches a point of logical deduction and can focus on the truth.

Oh, but wait a minute here. What if you, the author, arrive at some remarkably unexpected turn of events, decide to use it, and then have trouble justifying it as logical or even possible within the scope of reality? The answer is simple. You're living in your mind, remember? You're creating an imaginary scenario from your own creative experiences, fantasies, thoughts, hopes, dreams, and desires. In short, you, as the creative writer, can do anything. You can justify anything. You can make anything appear possible if you work long and hard enough at thinking through the potential problems with an event and creating a rational explanation for them.

And, if you're writing a mystery and you decide to raise a dead person back to life (I don't know why, but, hey, anything is possible), no problem. Even if you've wracked your brain for a logical rationale, go with the story. Just switch your work's genre from "Mystery" to "Sci-Fi/Fantasy," "Horror," or something else that fits better, and keep working. To hell with convention. Just keep the creative juices flowing. Remember that some of the world's most innovative examples of lasting literature evolved just that way.

Ever hear of *Frankenstein*, *The Lost World*, *Twenty Thousand Leagues under the Sea*, *Lord of the Flies*, or even *Moby Dick*? I thought so.

So, there you have it--your roadmap for creating more memorable "out-of-the-box" stories and your guide to how to handle things when your creativity runs wild.

Just remember: There's no such thing as a bad story, only a boring one. Similarly, there's no such thing as a bad writer, only a lazy one.

Get thinking; get writing; get asking; get answers. The rest should come easy.

Hope this helps, even *without* the "two elements" theorem.

Is it a book doctor's job to salvage a poorly written story? I've been told by some amateur authors that they only suggest solutions to problems, but then it's up to the author to fix them.

I would suggest (humbly, of course) that the book doctors to whom you and those amateur writers refer weren't doing their jobs. A doctor's function in society, no matter what his area of expertise, is to help cure what ails the patient. It's not to tell the patient what's wrong and suggest how that patient might proceed to cure himself.

It's the same with book doctors. Their goal, as I have seen it for more than half a century now since doctoring for Art Linkletter, Lawrence Welk, Ronnie Schell, Jimmy John Liautaud, Sammy Davis Jr., and others, is to get the job done. Sometimes, that begins with simple editing. Often, that's followed by consultations with the author before the doctor digs in and rewrites sentences, paragraphs, chapters, or even entire sections of that book as required.

Why on earth would a doctor of any caliber make suggestions to a writer who cannot comprehend what was wrong before the recommendations and most certainly isn't capable of correcting them after? *Uh-uh.* Don't make sense. Ain't gonna float. Unless, as I said, the doctor is shirking his responsibility, which should be to assist the author in turning the finished product into the best book it can be.

In that vein, book doctoring is similar to script doctoring, except that it's more demanding. That's because of the more complex nature of the novel's structure versus that of the screenplay. Script doctors don't come in and make suggestions to the original screenwriter about what needs fixing and how he should proceed to do it. Merely *knowing* how to fix something does not translate into an author being able to *do* whatever is necessary to fix something properly.

With all this said, my idea of ghostwriting is to take someone's (usually raw—*very* raw) written notes and create from them a beautifully marketable work of art. Or working from face-to-face, telephone, e-mail, or taped interviews. I've ghosted utilizing all five types of sources. The bottom line is that a ghostwriter doesn't have to "fix" anything because it's not yet broken.

A book doctor, on the other hand, inherits what is usually a completed product that sucks. His goal shouldn't be to mentor his client but rather to work with that client to do whatever it takes to turn a roughly written work into a great, memorable, and marketable piece of literature. Period.

Game, set, match.

But, again, that's been my experience, and those have been my guidelines. To me, it's less important how someone defines me as to how I salvage an otherwise surely unsalvageable work.

So, you're correct in saying that ghostwriters do more (original) writing than book doctors. I never suggested otherwise. But book doctors have to bring an entirely different set of tools to the job site. And, in my experience, doctors have to work a helluva lot harder to turn a silk purse into a sow's ear. (Or, hopefully, the other way around.)

Just my thoughts on the matter, and they're probably not worth much. After all, I'm just a poor country boy trying to scratch out a living from the clay-rich soil here in Duncan. What could I know about it all?

Time for a Sazerac. *Oops*, I mean a Bud Light.

As a beginning writer, should I hire a developmental editor?

Well, the answers you've received to this question to date range from the ridiculous to the absurd. Throw "ludicrous" in there for good measure. My advice? Never take guidance from a bad writer. Check out the writer's published work, evaluate his or her experience and credentials, and *then* decide for yourself whether or not that person makes sense.

The right response is always the best response. In this case, the best response to hiring a developmental editor is: *Absolutely.*

Maybe.

Several factors enter play here. First, do you want to become a better writer, to keep improving with everything you write, or are you satisfied with the concept of getting a book-length manuscript self-published before moving on with your life to something else? If the former, hire an editor. If the latter, don't waste your money.

Second, are you ready to accept the advice of an expert? To follow it and to learn from it? If so, hire an editor. If not, don't waste your money.

Third, can you find a qualified professional editor? In my experience both as a writer and an editor/publisher, I've met probably three or four top-quality editors out of a hundred working in the field. Those falling beneath the threshold range from "pretty good" but not perfect to absolutely pitiful. More fall along the latter line than the former.

Of course, that brings up the question of where to look for an editor to help with your specific needs. For that, I would suggest avoiding online "clearing houses" that supposedly vet their editors before hiring them. Most such agencies lack the skills and experience to determine the good from the bad. Instead, find an author whose work you admire, whose writing style appeals to you, and who makes sense, and contact him or her. Either search for that writer/editor online, or contact the writer's publisher or agent to ask for an introduction. If you need further direction, just let me know at http://www.djherda.org.

And, please, for your own sake, stay away from bad respondents with ridiculous answers. They'll only cost you time, money, and frustration in the long run

FOUR: The Secrets of Writing

As we draw down to the final chapter in the book, one of the least tapped and largest sources of information remains: my personal experience. If anyone sets out to be an author at the age of 14 or 15 and makes a go of it for the next half-century and more, he has some stories to tell. And some information to impart. And some inspiration to share.

Granted, I've done all that through teaching various writing courses, including Creative Writing Workshop, throughout the years, but I had never had an opportunity to place the wealth of information about writing, publishing, editing, and agenting into a single volume before.

Are there really secrets in the pages to come? Yes—some more so than others. But, everything you read about here, as well as in the other series books, is one hundred percent accurate and based upon personal experience. No hunches masquerading as truths. No realities hiding behind suppositions. As Sgt. Joe Friday used to say on the old television series, *Dragnet*: "Just the facts, ma'am. Just the facts."

So, here's what I have come up with in response to some of the questions asked of me over the years, based upon my own experiences and knowledge. I only wish I'd had a similar resource when *I* was struggling to get my sea legs as a young, beginning writer. That would have helped make my life a whole lot easier and my career a whole lot more productive. Here's what I mean.

I'm writing a novel set in medieval Europe but can't think of

ABOUT WRITING RIGHT

what might have taken place at a meeting in one of my scenes. Any ideas about specific issues of the time?

Hmm. I'm curious. *You're* writing a novel about medieval Europe and have to ask others for information on what to include in a scene? And not only what to include, but also what topics were "hot" during that time? Does the word, "research," mean anything to you? I'm not trying to be cute here (although it's awfully hard to resist), but I can't understand why you would surrender the creative process to someone else, not to mention why you'd undertake a period piece without knowing what on earth that period is all about. And, by the way, have you ever heard of the word, "outline"?

There's a term for that kind of slipshod investigative reporting at newspapers. It's called "You're fired!"

I would humbly suggest that you stop work on the book at once and, if you'd like to write it eventually, do so only after making an exhaustive study of the subject and time period. And drafting a synopsis and chapter outline. I mean, it shouldn't be that difficult. It's not as if nothing is known about medieval Europe. There's probably been more written, filmed, and staged about that locale and time than any others in history.

So, get busy!

Oh, and, by the way, you can thank me later. *After* you've completed the book.

Does writer's block apply to nonfiction as well as fiction?

First, let's get one thing straight. "Writer's block" is not a disease like cancer or diabetes. In that respect, there *is* no "writer's block." What there *is*, then, is a lack of motivation to write, fueled by insufficient organization and inefficient procedures.

Huh?

In other words, if you want to write, you write. Period. Perhaps not what you'd prefer to write (the Great American Novel, for instance), but something. *Anything.* The key to defeating this dreaded literary malady is to get your mind focused on writing. Summarize a weather report for the day. Write about the previous evening's dinner. Outline your impression of your neighbor. Again, write *anything.* Just write!

Once you train your mind on the specific tasks required to move words from your cranium to your screen, you'll find the words begin flowing like water through a mountain stream. Once the floodgates are open, you'll find moving from writing weather reports to fiction a relatively simple step. It's getting the mind ready to perform the mental tasks required for writing that's important.

With that said, you also need to have some idea of a story in your head if you hope to put it down on paper. A chapter outline would be ideal because it gives you a place to begin every time you sit down to continue work on your masterpiece.

And, getting back to your original question, "writer's block" can strike no matter what you're writing—fiction, nonfiction, letters, business correspondence, diary entries. The key is to write and work past it.

Try it. You'll be amazed at how successful you'll be in getting beyond those self-induced psychological roadblocks to which we ascribe the failure to create.

What was the turning point when you became a great writer?

First, any writer who can pinpoint the moment he became a "great" writer hasn't gotten there yet. When people ask me what book I think is my best, I reply, "My next one." When someone asks me when I became a great writer, I tell them I'll let them know when it happens. And that's the truth.

Writers aren't pieces of furniture. We're not thirty or forty individual sticks of lumber stacked in the corner of some warehouse, waiting to be assembled into a sofa. We don't sit around in anticipation of growing old and appreciating in value. On the contrary, we stay young by *working*. If not today, then tomorrow. If not tomorrow ... well, you get the point.

I did have a metamorphosis when I turned from being a writer wannabee to a genuine scribe, though (although far from a "great" one), and I remember the moment clearly. I had recently been named acquisitions editor of a large national magazine, and one of my monthly columnists was *L. A. Times* travel editor Jerry Hulse. I always liked Jerry's pieces because they read extremely smoothly and effortlessly and yet contained a ton of information. By the time you finished reading one of his features, you felt as if you knew him personally and believed every syllable he had written.

ABOUT WRITING RIGHT

As it turned out, Jerry wrote the way I spoke. But I didn't *write* that way. In fact, as a young developing writer, I suffered from a disease I call severe "Writerese," or the propensity to write the way writers think writers should write. Unfortunately, nowhere in my style was *me*! After six months or more of reading/editing Jerry's work at the magazine, I set out to write yet another of my own articles for sale, assuming it, too, would be unsuccessful—that is, it would go unsold and unpublished. Imagine my shock when the editor to whom I submitted the piece bought it.

And then something remarkable happened. I realized I had written that article not in my normal "Writerese" style but, instead, in my normal *spoken-voice* style. The same style, in effect, in which Jerry Hulse had been writing for years.

From that time on, I was able to hone my literary voice. *Not* to emulate Jerry's but, instead, to reflect my own spoken voice. Jerry Hulse's writing style had "piqued" my psyche into delving deeper into my subconscious until I finally managed to see what was under the hood. I realized Jerry was writing the way everyday people talk. He wrote the way *I* talked. No mumbo-jumbo. No Writerese. No stumbling around, looking for the right-sounding word. From then on, I never looked back.

That's not to say I never strayed from my voice and reverted back to my old habits. No, Writerese dies hard, if it dies at all. But the more I wrote in my authentic literary voice, the more quickly I came to recognize when I had strayed from it. Then, I'd go back and rewrite the piece until I'd returned to my *true* voice.

For that, I have thanked Jerry Hulse a million times. But never, unfortunately, to his face. He underwent surgery in 2002 at age 77 and died shortly after from complications. That was just about the time I left the magazine and never did learn of his demise until years later.

The moral of this story? No writer is great while still alive, because he's still hard at work trying to achieve greatness, aka literary perfection. Only years later will he be heralded as a "great" writer.

Just like Jerry Hulse.

How do I go about finding people to help write/publish a book for me, (of course they'll get paid for it as well) safely from a legal point-of-view?

Well, I'm going to start with a caveat. Don't go by anything you come across on the Web or from a Google search. So many falsehoods and outright lies (exaggerations, misrepresentations, and worse) are floating around cyberspace, no matter how good or bad someone sounds, take for granted that someone has a hidden agenda, and you're the recipient of that person's lies.

Next, get a *personal opinion or recommendation,* preferably from someone who has used that ghostwriter and has some thoughts on working with that person, pro and con.

Then, contact the ghostwriter to see if he/she is interested or able to take on your project within the time frame you're seeking. Go over the rough details, including timeframe and all charges.

Finally, work out the fine financial and other details, get a written and signed contract spelling out all aspects of your professional relationship and the duties and responsibilities of both parties (you and the ghost), and check with an attorney for possible revisions or refinements if necessary.

Now, the question of where or how to get a personal opinion or recommendation comes up, if not on the Web: How do you find such a person who is willing to recommend a qualified ghostwriter? Answer: Join the Authors Guild, the American Society of Authors and Journalists (ASJA), or some other bona fide writer's group, go on the group's forum, and snoop around. Ask for suggestions from people who have used ghostwriters before. Then contact the most likely candidate(s) and get recommendations. Some things to look for:

1. Consider only legitimately published (not self-published) authors, preferably with several books in publication or under contract with a conventional advance-paying publisher.
2. Give special consideration to ghosts with publishing knowledge, which means authors who have also worked as book editors somewhere along the line and know what publishers are looking for.
3. Follow up with a telephone conversation to get a better "feel" for the person you're considering hiring. If you seem to hit it off and all the right qualifications are there, "It's show time!"

After that, just sit back, enjoy the experience of working with a proven professional with a track record of success, and enjoy!

ABOUT WRITING RIGHT

How do you find an out-of-print book that you'd like to buy?
Quite often, merely searching on Amazon will turn up titles of out-of-print books. That information doesn't do you much good if you're looking to acquire the book. Still, you may also find on that Amazon book page a list of non-Amazon (independent) sellers who have copies of the book for sale in a range of prices, depending upon the book's condition.

If that doesn't work, here's a list from Biblio of dealers in rare and out-of-print books that might prove helpful. You'll find the list at *Bookstores Specializing in Out of Print Book*, which you'll find at https://www.biblio.com/bookstores/out-of-print/188. Even if a person you contact can't help you out, he may be able to suggest someone else who can. Don't hesitate to ask.

And please remember that most of these people are in business because they love books, not because they hope to get rich. They also enjoy helping people out. Treating them with a little courtesy and respect will go a long way toward finding you what you want.

Happy hunting!

Is it easier or harder to get a book published these days than before the growth of the internet?
This question is a bit difficult to answer as framed because Internet growth wasn't exactly synonymous with the cosmos' Big Bang. Not everything happened all at once, and not everything affecting book publication occurred simultaneously.

For starters, the Web development that led to personal e-mail made landing a contract from a conventional book publisher *far* easier than in the past because it made multiple submissions an economic reality. Originally, a writer had to physically type a manuscript on a typewriter (perfectly, I might add); make a photocopy of it to send out via snail mail (except to those publishers who *demanded* originals, no photocopies allowed), and include a costly self-addressed stamped envelope (SASE). Then he had to wait several months or longer for a response. With the Internet, that same writer could suddenly send copies of his manuscript to as many different publishers he wished--virtually free of costs! Instead of sending out copies of his document to three or four publishers a year, a writer could at last send that same manuscript to three or four hundred!

D. J. Herda

This concept didn't "fly" with the vast majority of publishers in the early days of the intersection of Web technology and the book industry. Publishers outright refused to read digital submissions and chastised writers and agents for submitting them. I know because my own agent was among the first and most determined to force publishers to accept the switch from regular mail submissions to e-mail. Her persistence, as we now know, paid off. In time, everyone recognized the value of digital submissions. They were less costly, easier to handle, simpler to distribute to other editorial board members for input, more conducive to following up with the author, and even easier to turn down, alas. Before long, only a handful of publishers held out until today, even *they* have mostly succumbed to the changing of the guard.

So the advent of e-mail made the prospect of getting a book published easier. *But*, the introduction of e-mail submissions with their vastly easier means of approaching publishers created an entirely new generation of authors, all competing for the same number of publication slots that had been available before. Suddenly, instead of an editor having twenty or thirty manuscripts to consider in a week, he had two or three hundred! Naturally, no one person can read and evaluate that many manuscripts in a week; so, many editors summarily dismissed the works of "new" and "untested" authors, relegating them to the slush pile. In effect, the technology that had made getting a book published more easily evolved into the same technology that had just the opposite effect.

Then, most recently, came POD (Print on Demand) publishing. It allows authors to create printed and digital books quickly, easily, and inexpensively. The result was predictable: an explosion of words and a glut in the marketplace. In turn, that created a backlash against self-published authors whose works were mostly awful. As proof, various industry statistics show that the average self-published book today sells far fewer than 100 copies, and many of those are purchased by the author and his friends and relatives!

Of course, in light of all this bad news, authors have a glimmer of hope to which to cling. It's called "best seller." All you have to do is become an extraordinarily talented wordsmith, develop a can't-put-it-down storyline, and reach the right editor with your book proposal.

ABOUT WRITING RIGHT

Then, if he or she can't wait to read it, ends up buying it, and places it in print at just the right time, you're halfway home. The rest could well be, as they say on TV, "history."

When buying a book, in which situation do you personally buy a hardcover or paperback, and why?

As a writer, I often buy books to use in my research. Since I need them only as long as I'm double-checking my facts against those in the books I purchase, I usually go the least costly route—eBooks, paperbacks, or used books in good condition or better. The one exception to my buying books for research is if the book is a classic or something I'm going to want to keep around after completing my work. Most likely that's because I anticipate doing research for another book on a similar topic later.

If, on the other hand, I'm buying a book for my personal library (such as it is!), I often buy hardcover for one of several reasons. One is that it holds up better to everyday wear and tear than a paperback. Another is that it feels "heftier" and thus imparts a greater sense of value than a paperback. Still one more is that it can be gifted or passed along to future generations for inclusion in *their* libraries (or to sell on eBay, if that's what they decide).

As for eBooks, I buy them strictly as ultra-short-term, inexpensive sources of research. As a growing number of people are learning, you never really own an eBook. It can be "snuffed out" in a heartbeat by whomever initially issued it, leaving you holding an undecipherable mass of gibberish or, worse, blank pages. Try willing *that* to the grand kids when the time comes!

What motivated you to become a book editor?

I chose to become a book editor years ago for two reasons. First, I was relatively young, and I needed the money. A publisher not too distant from me needed some editorial help, so it seemed as if it were a marriage made in heaven. Second, I wanted to see what life on the other side of the desk was like. I'd already been writing for a decade or more, and I thought the experience of seeing book publishing from the editor's side would be helpful. It was.

By the way, I left the world of book publishing because I didn't think the publisher's editorial standards were high enough to suit me, and I wasn't willing to compromise. I received more personal gratification working for other publishers in the magazine and newspaper industries.

Still, there were some things I enjoyed as a book editor. Working with various authors' manuscripts was satisfying, something I do to this day on a book-by-book basis as a professional, independent book doctor. I also enjoyed the enormous sense of power an editor feels. Less so as a junior editor, of course, than someone higher up on the food chain. Still, it was a unique experience and one I tried to keep from going to my head.

How can I find a really good research writer?

I think the best way to find a writer who's a good (or even great) researcher is to explore some nonfiction books that appeal to you, particularly in the area of expertise you're interested in pursuing. You can browse Google or Amazon, or check out your local bookstore. Find a tome that complements whatever it is you want researched and contact the writer. You can do that by running a search on the Internet or by contacting the publisher. If you give the publisher a short note to pass along to the author, you should hear back promptly.

Most authors are pretty good about returning inquiries from their readers. After that, you can feel out the author on his willingness and availability to work with you.

Are good writers good teachers?

Good writers don't automatically translate into good instructors. Teaching is both a science and an art. It requires a knowledge of the different ways in which people learn plus the ability to be empathetic while relating to one's students.

Writers, on the other hand, possess an entirely different skill set, so although one person can have both sets of skills and be able to employ them successfully, that person is a rare discovery. The two do have one thing in common, however. Practice. Writers become better with practice, and so do teachers.

How can magazine publishers afford to use so much color when my color ink cartridges are expensive enough to bankrupt me?

Magazines and newspapers can afford to run big, splashy color sections because they get discounts from their printers (usually one of several mammoth companies that do nothing besides provide printing for publications)—the greater their circulation (the more printing involved), the greater the color discount. Even at that, publications couldn't afford to run color, or even black-and-white for that matter, if it weren't for advertising revenue.

Advertisers specify when ordering their ads whether they want them to run in b&w or color. The ad rate for color is always more costly. The income from a color ad usually pays not only for the color ad on that page but also for color availability on multiple additional pages. That means that, if a publication sells one color ad, it can run several more color pages within that color section at no additional expense to the publication (except a minimal ink expense, which is often absorbed by the printing company).

In short, once the color section is paid for by a single advertiser, all the other color charges the publication makes for additional color ads are gravy. It's how publications stay in print. It's not circulation driving a publication's financial well-being (except that larger circs make charging more for advertising possible). It's ad revenue.

The same is true for television and radio, by the way. Viewership (listenership) drives the price of ad time, which helps defer costs and generates a profit for the station.

Obviously, whoever said capitalism doesn't work doesn't know much about the system as it functions in the real world. It's called supply and demand, and it has worked pretty well for humanity nearly since the origin of humankind.

As for why you have to pay an exorbitant price for your inkjet color ink, figure it this way: What's more attractive to a manufacturer, someone who spends $100 once every four or five years, or someone who spends thirty dollars every six weeks? My suggestion to minimize your costs? Read the printer reviews on-line, weigh the comparative cost of color ink, and make your decision based upon your findings. All printers—just like all ink cartridges—are not the same.

What are the chances that my book will be turned down by a major publisher?

My initial response to the chances of a book getting turned down by a publisher was my gut response: nearly 100 percent. But that answer needs some tempering.

When I began writing at age 14 or so, I sent my manuscripts out based upon publisher name recognition: If I'd head of them, I wanted them to be my publisher. It was that simple. And also that fruitless. I had no idea that publishers had preferred genres, and I couldn't believe at that age that any publisher anywhere wouldn't *leap* at an opportunity to publish my work of genius—no matter what its genre. Needless to say, I collected enough rejection slips to wallpaper a large bathroom.

Now, nearly half a century later, I know the score. I also have an agent who knows the score. So when I write a book pitch now, it's not long before one of our *targeted* publishers picks it up. Perhaps one or two or three will turn it down for various reasons, including that the publisher already has a similar title in its catalog and can't see publishing a competing book. But the fourth or fifth will pick it up. That's with oddball genres and things I don't write regularly. (These days, I write just about whatever I want, understanding that no one publisher is going to be suited for all my book pitches.)

If I want closer to a hundred percent acceptance rate, I gear my pitches to a specific publisher. That means western books to western Americana publishers, mysteries to mystery publishers, etc. I also call upon publishers for whom I have written before. A big part of an acquisition editor willing to take a chance on a writer is a belief in that writer that he can get the job done: He'll deliver what he promises when he's supposed to, and nothing less. By pitching editors with whom I have worked before, I immediately have that "trust factor" working for me. My chances of a contract, then, are significantly greater than when pitching an editor who doesn't know me from Adam.

Bottom line: Do your homework to increase your chances of success in landing a publishing contract. That's what it all boils down to. (Assuming your work is of a high enough caliber professionally to merit publication—which should go without saying.)

An agent asked to see a two-page synopsis of my book. I have already cut it from six pages down to two and a half. There is physically nothing left I can cut without ruining the story. Is this okay? Or should I cut more?

You're wrong. If you're professional enough, you can cut your six pages down to one or less. It's all a matter of linguistics, knowing how to put thoughts into words, and understanding how to economize. That

ABOUT WRITING RIGHT

is a challenging thing for inexperienced writers to do. If you've ever worked as a newspaper stringer, reporter, or editor, you understand what I'm saying. If you write a newspaper story that's 3,000 words long and your editor says you need to cut it down to 500 words to fit into its slot, you cut it down to 500 words to fit into its slot. Period.

So, yes, I suggest you keep working at reducing the wordage. Generally, the fewer words you use to convey a storyline, the stronger the result. There is a limit, of course. But even *Gone with the Wind* can be summarized adequately in twenty-five words or less. Really. Remember that everything you feel *must* be included in the pitch is influenced by your personal biases and your closeness to the story. You want to explain every nuance to the reader so nothing gets missed. Understandable. But an outside editor, without those biases, could do the job in a heartbeat. So, I have a feeling you're nowhere near approaching the "trim limit." My suggestion? Get back to cutting!

How do you feel about the shrinking number of bookstores?

Not good. To a writer, dwindling bookstores are like a shortage of oxygen. Readers need books to research and inspire themselves. They also need them to sell to others for the same reason and, not coincidentally, to survive financially.

As a teenager, I discovered bookstores to be a fantastic source of information. Even better, *used* bookstores filled me with gratitude and inspiration. The gratitude came from those authors who preceded me. The inspiration came from the remarkable wealth of subject matter, research, sweat, toil, and tears I found in those ancient tomes. More than anything else, I longed to see my own volumes upon those dusty shelves one day.

And I did. Thanks in good part to those miraculous oases of sanity. It's sad to see bookstores falling by the wayside. Hopefully, one day, through one means or another, the dwindling will stop, and we will experience a resurgence of bookstores, booksellers, and book lovers. I have faith in the future that this will be the case. Until that day comes, all we writers can do is to keep on pounding the keys. And cranking out worthwhile books.

Do you create your book covers before or after writing your book?

What one cover designer already told you rings closest to reality. How can a publisher (or anyone else) design a cover without having read the complete manuscript? It's a ridiculous notion. I have been published by probably twenty or more different conventional publishers, and every one of them has had the completed manuscript in hand before commissioning a cover based upon the book's content. Doing anything else simply isn't rational. After all, you don't bake a cake before reading the recipe!

By the way, I nearly always work up my own cover designs for my books, as well as those for some other authors. But, even when I submit a design to a conventional publisher, the publisher very rarely ends up using it. As in *never*. Some publishers accept input from their authors—particularly those with visual art experience—regarding general cover layout. After that, they pretty much leave the design process to their assigned freelance artists, who usually submit three or more drafts for the publisher's consideration.

After a lot of editorial haggling, everyone (often except the author, forsooth) agrees on the best cover mockup, and that's what the publisher usually goes with. The reason that all conventional publishers retain control over final cover selection is simple: they supposedly know the book-buying market better than most authors; so, they're better suited to decide what's likely to sell and what's not.

Think of it this way. Book covers come in two distinct flavors: What the author envisions as representative of his story and what the publisher thinks will sell the most books. The two are rarely synonymous. In the end, the publisher gets to make the decision.

Is that decision *always* best for sales? Unfortunately, no. Is it *usually* best for sales? Probably yes, but who can say for sure without publishing the same book with two different covers and pitting them against one another?

Simple, no?

No.

Still, that's the way the real world operates. At least the real world of publishing.

What locale is the best in the world for becoming writer?

Nowhere. And everywhere. The truth is, you should live where you want. If you're a writer, you can live anywhere on earth and still write.

ABOUT WRITING RIGHT

I'm tempted to say that you'll be a more proficient writer if you're happy than if you're sad, but even that is an overstatement. I've known plenty of unhappy writers who escaped through their writing, and I've known several dozen more who write best only when they're happy.

Me? I write all the time, home or away, happy as a lark are glum as a sad sack. But I learned to write under deadline for newspapers. That means I believe there's no such impediments to writing as writers' block, the best place to write, a perfect time to write, a preferable genre in which to write, or any other rationale.

When you're writing to put food on the table, it doesn't matter where you write—only that you write.

What writer would be willing to write a book if I provided all the facts?

"Be willing to" is different from "be willing to for money." If you're looking for the best there is, you'll need to shop your material around before settling on the right writer for you. Expect to pay, though, because outstanding writers aren't a dime a dozen, and they don't work cheap.

Remember: writers are almost like regular people in that they need a place to live, clothes to wear, cars to drive, food to eat, and miscellaneous expenses such as computers, monitors, and printers. If you can find a great writer willing and able to write for no money down, count yourself among the blessed few. Basically, that writer doesn't exist.

Why do book authors and publishers sell their books on Kindle?

Okay, I'm going to take a stab in the dark here: How about too make money? Amazon is the leading seller/distributor of eBooks in the world. If anyone is interested in making money from his work, he'd better make sure it's available as an eBook through Amazon. Love 'em or hate 'em, where eBooks are concerned, Kindle reigns supreme.

If you ask great questions, will you eventually become a great writer?

The answer to this one is simple: *No*. But asking great questions does make you a great questioner. After all, repetitive experiences usually result in increased effectiveness, whether you're talking about questioners or brain surgeons.

D. J. Herda

Of course, you can conjecture that being a great questioner makes you a great "interviewer," which may or may not be correct. If it is, you can also speculate that being a great interviewer may someday lead to becoming a great writer. But that's not going to happen simply by asking questions. Becoming a great writer takes practice, knowledge about the art and craft of writing, and experience.

So, is the leap from questioner to writer guaranteed? Absolutely not. Is it possible in rare instances, given the questioner's desire and ability to learn? Sure. But don't bet the bank on it.

I have a great idea for a book but can't write. Could I find someone else to write my novel for me?

Great question. Unfortunately, I've seen some really bad and totally inaccurate responses to it. As a ghostwriter/editor/author/publisher's book scout, I'll try to set things straight.

For starters, you have to be realistic. If you're planning on schmoozing an accomplished author into working to bring your "baby" to life, based upon a share of future earnings, forget it. No author worth his salt can afford to work under such conditions. Like everyone else, authors require a steady cash flow with which to pay their living expenses.

With that said, if you're seeking to hire a professional novelist/ghostwriter to write for you, solicit applications from as many different sources as possible until you have at least three or four applicants. Get their qualifications, read their writing, and share a rough concept of your story idea with them, asking them how they'd proceed. Also, ask how much they'd charge, how long they estimate it would be before completion, and what kind of payment schedule works for them.

As a ghostwriter for novels, I require six months' time to complete the book with no "hitches." I also require unfettered contact with my client by telephone and/or e-mail so that we can track the progress of the novel chapter-by-chapter in a reasonably productive manner. That also makes sure that I'm going in the same direction as the story's creator. I ask for 1/3 of my total fee down (flat rate *always* so there are no surprises at the end), 1/3 approximately midway through the writing, and the final 1/3 upon completion. I also issue a contract committing all elements to writing. The author would receive total

ABOUT WRITING RIGHT

credit, and the ghostwriter would sign a nondisclosure agreement to remain totally anonymous. After that, it's show time!

Of course, all this costs money, which you can expect to range from the mid-to-upper five-digits (that is, $40-$80K, depending upon the complexity of the writing involved and other factors). This is determined by taking the author/writer's annual income, halving that (for six months' work), and the result is what you can expect to pay for the job.

Why can't you expect an author/ghost to work for a percentage of profits, considering your idea is *fantastic*? The answer to that is simple. Fantastic ideas are a dime a dozen; great novels are rare. Also, fantastic ideas don't pay the rent. If you run across an author willing to work for a percentage of the eventual profits, you'd better turn and run because there's a con afoot somewhere. No one works on a hunch, which is all sales projections are in publishing, anyway.

So, yes, hiring someone else to write your novel for you can be done and is done more frequently than most people realize. Hiring the right person, though, is critical. If you need help locating someone, let me know, and I'll assemble a list of available ghostwriters for you to contact.

Is publication the ultimate goal of a writer during his life on earth?

No. Death is.

At my advancing age, people often ask me if I'm retired. I tell them, "No, I'm a writer." If pressed, I explain that a writer writes with his mind; so, as long as his mind is functional, he can't retire. After all, no one can turn off his brain, can he?

You see, writing is forever. A writer is a writer for a lifetime. He's not like a plumber who can't kneel down anymore or a surgeon whose hands aren't steady enough to wield a scalpel. Some writers, such as Tom Wolfe, are comfortable writing until they stop breathing and go out with a satisfying whimper. Others, such as Hemingway and Virginia Woolf, have a tougher time facing reality.

It all depends upon one's personality and psychological makeup, I suppose.

How do I plan on going out when my mind finally tells me the writer in me has died? I'm not sure that will ever happen. If it does, I'll let you know.

Meanwhile, forgive me, but I have to go write now.

Is writing a book with witches, demons, and ghouls in it a sin?

Only if you have connubial relations with them.

Seriously, it's not a sin for me in my personal judgment, having been raised in a traditional Christian methodology in which I am the ultimate arbiter of whether or not I have sinned based upon my intent. I suspect a Judeo-Christian God would not hold people accountable for the "sin" of writing about certain people's realities, thoughts, histories, fears, or projections either. But, unlike someone with "three years of Bible school" under my belt, I'm really nowhere near as qualified to answer that question as your own religious or spiritual leader might be. Tempered, I imagine, by your own true conscience.

But, just to be sure, keep your pants zipped up tight at all times.

Can a straight woman write about a male homosexual relationship accurately?

I assume from your question that you think a straight woman can't write about a male gay relationship because she's never experienced one. You know the old axiom: *Write only about those things you've experienced.*

Given that premise, no one but an astronaut would ever be able to write about space travel, and no history buff could ever record an event that occurred during the American Revolution. And on and on and on.

My answer, then, is not to *Write only about those things you've experienced* but, rather, to *Write only about those things you can envision.*

The human mind is a miraculous invention, discovered, I believe, by Alexander Graham Bell back in the 1800s. Regardless, it's capable of imagining all sorts of things. It's also capable of deductive reasoning, generational thought, and other advanced mental concepts. That means that, if you can picture it in your mind, you can write about it in such a way that your readers will also be able to picture it in *their* minds.

ABOUT WRITING RIGHT

Getting back to your question, then, yes, a straight woman can write about a male homosexual relationship as long as she takes the time and effort to picture it, to hone in on the details, to drill down into the characters' psyches, and to relay all that information accurately to the reader. For a writer to be successful in writing about *anything*, that writer must succeed at projecting every aspect of the event and the feelings of those participating in it. You know: *See it; don't say it.*

Now, it's possible that the mind of a straight woman trying to write about a gay male relationship would throw up all sorts of roadblocks based upon social taboos and religious precepts preventing her from envisioning it. That would be an impediment that might negate her ability to relay an accurate image of the relationship. In that case, she would probably have to get someone else to write that passage, cut it out of her book, or begin a long and costly program of psychotherapy.

Writing is not a "piece-of-cake" endeavor. It can be a cathartic and often painful journey, depending upon the subject matter. A writer unaffected by social dictum and mores is a rare commodity, indeed. But that writer does exist and is often among the most successful examples of the breed.

In short, a good writer writes with his mind, not with his fingers.

How can a writer spot those places in his book's plot where things just took a turn toward the absurd?

I've read several responses to your question, none of which actually *answers you* accurately. If you want to run a reality check on your own (which, I believe, is far better and more accurate than relying upon beta readers and such), here's how.

Put your writing aside for a day or more. That will give you a pair of "fresh eyes" when you go back to review it.

Return to your story and *print it out*. The reason for this is that people read more accurately from the printed page than from an LED screen. We've had thousands of years of practice doing so as opposed to a couple of decades of digitally enhanced technology.

After that, take the printed story, close the door to the room you're in, and start reading out loud. It won't do to read to yourself because your human ears "hear" better than your mind's "ears" do. If you read silently, you fall victim to the same shortcomings you did when you were writing the piece: Your mind takes the weak parts and "strengthens" them so that you won't notice. It "forgives" your shortcomings, hiding them from scrutiny. That's not the case when you hear things that you're reading out loud.

Make a note with a pencil, pen, or crayon (in case you're prohibited from handling sharp objects) wherever something sounds "off" or implausible. Also, note those typos and grammatical errors you're bound to discover.

Go back after you've finished reading out loud, and analyze the areas your ears found to be lacking in substance or reality. Make the necessary changes.

Rinse, dry, and repeat. Do this routine as often as it takes until you can find no more weak spots, and your work is ready for release.

Easy? Simple? Enjoyable?

No, no, and not necessarily.

Necessary?

Well, let's just say it's the absolute surest means of correcting weaknesses in your writing. ALL your writing. Whether we're talking about epic novels or e-mails to your favorite Aunt Tillie.

You can thank me later. (Money is always nice, but a good Shiraz is also appreciated.)

What compels an author to have to write a book?

Good question, Graham.

I *hate* good questions; so, *stop it*!

Okay, okay. Actually, I like good questions almost as much as I like a couple of the answers several other respondents gave you about needing to pursue something from a germ of an idea to a finished product or having voices in your head that you have to let out. And someone else nailed it by saying every writer is different and has a unique reason for cranking out books.

Me? I write for several reasons. First, it's far less messy than painting or sculpting, and you don't need any ancillary equipment. Second, the money I've made from writing over the years has sustained me like, perhaps, no other art form could have. Third, I'm still chasing the illusory ghosts that haunted F. Scott Fitzgerald, who once said that writers write for fame, fortune, and the love of beautiful women. I'm not sure how he would have amended that to account for female writers, but I'm sure he would have come up with something. Or Zelda would have.

Finally, there's a little unseen, hidden man deep inside my soul that makes me want to create. Painting, photography, composing, acting, performing music. All of them can put a damper on the little guy for a day or two or maybe even a week as I immerse myself in the freedom of creation. But after that, the demon pops up again, and nothing will satisfy him short of a big, juicy, literary steak. So I turn the broiler up, sit down behind my keyboard, and start cookin'.

Ahh, that's satisfaction!

Even when an author isn't writing, he or she is writing. *In the mind.* That's where all good writing begins and ends. It begins in the writer's mind with the germ of an idea and ends in the minds of his readers with the thundering bang of personal realization.

Tough to beat a feeling such as that—knowing that you've influenced someone positively, possibly for life.

Give me that feeling every day of the week!

Will I receive backlash from others if I write an atypical script about Satan who is traditionally treated with disdain?

Let me answer your question with a couple questions of my own:

Why should you care? Are you a writer or a backyard gardener? Do you create your stories to educate, entertain, enlighten, awaken, and inform your readers? Or do you write your stories to please them?

If you're a writer, you don't have to ask other people's permission to write—at least not in a democratic society. And, you don't need to be worried about how others might react to your writing. Besides, what makes you think anyone you're asking would be able to give you an accurate answer to your question, anyway?

People are people. No two are alike. You can write a modern-day sequel to Cinderella, and I guarantee that half of you readers will take offense at it while the other half will be petitioning the awards committee to give you the Pulitzer.

So, I ask you again: Why should you care? If you're a writer, write. Write the way you want to write. Say the things you need to say. And let the chips fall where they may.

They will, anyway, regardless of how you approach—or avoid—your subject.

D. J. Herda

Which was the better writer, Truman Capote or Tennessee Williams?

That's an interesting question without a credible answer. It's like asking which is better, apples or oranges? You'd might as well ask what color do you like best, red or orange? Which brings up the question: If oranges are *orange*, why aren't apples *reds*? Or bananas *yellows*? Or grapes ... Oh, hell. Never mind.

I'd think a lot of people would have difficulty answering this question because both writers painted with an imagery-rich brush. Williams had to do so as a playwright; Capote had to do so as a tortured soul.

Not that both men didn't suffer; both didn't drink to excess; both didn't destroy their careers and their lives in the end. Both did. In that, they weren't alone.

But, returning to your question, which do I think is best? Easy-peasy. Catfish. I'll take a really good breaded catfish plank over a tuna steak or a salmon filet any day of the week. Unless the tuna steak is really extraordinarily well done, in which case it wins out. Unless, of course, the salmon filet is sprinkled with dill and mesquite salt and steamed to perfection, in which case it takes home the gold medal.

Am I wandering? So are we all when we stop to consider such a question. If you really need an answer, Williams was a better playwright; Capote was a better novelist.

Game, set, match. And let the chips fall where they may.

What do authors do wrong when they try to add diversity to their books?

Authors make a mistake when they paint with too broad a brush. A racially defined character must *belong* in the story to merit a personality. That means the author has to understand that person inside and out. To do so, he must "see" the diverse person's background, history, educational achievements, work experience, home life, relationship to others, love or hate toward animals, prowess in the kitchen (and/or bedroom—author's choice), expertise at driving a car, hobbies, medical history, and more. Put all that down on paper if necessary, and study it until you know the character intimately.

The *only* exception to this is if the diverse character is a cardboard cutout or a throwaway character. That would be someone who makes

ABOUT WRITING RIGHT

an entrance to the story, contributes whatever necessary, and exits just as quickly. You definitely don't want the reader to invest time and energy getting to "see" the character is fully as you do only to have the guy disappear forever after four paragraphs.

Most authors who insert diverse characters fail to study them first, so the characters become a stereotype. If that character has a major role to play in the book, that spells disaster. Readers get even more tired of shallow, predictable characters than do their creators—the writers. If you're going to do it, do it right. Otherwise, stick to whatever you can see in your mind and describe best.

One more point. Anyone can learn about other races by doing research. It's that simple. Look up, find out, read, learn. *And think.* Somewhere along the line, you knew a person of a different race than you. Dig up your impressions. Expand upon them. *Run with them.* Before long, that black kid from the slums of Atlanta will be a living, breathing human being with a world of history and promise to bring to a book. Likewise, the white horse-racing addict, Native American, Hispanic, Asian, Pakistani ... well, you get my point. Just as a writer should never try to explain what it's like drifting through space without studying it and thinking about it enough to "see" the experience, he or she can't describe a diverse person without similarly "seeing" him. Envisioning him. Knowing him well enough to recognize him in his sleep.

That's my take on it, anyway.

Why would authors write newspapers?

I hope you're not the author in question. If you are, good luck getting published anywhere. Reading between the lines, I'm guessing you meant why would "book" authors write "for" newspapers. If I'm correct in my assumption, there are several reasons.

First, the publicity. Newspapers (particularly dailies) offer high visibility for their writers. That could prove beneficial to a writer with a new book about to be published.

Second, the excitement of regular exposure. There's still something magical about seeing one's by-line in print, even in a newspaper of the diminishing quality of, say, *The New York Times* and *The Washington Post*. And, yes, I know. I wrote a column and feature pieces for the *Post* back when they were a legitimate news organization.

Third, the weekly income. What's that they say about every little bit helping? Particularly in this age when book publishers are paying lower advances to their authors and providing little or no marketing and promotion for new books, money for even a popular and a talented author can be a little tight.

Fourth, the prestige, although there's less of that when writing for the mainstream media today than there used to be. If anyone thinks journalism isn't dead, let me know upon what you base your premise. I could use a good laugh.

Hope this is what your cryptic question meant and that this helps a bit.

Why did Joseph Pulitzer cross the Atlantic in 1864?

That's easy: "To get to the other side."

Oh, wait a minute. Wrong question.

Actually, Pulitzer came from a wealthy family in Europe. In 1853, his father, Fülöp Pulitzer, retired and moved the family to Pest, where he enrolled the children in a private school where they learned French and German. Fülöp died in 1858, and his business went bankrupt. Suddenly impoverished, Joseph attempted to enlist in various European armies before emigrating to the United States. His passage was paid for by Massachusetts military recruiters looking to sign up soldiers to fight in the American Civil War.

After several years of fighting and bouncing around the country in search of employment, young Joseph finally found success—not only in publishing but also in politics. He died a wealthy man on October 29, 1911, aboard his yacht, *Liberty*.

And that, or so they say, was that.

What's the most effective media for getting reputable information on different subjects?

Okay, discounting the partisan "whack jobs" who responded to you and the people who missed the object of your question entirely (No, Trump didn't destroy the universe, and, no, he didn't elevate Rudy Giuliani to Pope), here's the truth. There is no one *media format* that's more reliable for accurate information than another. I assume that's what you're asking in your somewhat nebulously phrased question.

ABOUT WRITING RIGHT

If I'm correct, the truth is painfully evident: The press is dead. Period. End of discussion. Deny it if you will, but if you do, you'll only be harming yourself.

When I began reporting as a cub stringer for a weekly newspaper in suburban Chicago back in the early seventies, accuracy was *everything*. Editors *stood* for something. Sure, papers were slanted left or right, but only marginally. The *Chicago Tribune*: Left. The *Chicago Sun-Times*: Right. And on and on throughout the country.

When I moved up to become the second most widely syndicated columnist in the world after Ann Landers, accuracy was still *everything*. Today, it is nothing. Today, journalism is the exclamation point on partisan politics. Journalism is pimping for a candidate or a political party. A *liberal* party. And the truth be damned. Sad to say.

So, where can you get the "most effective" form of media for "reputable information"? You tell me.

If you're serious about obtaining unbiased information, get feeds from *The Jerusalem Post*, the *New York Post*, Fox News, Newsmax, CNN, MSNBC, and *The Wall Street Journal*. Then, do what we used to do as a daily exercise in Journalism School. Compare the same story as told by different news outlets with different slants. And, in the end, evaluate all the stories with all their biases and make up your own mind as to which is most accurate and which is less.

Sorry I can't offer a simpler answer. But the truth is, there is no simpler answer.

God save the Queen!

I'm writing a book about people's most dangerous skills and need a two-word explanation of what they're skills are.

Sorry to be so blunt, but if you can't even ask a single question in grammatically correct English, why on earth do you think you're qualified to write a book? And need help to get it going, as well? I understand there may be extenuating circumstances, such as someone paid you to ghostwrite a book, or someone told you a market for such a book exists and you should rush to fill it. But, getting back to my initial observation, are you deluding yourself?

Writing a book is a tremendous undertaking in time, energy, and often money. If you do everything along the way *perfectly*, you may stand a chance to lose only a little bit of equity. As for the possibility of making millions—forget about it.

And if you *don't* do everything perfectly? Well, there goes the old investment. *Guaranteed!*

Before falling asleep, I get fancy ideas for a novel but don't know how I can sell them without writing the book myself.

Before sleep, *everyone* gets fancy ideas for a novel. Ideas are a dime a dozen. Novels (which we can compare at, say, a dollar a dozen) are much more difficult to create than ideas, which are usually nothing more than mental sketches and not very well detailed or developed. Certainly, they're not usually marketable anywhere I know of on Planet Earth.

"Usually"? Did I say "usually"?

Yes, I did. About the only shot in hell I can think of for your selling an *idea* and actually making some money off of it is to form a working relationship with a professional writer who is well-connected to Hollywood or New York. A scriptwriter who has a steady job providing copy for production would be perfect. If you can find someone such as that who just happens to *love* your ideas, you may be able to form a co-writing relationship that could net both of you a string of steady income.

Not likely, by the way, because even the most pressured screenwriters and scriptwriters either already have a co-writing partner or don't need one, preferring to go it alone.

So, until you can convince yourself that writing might be the most profitable way for you to turn your ideas into cold, hard cash, you're most likely doomed to seeing them reach fruition only in your dreams.

How can I hone in on what's unique about my style of writing?

Hmm. I wish you were kidding with that question, but I have a feeling you're not. It sounds as if that's a query that should be asked in a creative writing workshop setting or somewhere where at least someone—make that *anyone*—has seen and read some of your work. Without that, how can anyone possibly comment intelligently on what's unique about your writing style, let alone how you can use that uniqueness to your advantage?

Conversely, if you expect someone to seek out your writing on allpoetry.com, whatever that is, you're expecting too much. What qualified literary analyst is going to run around the Internet, risking all sorts of infections from unknown sites, trying to track down your writings just to analyze them because you asked him to? That doesn't make sense.

If I've learned anything from my half century of writing for a living, it's this: Make things as easy as possible for those from whom you're seeking help. You'd be amazed (or possibly not) at how often I still see neophyte writers pitching an agent or a publisher while asking them to check out their material at XYZ.com-something site. Sure they will. It's tough enough to get help when you lay everything out in front of someone let alone making that person jump through hoops and then find out, in the end, that he wasted his time.

I wish I could be of more help, but without a ton of additional information laid out at my fingertips, I'm afraid we're at a loggerhead.

As the CEO of a nearly broke publishing firm, what book would you choose to publish to make you millions?

That's simple: the next *New York Times Review of Books* number-one bestseller. Hopefully, one that retains that slot for five or six weeks running.

What book, exactly, is that? *Hmm.* I was hoping you'd tell me.

Seriously, it's as easy and as difficult as all that. Want proof? Hunter Biden's bomb that cost its publisher dearly. It hasn't come close to earning back the advance the company paid Biden in exchange for cashing in once again on his father's name. Shouldn't the publisher have anticipated that the book, in light of the author, would fail? I'd like to say *yes*, but in publishing, as in life, there are no sure things, and no one knows what the next big hit will be.

No one.

Oh, and, by the way, if the CEO of that near-broke publishing company is serious about that million-dollar bestseller, have him give me a call. I don't work without an advance, but I can be flexible.

Should I have my novel's main character leave their toxic girlfriend?

I think the first thing you should do is to learn to write. A character doesn't leave "their" toxic girlfriend. "Character" is a singular noun, and "their" is a plural pronoun. No-no. Can't mix them. *Big* no-no. *Major* no-no. *Huge. Massive. Gigantic.* That is, it's a big deal if you hope one day to get your novel published. If you're just writing it for therapy, well, then, it's not to worry.

As for your question, sure, have your character leave his toxic girlfriend—if that's what works best for your novel. As an alternative, have your character remain with his toxic girlfriend—if *that's* what's best for your novel. No one can answer that question other than you, given the amount of information you have provided here.

Now, anything else I can't help you with today?

Seriously, you're the creator of this story. I suggest you sit down, consider your story's plot (and if it doesn't have one, *create one pronto!*), and toy with some options open to you. Character leaves girlfriend, character doesn't leave girlfriend; girlfriend leaves character; girlfriend gets run over by a bus; character gets run over by a bus; *oops*, but that would be the end of the novel! (Forget that one.)

Once you've envisioned the *entire story* in your head, take some time to write out a summary or a synopsis. After that, go through the summary and find jumps in the time, setting, or action that could serve as chapter breaks. From there, create a chapter summary. It should look something like this:

1. John meets Cherry at the Museum of Science and Industry and falls in love. Cherry agrees to join John at the local soda joint for a soda (or a joint).
2. Cherry stands John up on their first date and runs off to Terre Haute with Dick.
3. John hops in his car and heads to Lake Michigan, where he finds Cherry and Dick working at a fish farm in southern Indiana.
4. Cherry immediately realizes her mistake and begs John's forgiveness, but, before he can give it to her, she gets run over by a bus. John asks a sanitation worker who witnessed the event for directions to the nearest Catholic Church. The sanitation worker points down the street.
5. John oversees Sunday Mass at St. Adalbert's Church where he has just been ordained, and he asks his parishioners to pray for all the Cherrys of the world.

Hey, not bad, *huh?* Once you finish your chapter outline, you can go back and start fleshing-out each chapter until you arrive at the last chapter and a completed book.

ABOUT WRITING RIGHT

Of course, you may decide as you flesh things out that new characters and plot twists that you hadn't originally foreseen create a need for some outline changes. In the end, perhaps John *doesn't* become a priest but runs away to join the circus. (John always was a little squirrely.)

Remember, this is your book; you can do with it what you want. But you won't do much of anything with it until you have the story organized in your head and then transcribed to a chapter outline on paper. That's when you'll see more clearly where to go and how to get there. Just follow the roadmap you drew from your mind.

Is it normal for literary agents to ask for "upfront money" for query writing before representing an author?

First, there is no such thing as an "introductory" literary agent. A person is either a literary agent or he or she isn't.

Second, agents make their money by selling your work. On average, they receive 15 percent of every dollar the work earns during the lifetime of the author-agent agreement.

Third, although agents may legitimately respond to *authors' requests* for editors, re-writers, ghostwriters, book doctors, and other professionals to help hone their works prior to representation, they cannot make a *stipulation of payment* from an author to any recommended professional as a requirement for representation of that author. In other words, there's no "pay to play" involved in a legitimate author-agent relationship.

I have had six literary agents in my career. (I keep outliving them!) Not one of them has ever violated that author-agent understanding. If any of them had, I would have fired him or her on the spot. Period.

And you can take that to the bank.

So, if an agent asks you for upfront money to write query letters (which is part of a literary agent's job in return for earning 15 percent of all revenues received from properties sold), you'd best close the book on that agent. I'll be happy to recommend some *legitimate* agents for your consideration if you'd like.

Should I take George R. R. Martin's advice about writing and selling short stories before trying to write novels?

Well, I've seen some *relatively* good responses to your question, and I've seen some pure, unadulterated *crap*. Most of the latter falls into the "short stories are easier to write than novels" category. Malarkey! They're not. In fact, in many respects, they're infinitely more challenging to write than long-form fiction.

There are numerous reasons for this, the most apparent being that everything you do in creating a novel of 80,000 words you must do in creating a short story of 8,000 words. except more expeditiously. That means no wasted language. No wasted turns. No false leads. No flowery descriptions. None of the things you can get away with in a novel—which by its very length should be leisurely and pleasant reading—works in a short story.

If I had to use one word to sum up the skill most necessary in creating a compelling short story, it would be *efficiency*. Images must be crisp and sharp, pointed and effective. Character development must be rapid and precise. Storylines must be pointed and unwavering.

Yet, the writer has to do all this in a manner that's both unpredictable and believable.

So, for all the respondents to your question who think that writing a short story is easier than writing a novel, I beg to differ. You can argue with me all you want—*after* you've published to acclaim several dozen of each—short stories and novels. Until then, I suggest the most accessible form of logical conclusion isn't always (or often) the best.

Are novels, then, actually easy to write? Nothing worth reading is easy to write. One advantage a newbie writer has in creating a short story rather than a novel is the very construction of the former. It's *soooooo* easy to get lost in writing a novel unless you're a precision-oriented, well-organized, Type-A personality with a strong masochistic streak. With so many words available to a novice writer, the temptation is great to lose focus of the goal and wander everywhere except toward the finish line.

On the other hand, a short story forces a writer of any age or experience to color within the lines. There's no room for wandering hither and yon. (Thither and yon? Whatever!)

But, easier focus on the goal doesn't get a writer home more quickly or easily. Every little mistake—every misplaced modifier or wasted descriptive passage or unnecessary verbiage in a short story—is magnified tenfold. Or more!

ABOUT WRITING RIGHT

So, are short stories easier for a novice writer on which to maintain focus than novels? Absolutely. Are they, therefore, easier to write than novels? Absolutely not. For every commercially successful short-story writer, I can point to dozens of successful novel writers.

And, in case you're wondering, given the two, I happen to like writing novels best. Except when I'm in the middle of creating a dynamite short story, which I then like best. Until I start my next novel, which …

Well, all I can say is thank God for both forms of fiction. And more power to those writers who have taken the time and invested the energy to perfect the writing of both. If you haven't yet tried writing both as a necessary learning experience to the development of your chosen craft, I highly recommend you do so. *Now.*

And, just as an aside, taking George R. R. Martin's mandate for developing young writers to improve their craft is a little like turning to Dear Abby for instructions on wiring a new home for electricity. It may look fine from a distance, but don't hit that switch! If you've ever read any of Martin's stuff, you know what I'm saying. As a good writer, he's made a lot of money off whatever talent some people think he has.

Are there some good writers here I can chat with to help with my novel?

You don't need "some good writers" to help you write your novel. No one writer you meet online is likely to be able to inspire you or guide you through to your goal. What you need is a professional analysis of your writing based upon samples plus a look at your proposed novel, what you've already done, what you plan to do, and how you plan to do it.

To find such a professional, often referred to as a book doctor or a literary mentor, you'll need to do some research. Find someone whose writing you admire and who seems to be approachable. Preferably, it should be someone with extensive personal novel-publishing and teaching experience.

After that, you'll need your mentor to give you feedback on your problem areas and his or her best advice on how to correct them. Following that, you'll need at least one more round of give-and-take, showing what you've done after receiving the advice and how you're progressing in your novel writing. Chances are you'll need more than that additional round and, perhaps, ongoing feedback from the start to the finish of your opus.

It's difficult to speak authoritatively without seeing your work, but when I work with an upcoming new novelist, that's usually the way I start out.. Once underway, I offer additional exercises, advice, corrections, and suggestions as warranted. Not all problems in a writer's repertoire are corrected by the same advice, just as no two illnesses are likely to respond positively to the same treatment.

Of course, all of this takes time, and time to a writer is money. You'd be looking at paying a professional capable of helping you through any problems you might have or run into upwards of $10K or considerably more, depending upon the length of mentoring and the efficiency of your progression as a novelist.

Does that sound like a lot of money? It may well be. But, remember: Nothing in life that's worth anything comes free. Well, few things, at least.

Can kids write serious philosophical and/or historical works, just as others have written fantasies and romance novels?

Oh, absolutely. Children today—thanks mostly to the influence of Facebook, Twitter, and other universally acknowledged, advanced-level educational resources—are nearly universally equipped to write serious philosophical works and history books. The philosophical works are mostly a product of intense, advanced mental-acuity training made possible only by the closure of our antiquated, traditionally orientated educational facilities and their replacement with the Fauci Doctrine of Advanced Dining-Room-Table Learning Facilities during the COVID-19 lock-down. The historical works are made possible by the intense interaction of our youth within the frameworks of Cancel Culture, the 1619 Project, and the creation within our kids of an overwhelming desire not only to study history but also to *create* it.

Now, do you have a serious question, or was that your best shot?

Understand that I'm not implying that teens (and preteens, although rarely) aren't capable of advanced philosophical thought. They are. What I'm wondering about is what have all these super-accentuated preadolescent authors to which you allude accomplished. I mean, I read *The Two Cultures* by C. P. Snow when I was in grade school.

ABOUT WRITING RIGHT

And understood it. And I read Margaret Mead's works a year or two later. And understood them. What I failed to do was to follow up by writing my treatises on life and lore on Planet Earth while still a developing child. Silly kid.

So, yes, I'm sure that, although I, a precocious reader and avid learner, wasn't equipped to write the philosophical and historical tomes to which you refer, some of "us" were. Surely. Unfortunately, I don't happen to have a list of their names at my fingertips.

More the pity.

When looking for an agent, is it the author's responsibility to query the agent with a proposal?

Absolutely. First, you have to "vet" the agents you contact to make sure they handle the type of work you want to pitch. To do that, run an online search of agents, and check out each agent's Website.

Once you've found a few suitable candidates, you'll want to send out your best four-paragraph pitch. First graf: A teaser for the book to grab the agent's attention. Second graf: Background as to what the book is about, where it's going, and any potential sales it's likely to receive (and from where). Third graf: A little about you, your devotion to your craft, your research of the agent, and your belief that the agent might enjoy checking you out further because you seem to have a lot in common. Fourth graf: A *sincere* thank you for the agent's time.

If that doesn't work with the agent behind Door Number One, move on to Door Number Two. Oh, and you can pitch more than one agent at a time, as long as one of the agents doesn't require an exclusive. Most agents understand that it's a competitive world, they're notoriously slow in their responses, and you can't wait around forever to see whether or not one agent will respond to you after three or four months. (Some *never* write back, sad to say.) Most agents expect multiple submissions and ask only that, if you reach an agreement with another agent, you let them know so they can remove you from consideration.

Can a PhD help an author write history books for the general public?

Contrary to one respondent's answer, there are no "valid perspectives regarding whether having a PhD will be helpful in writing a history book for the general public." Disregarding the respondent's lack of grammatical precision, a PhD is not a license to write and not a blue ribbon for writing. It's an acknowledgment that the participant achieved a certain degree of educational proficiency as defined by a particular institution of higher learning and, thus, can legally and ethically refer to himself as Dr. Jill.

As for writing? You've got to be kidding. Not even writing degrees translate into writing prowess. Writing comes from within, not from without. Writers develop regardless of educational degrees or histories of educational participation. Or they don't. It's either one or the other, and no degree can ever change that dynamic.

But, can appropriately designed creative writing workshops help a writer in his or her development? Absolutely, if taught by the right person or persons. Absolutely not, if not.

So, in response to your question:

What was the question, again?

Oh, yeah. And, I think you already knew the answer to your question before even asking it. I mean, *no one* could ever believe a PhD entitles anyone to anything other than a title and be serious about it. No one.

How good a writer is J. K. Rowling really in your opinion?

I think she's, *umm*, not great. Just my opinion, of course. But, given the fact that she has some of the best editors/rewrite people in the world cleaning up her copy before it goes to press—and that the one time she tried pushing through a novel under pseudonym (her true identity unknown even to her publisher), and it universally panned—that's not a good sign.

Granted, she is wealthy. You've got to give that to her. She has some creative ideas. But, then again, so do you. And I. And millions of other writers. Many of whom are better wordsmiths than she—by far. By anyone's favorite marker.

It's true: she *was* in the right place at the right time with the right property. And the rest, as they say, is history. That, ladies and gentlemen, is the story of how many "great authors" have been created throughout the last several millennia.

Cheers!

Is journalism difficult today?

Well, let me ask *you* a question: How cool is "drinking water"?

ABOUT WRITING RIGHT

Assuming, despite your lack of credible syntax, you mean how difficult is it to be an ethical journalist, it's very difficult. Extremely difficult. Nearly impossible in this era. Journalism, as those of us who are old enough to have studied under the tutelage of working, professional, unbiased journalists of reputable, unbiased publications can attest, is dead.

It's been replaced by political partisanship. Exactly the persons journalists were originally charged with overseeing and reporting upon for *more than a century* are today the same persons paying the "mainstream" journalists' salaries. Oh, not weekly or anything as banal as that. But by promoting them, hyping them, pitching them, congratulating them on their anti-journalistic accomplishments, and rewarding them with *huge*-paying political jobs at every possible opportunity.

Let me repeat. Journalism today is dead. You want to debate me? Please, feel free. But you'd better have more than the obvious hackneyed partisan politics in your arsenal, or you lose. *Period*.

Let me backtrack a bit. I used to write regularly for the *Washington Post, Boston Globe, L. A. Times, Minneapolis Star-Tribune, Chicago Tribune*, and more than 1,100 other newspapers throughout North America. And there wasn't *one* for which I wrote that I was ashamed.

Today, I can't name one for which I *wouldn't* be ashamed. That's a big shift in a matter of a couple of decades. No, it's a *huge* shift.

So, getting back to your question of how difficult journalism is. From every conceivable standpoint, it's extremely difficult to conduct ethically today. Almost impossible. And if I haven't yet convinced you of that, contact me through my Website. We can continue the conversation there.

Where can I find writers who would be interested in hearing my story?

You can't. At least, not if you're looking for writers to hear what you have to say so they can rush off to write about it. *Uh-uh*. It doesn't work that way. Writers (we're talking professional-caliber here) have far more ideas than they'll ever have time to put down on paper. The last thing on earth they need is, "Can I tell you my story because you're going to fall in love with it and want to turn it into a book."

Now, if you're talking about *hiring a ghostwriter* to take your story and develop it into something publishable, that's a different matter. Ghosts are available everywhere. Run an Internet search for a sampling of who's out there. Or work through a professional writers' group such as the Author's Guild. Just be aware that ghosts run the gamut from a total waste of time and money to absolute literary magicians who can turn any project into a four- or five-star book, regardless of how "rough" the story might be. Look over their contracts and ask questions before you sign on the dotted line.

As a Christian author, is it wrong to write books based upon ancient Greek mythology?

Yes, it is. It's every bit as bad as authors writing about Hitler and outer space and black holes and racism and holocausts and pandemics and slavery and starving people in Africa where I once told my mom to send my cauliflower, because I sure as all hell didn't want to eat it.

Authors should write only about sunshine and cancer cures, about pixies and fairy dust, about wishes and dreams come true. Get it?

Next question.

How many words will fit into three single-spaced pages?

Wait. This is a trick question, right? I mean, you can't really be asking this with a straight face, correct? Because you *know* that the answer would depend upon the type font, the font face, the type size, and the type spacing used. It would also depend upon the size of the pages, the leading between lines, the kerning or tracking, and the width of the margins all the way around. It would depend as well upon the length of the words (how many words are "is" and how many are "Incomprehensibilities"?), whether or not you use indented paragraphs, and if the copy is flush left/ragged right or justified, plus a few other variables.

So, it really *is* a trick question, right?

Right?

Can I sell a 10,000-word eBook for $2.99 for a 10,000-word eBook?

I would say it's possible only if the book proves to be in demand. In other words, it has to be something of value to the reader. What puzzles me, though, is why you'd pick that price out of a hat. If the same book sold twice as well for $1.99, thus increasing your profits, wouldn't you be smarter to price it there? Would $.99 sell five times better, thus sending your profit line and your spirits soaring?

Do some research, and remain flexible. If testing for pricing means adjusting your price and keeping tabs of sales for each price point from month to month, do so.

Is self-publishing a step back for serious writers?

Yes. The key word here is "serious." There are *millions* of authors who aren't serious. That, to me, means they're not intent upon earning their living from writing books for the next thirty-to-fifty years of their lives. For those who *are* serious about doing so, be aware that self-publishing remains a stigma with many conventional-house publishers. And for good reason. *Anyone* can self-publish. Not just *anyone* can publish conventionally. In fact, far from it.

So, what's a person to do? Whatever is possible. My advice to first-time authors is to try the conventional publishing route first. Research the markets. Then Query. Wait. Accept the rejections. Query some more. Accept more rejections. And wait until there's no one left to query.

Then, and *only then*, consider self-publishing.

Just my thought on the matter.

Which technology helped writers the most, the typewriter or word processing? And do you think students don't place enough value on the art of rewriting?

Great questions. Which college professor asked them? And don't you think you should put in a little brain work of your own instead of hoping for someone else's inspiration to see you through life?

Even if these weren't questions on an assignment, why would you think the technology leaps for writers would equate to students underestimating the value of rewriting? It's a little like asking, "Which is better, cows eating in the morning or cows eating in the evening? And, while we're on the subject, who won the Fifty-Seven World Series, anyway?"

Good luck. Until you change your approach to life, I think you may need it.

Ciao, bella!

Why did authors who used to appear at book signings stop doing so?

D. J. Herda

Most authors stopped doing book signings long ago for one of two reasons.

First, they don't work. The primary goal of a book signing is to sell books. The secondary goal is to create "buzz," which in turn feeds into the primary goal. Most authors who do book signings fail to meet either one. A book signing is scheduled, the author shows up, and the store manager sets up a poster and a book dump. A few potential admirers may stop by to chat and get an author's signature on their books. Very few.

Second, publishers know about the first reason, and most have stopped promoting and funding signings. The few who still do are generally major publishers (you know their names) and a few A-List authors (you also know *their* names). Those people draw crowds no matter where they appear or for what reason. They create both news and sales by their mere presence. They are the celebrities of the book world. So, publishers will most likely continue to fund them, sending them on what amounts to promotional tours around the country. But, for an author who's anything less than A-List, well, he's out of luck.

Or, he's incredibly lucky, depending upon your point-of-view. Either way, book signings are far more trouble and expense than they're worth. And nearly everyone in the industry knows it.

Can you relate the social issues of *Les Miserables* to society today, with references?

I can, yes. Can *you*? And, if so, why are you looking for someone else to complete your homework assignments? Furthermore, if you can't answer your own test question, *why* can't you?

Let me tell you a little story about slugs. You know, those slimy little creatures that crawl along the ground, avoid sunlight, live in filth, and devour their hosts until their hosts no longer exist? Although not parasites themselves (living off the lives of others), they provide hosting material for other parasites as the slugs slither across the ground. Most feed on a broad selection of organic materials, including leaves from living plants, lichens, mushrooms, and even carrion (look it up). Some slugs are predators and eat other slugs and snails or earthworms. Slugs can feed on a wide variety of vegetables and herbs. These include flowers such as daffodils, chrysanthemums, petunias, daisies, lilies, primroses, tuberous begonias, and hollyhocks. They also include fruits (particularly low-growing strawberries) and vegetables such as peas, carrots, and cabbage.

Slugs from different families are fungivores, meaning they feed on slime molds and mushrooms.

Toward the end of their life cycle, they perish naturally but not before laying more eggs and creating more slugs (they're hermaphrodites—look it up). Or they run out of moisture and are burned up by drought and the sun. Or they succumb to the debilitating treatment of salt, vinegar, or commercially available pesticides. Or, even more environmentally friendly iron oxide or diatomaceous earth. Or maybe even a bowl of stale beer, which seals their fate just as effectively, although perhaps more pleasantly.

In short, without slugs, a gardener's life would be so much more pleasant—and rewarding. Still, slugs serve a purpose in the overall scheme of things. They provide food for some birds, snakes, frogs, toads, and fish. But, their negative contributions to society far outweigh their positive. Some species of slugs are serious pests of agriculture and horticulture, destroying foliage faster than plants can replace it, thus killing even the largest of plants. They also feed on fruits and vegetables before harvest, making holes in the crops, which become unsuitable for sale for aesthetic reasons while making the crop more vulnerable to rot and disease.

Sound as if all this hits a little too close to home? You know, *things* that live off of other things' well-being while providing little or no benefit to society on their own? If not, think a little harder. And decide whether or not you really want an answer to your question.

Or, if you'd rather do the research and come up with that answer on your own.

Would you cite modern authors such as J. K. Rowling and Zadie Smith going down as among the twentieth-century greats in American education?

Absolutely, given the fluid state of education today. Both Rowling and Smith will be Gods. Or goddesses.

From an objective point-of-view, however, not on your life. At least not for the two authors you spell out.

J. K. Rowling is no Herman Melville, and Zadie Smith is a self-absorbed hack. Just my point-of-view. Take it or leave it.

D. J. Herda

As for the other twentieth-century scribes, yeah, you've got a nominee or two. Harper Lee, Huxley, Hesse, Fitzgerald, Nabokov, Steinbeck, Orwell, Kafka, Salinger, Bradbury, Golding, Capote, Vonnegut, Atwood, Sartre, Hemingway, Tolkien, Faulkner, Pynchon, Joyce, Kesey, Graham Greene, Steinbeck, Beckett ...

Well, let's stop there, shall we?

Now, what was your original question again?

Rowling or Smith?

Uh-huh. Sure.

Do series authors put all their efforts into their first books and less into the sequels?

Actually, that may be true. With *hack* writers. You know, people who want to be writers for whatever reason (and there are millions of them!) but have never bothered to put in the time to learn, study, practice, perfect, and analyze everything they do and everything every other writer they've ever read did. Both the good and the bad, the effective and the utter waste of time.

But with *professional* writers for whom the writing profession really means something special, it's just the opposite. The first book in a series is the *sweat-bullets* book. It's the one where you as the author are going out on a limb to see whether or not the branch will break—with you still clinging to it!

Subsequent series books have a roadmap for the author to follow. The author knows who the main characters are, what their characteristics are, how they talk, think, and act. With all that knowledge "in the bank," it's easier to write subsequent series novels but also mandatory to demand more from yourself. You *know* what you know about the series, and so does your reader. So, you have to crank out something extraordinary to catch the reader napping, to take him or her by surprise, to blow his mind. And that's where that extra mile comes in.

Good writers walk the walk; bad writers take shortcuts.

Just my thoughts on the matter. Hope they help.

What do new magazines have to do to get published in stores?

Nothing because they don't get published in stores. They get published in print shops, such as R. R. Donnelley based out of Chicago. Then, they get *distributed* to stores. If what you're asking is how do new magazines find their way to store racks such as those in grocery stores, chain stores, drug stores, and elsewhere, the answer is simple: It ain't easy.

First, a new magazine has to prove itself with circulation and advertising revenue. It's tough getting one without the other, but it's part of the game. Once a periodicals distributor catches wind of your publication and is convinced it's a good, reliable seller capable of generating strong monthly earnings (or whatever the print schedule), they'll approach the publisher with a distribution contract. After that, it's smooth sailing! (Well, not really, but we can dream.)

Can you advise me on how I can become a paid reviewer of various authors' books?

If you're asking for a pathway to earning enough money as a paid book reviewer so that you can sit around all day, reading to your heart's content, and then write a few dozen words about your experience, sorry. Book reviewing hasn't been that lucrative for a couple hundred years. One of the reasons, as with damned near everything in society today, is Amazon. Why would anyone pay readers to provide book reviews when the King of Retailers, merely by its existence, can provide them free of charge all day long?

As someone mentioned, there *are* sites that pay book reviewers nominal amounts for their reviews. In order to recoup their outlay, these sites charge a healthy fee to the authors for whose books they provide the reviews. Kirkus is one of the oldest and most notorious of such sites. Naturally, the ethics of paying a site to provide a review of your book leads to all sorts of speculative ethical breaches, whether true or merely imagined. Still, the questions persist.

But, back to your initial question: How do you become a paid book reviewer? I'd ask in return: *Why would you want to?* If it's for a lark, I'd say go for it. If it's to earn a living from writing reviews, I'd suggest you'd be better served writing kids' books or YAs or cranking out an occasional article or two for a magazine or even working as a "stringer" for a local community newspaper. At least you'd be sure of making a few bucks, although none of those things would pay enough to see your way through college.

Sorry I don't have better news, but I hope the information helps.

Can you recall what the most moving or inspirational

inscription was that any author ever wrote inside a book to you?

Hmm. There have been so many! (Wink, wink.)

I did receive an autographed copy from an author for whom I book doctored, turning what began as an unpublishable work into a genuine page-turner. The author wrote, "Thanks for all your help. I couldn't have done it without you."

It felt good knowing that someone of worth noted my contribution to the book's publication, as well as to the writer's dream of becoming a conventionally published author.

Should I pursue a career in the arts as I want or in the sciences as my parents want?

Hmm. "There is the goddess, standing next to Charlie in her negligee. And you are there on your knees, begging. Poor Charlie. Tough decision."

First, you don't say *why* your family argues for a career in science for you, although I assume it's money-oriented. If that's the case, they're probably right. I believe it's far easier to earn a six-figure income in one of the sciences (not the social sciences, of course!) than in the arts.

That said, the next question is for *you*: What's more important—happiness or income? And don't downplay the question. It's critical in determining your decision.

And yet another question: Are you "beholden" to your parents and averse to crossing them, or don't you give a damn about their beliefs? That could mean a lot to you either way.

Finally, one last question. Why on earth are you considering what your parents want for you, who I assume are a grownup human being, when you should be considering what *you* want for you?

'Nuff said.

Hope this helps.

Oh, yeah, and if you choose the arts, plan on struggling financially for most of your adult life. Just FYI.

And, also just FYI, it ain't the worst thing on earth.

Is Adolph Hitler's book, Mein Kampf, which I'm going to try to find on Oxfam, one long, neurotic rant or a brilliant piece of political science, as some have claimed?

Well, I must disagree with several respondents to your question

ABOUT WRITING RIGHT

who found fault with the book. Hitler's *Mein Kampf* is, indeed, a brilliant piece of political science literature—no doubt about it. At least in the mind of its author. Only one man could have written it. And that man proved his brilliance and political acumen by disenfranchising himself, his nation, and his people in less than a generation. He did so by launching a world war that had no justifiable rationale, proved impossible to win, exhibited no moral compass as a guidance toward its inevitable conclusion, and cost the lives of an estimated eighty-five million people. Seven million of them were German, and another five-and-a-half million were Jews exterminated in concentration camps.

But never mind that. The book is unique in that it laboriously and tediously documents the period as if written by someone with little or no formal education in literature, which as it turns out, is true. That makes for tiresome reading with a solid emphasis upon promoting the legitimacy of a new Aryan socialist state. Toward that goal, Hitler's writing is quite expressive, and his conclusions, irreversible. He accepted dogmatism as truth and mistook his unyielding lunacy for logic.

Admittedly, the man's festering hatred of Jews is somewhat slow materializing, not appearing in the book until the fifth page. After that, his attitude manifests itself as a zealot's rage and a harangue ad nauseam throughout the work. Hitler was, as anyone with a brain and a grasp of the human psyche already knows, a genuine mad man. Far before his egomania took hold and exploded upon the world, it existed minimally shielded, operating under the guise of political rationale and expediency.

But, let's be clear here: There is nothing either rational or expedient in this labored work or, for that matter, in the man. That makes itself clear from page one.

As for getting a second-hand copy from Oxfam, you'll have to find out for yourself if that's possible. My only question would be *why?* You'll learn little about Germany, world politics, or the malformations of the Nazi Party whose every step was engineered or approved by Hitler's deviant mind.

Admittedly, everyone should read as much literature as possible, pertaining to both sensible thought and its counterpart, if for no other reason than to broaden his or her base of knowledge and understanding. But, there must be some works more worthy of your time, attention, and consideration than this. Lewis Carroll's *Through the Looking Glass* comes immediately to mind.

Now, on the other hand, if you're looking for a revelatory study in the exploration of the deviant human psyche, this book might be just what the doctor ordered.

So to speak.

Does analyzing a work's geographical, ethical, and linguistic dimension help a person to understand a literary work?

Okay, now, I have a question for *you* before I provide you with an answer. How does going to Quora to get a response to your college-course question benefit you in any way imaginable? How does doing so enable you to expand your mental capacity, to solve problems, and to think creatively and grow in mental acuity?

Okay, I'll give that much to you. You're right. It doesn't.

But, wait a minute. Let's stop there for a moment and turn in another direction.

What does the question your college prof asked you matter in real life? Oh, sure, I know. It matters in academia because academia is so far removed from reality that it functions only in its particular universal sphere. You know, with its own universal relevance, moral code, political advocacy, social relevancy, and even language? I mean, "the literary text's geographical, ethical, and linguistic dimension"? Are you kidding me? That's what I call "Writerese" when I encounter it from a writer. It's what I call "academese" when I encounter it from a professional academic.

I'm a professional wordsmith of more than half a century. I studied and taught analytic grammar for five decades. I've written and had published a hundred books and thousands of short pieces in my career. I've published with every type and genre publisher imaginable. And I don't have a clue as to what those words mean. Not a *clue!*

And that's the sad part of it all. Our children are being taught academic gobbledygook in exchange for a piece of paper that, in all likelihood, won't affect their lives one iota in the end except, perhaps, *negatively* after taking into account the cost in money, time, and energy invested in obtaining that scroll.

ABOUT WRITING RIGHT

Now, I'm laying myself out here for all those offended by what I just said. You know, the ones who fit the age-old maxim: Those who can, write; those who can't, *teach*. Also, the ones who believe that attacking liberal orthodoxy is tantamount to harikari? So, take your best shots. But, please, do so in comprehensible English and not in academese. Then, more than mere academicians will understand what you're saying and, perhaps, be able to join in the conversation.

But, keep in mind that I have nothing against the teaching profession. I taught independently, privately, and at the public and private college level for most of my adult years on earth. But I did so in a way that touched my students, affected them, reached them, educated them, inspired them, and *taught* them.

Yes, it's true.

I taught analytic grammar; I taught literature; I taught creative writing workshop; I taught music; I taught photography; I taught downhill skiing; I taught editing; I taught gardening; I taught organic living. I did so because I'm a natural teacher. You know, someone who understands the different modalities in which different students learn most effectively and how to recognize them? And someone who adjusts his teaching methods to reach each of those students? Got it? And I never once relied upon a "geographical, ethical, and linguistic" dimension to move my students forward.

Oh, yeah, and for that answer to your college prof's question that I promised to give you in the first paragraph? *How does analyzing the literary text's geographical, ethical, and linguistic dimension help in appreciation of literary works?*

Answer: It doesn't.

Each specific concept (i.e., *dimension*) mentioned in the question is of such wide variance in meaning that no one answer could possibly apply without eliciting innumerable exceptions. Therefore, any meaningful analysis would be fruitless and, thus, invalid.

Thanks for asking.

Does people with a high-school degree ever succeed in writing books?

Not if they don't understand English grammar any better than you. Did you actually read this question before hitting the "Post" button, or did you just slap it together and move on to something else?

D. J. Herda

Writing is a serious business, and the field of writers looking to "make it" is glutted. The landscape is littered with lost and departed literary souls. The powers that be (that is, the pool of readers looking for something to occupy their time) are relatively unforgiving. Show them any sign of incompetence, and you're toast.

Why do some authors use nom de plumes when writing their novels?

Yeah, yeah, yeah. Great responses, one and all. A priest who writes erotica. *Duh.* A youth counselor who writes about Hannibal Lecter. *Ohh.* A government official who writes about UFOs. *Wow*! Do those authors really feel the need to disguise their true identities? They do? They really *do*?

Okay, I get it. You get it. Now, let's get real.

Authors use nom de plumes (sometimes referred to as "pen names" and sometimes as "naughty-naughties") for several reasons. Anne Rice wanted to protect her romantic reputation by venturing into the world of the never-dying without revealing the truth. But how about some other reasons? J. K. Rowling wanted to see if she could prove all her critics wrong by publishing a book under a pseudonym and selling a million copies without her *Harry Potter* influence to fall back upon: She couldn't.

There are a vast number of reasons authors use pen names. Some authors don't want to appear as if they're publishing *too much material* under one name to be taken seriously. (You know, if an author is prolific and getting published monthly, he can't be very "deep.") The solution? The author assigns some of his or her work to a fictitious name.

Some authors have to disguise their real identities because their employers forbid them to publish under their real identities. Some authors do so because their past sales figures are paltry, and they want to shed that stigma with future publishers and readers. Some do so to disguise revenue from prying eyes—the government or an irate ex-spouse or whomever. Others do so because they're writing from the point of view of the opposite sex. *I, a Woman* by Frank Lovejoy would raise more eyebrows than the same book penned by Penelope Stillwell. Still more do so because they think their real names are too hum-drum for the marketplace. *Forever Amber* by Jane Jones sounds a little flat

ABOUT WRITING RIGHT

when compared to *Forever Amber* by Monica de la Cruz or Hank Hunkjoy. Get it?

Come on, Quora respondents. It's time we stopped spitting out answers from inside the box and began considering *all* options in responding to a query. Think more things through, as Kara Krelove did in her response to this question, before rushing to be first to the keyboard.

Let's consider things to their logical conclusion before spitting out answers like so much popcorn from a popper. And if your experience is limited in the realm of the question, maybe you'd be wiser just to let it pass.

Just my thoughts on the matter. I wish they were wrong.

But I doubt that they are.

Which do you prefer for a reference book, Style: Ten Lessons in Clarity and Grace or William Strunk's The Elements of Style?

While I don't often comment on books I haven't read (that is, *Style: Ten Lessons in Clarity and Grace*), I think I can safely say I would prefer William Strunk, Jr.'s, *The Elements of Style*. There are several reasons for my choice: It's concise—both short, and sweet. It's easy to reference. It's affordable. It's a classic that has been around and helping writers forever.

Here's what the publisher has to say about the very first edition (of which there are now dozens) on Amazon:

"The original edition of the most trusted writer's guide to American English, this is the book that generations of writers have relied upon for timeless advice on grammar, diction, syntax, sentence construction, and other writing essentials. In brief and concise terms, author William Strunk, Jr., identifies the principal requirements of proper American English style and concentrates on the most often violated rules of composition."

Originally published in 1918, *The Elements of Style* is generally regarded as one of the most valuable and reliable writer's reference books written. It's one of five or six such books on my library shelf.

'Nuff said.

AFTERWORD

After expending so much time and energy on the body of this book, I should be exhausted. Empty. Nothing but fumes in the tank.

Not so. In fact, I could go on writing for another hundred thousand words or more. That's how many unanswered questions about writing right that remain. Whether for publication or pleasure, as a hobby or a career, questions about writing, publishing, and editing (okay, let's not forget the unsung heroes of this book, the *literary agents*) pop up constantly. Most have been driven around the block a few times; some are new. All are important. Although I have attempted to cull those questions of the widest possible interest or the most valuable resources to the writer today, new ones keep popping up daily.

Partly, that's because new technologies place new demands upon our industry. A mere ten years ago, I wouldn't have heard more than a question or two on self-publishing or Print-On-Demand (POD). Today, nearly one out of every three or four writers has a question he'd like answered. As for tomorrow ... who knows?

For those of my readers whose questions I somehow failed to answer, I'd like to extend an invitation to drop me a line. You can always find an e-mail contact link on my Web page at http://www.djherda.org. Or you can reach me through one of my publishers, as detailed on Amazon, B&N, and elsewhere. I'd love to hear from you, and I'd love even more answering the questions that claw at you the most.

ABOUT WRITING RIGHT

Until then, keep writing, keep up those good spirits, and keep in touch. I'll look forward to hearing from you at www.djherda.org or at www.djherda.substack.com, and I'll get back to you. Guaranteed.

BIBLIOGRAPHY

The Chicago Manual of Style, The University of Chicago Press Editorial Staff (Chicago: University of Chicago Press), 2017.

A Dictionary of Modern American Usage, Garner, Bryan A. (New York: Oxford University Press), 2016.

The Elements of Style Fourth Edition, Strunk, Jr., William J., and E. B. White (New York: Longman), 1999.

Fowler's Modern English Usage, Fowler, H. W. (New York: Oxford University Press), 2010.

Merriam Webster's Manual for Writers & Editors: A Clear, Authoritative Guide to Effective Writing and Publishing, Ed. Merriam Webster's Collegiate Dictionary (New York: Merriam Webster, Incorporated), 1998.

On Writing Well: The Classic Guide to Writing Nonfiction, Zinser, William (New York: St. Martin's Press), 2006.